Cybercrime and Cybersecurity Research

nova
science publishers
www.novapublishers.com

Cybercrime and Cybersecurity Research

Information Systems Security in Small and Medium-Sized Enterprises: Emerging Cybersecurity Threats in Turbulent Times
Kennedy Njenga
2022 ISBN: 979-8-88697-390-7 (Softcover)
2022 ISBN: 979-8-88697-450-8 (eBook)

Cybersecurity and Digital Forensics: Challenges and Future Paradigms
Abdulrahman Yarali, PhD, Faris Sahawneh, PhD and Randal Joyce, PhD
2022 ISBN: 978-1-68507-810-2 (Hardcover)
2022 ISBN: 979-8-88697-013-5 (eBook)

Global Cybercrime and Cybersecurity Laws and Regulations: Issues and Challenges in the 21st Century
Shahid M. Shahidullah, PhD, Carla D. Coates, PhD and Dorothy Kersha-Aerga, PhD
2022 ISBN: 978-1-68507-755-6 (Hardcover)
2022 ISBN: 978-1-68507-854-6 (eBook)

Cybersecurity in the Current Framework of the EU and Italian Criminal Justice Systems. A Focus on Digital Identity Theft
Clara Pettoello-Mantovani
2022 ISBN: 978-1-68507-583-5 (Hardcover)
2022 ISBN: 978-1-68507-688-7 (eBook)

Cybersecurity Risk Management: An Enterprise Risk Management Approach
Bruce Ho, PhD and Kok-Boon Oh, PhD
2022 ISBN: 978-1-68507-428-9 (Hardcover)
2022 ISBN: 978-1-68507-505-7 (eBook)

More information about this series can be found at https://novapublishers.com/product-category/series/cybercrime-and-cybersecurity-research/

Gunikhan Sonowal

Social Engineering Attack

Rethinking Responsibilities and Solutions

nova
science publishers
www.novapublishers.com

DOI: https://doi.org/10.52305/KSOA7898.

Library of Congress Cataloging-in-Publication Data

ISBN: 979-8-88697-739-4

Published by Nova Science Publishers, Inc. † New York

Contents

List of Figures

List of Tables

Preface

The social engineering attack is presented in the first chapter of the book. It covers the definition, background, motives, and outcome of the social engineering attack.

The life cycle of a social engineering attack is covered in the second chapter of the book. Attack formulation, information collecting, preparation, cultivating relationships, exploitation, and debriefing are the six phrases used by social engineering attackers throughout the life cycle.

The basic concepts of social engineering attacks are covered in the third chapter of the book. The six principles of social engineering include scarcity, commitment, authority, social proof, reciprocity, and liking.

Various forms of social engineering attacks are discussed in the fourth chapter of the book. The physical method, social approach, reverse social engineering approach, technical approach, and socio-technical approach are the five main forms of social engineering attacks.

Identity theft is discussed in five of the book's chapters. The purpose of the information that attackers stole from users is explained in this chapter.

Social engineering tools are covered in the book's six chapters. Organizations deploy a variety of toolkits to informally teach their staff members and identify organizational weaknesses.

Chapter Seven of the book covers the countermeasures for social engineering attacks. There are three ways to counter the social engineering attack including policy and procedures, education, and technical methods.

The eighth chapter of the book covers the laws that are related to social engineering attacks. Many governments proposed many laws which directly or indirectly related to social engineering attacks.

The future of social engineering attacks is covered in the ninth chapter of the book. Some of the technology that will be utilized in the future for social engineering purposes is covered in this chapter.

Acknowledgments

My family is the most significant source of my strength in life; thus, I'd like to celebrate this joyous occasion with them. I received a lot of help from my Ph.D. advisor, Dr. K. S. Kuppusamy, in finishing this work. My wife, Mrs. Gitimoni Chutia Sonowal, was staunch in her support. Without the constant support of my parents, Mr. Nandeswar Sonowal and Mrs. Nilima Sonowal, and sisters, Jimpa and Simpa, it would have been challenging for me to fulfill this assignment.

Chapter 1

An Overview of Social Engineering Attacks

People, as individuals, are more vulnerable today than ever before in the cyber world. The present digital world is significantly more complex, large online firms spend more money, and as a result, security problems are more varied and advanced. Users at both homes and businesses have considerably grown. Social engineering is one of the most prevalent and successful dominant attacks at the moment since these exploits are so powerful that they underpin the vast majority of cyberattacks. It is the practice of exploiting human flaws to achieve their intended goal. It was previously associated with the social sciences, whereas it is now widely used by computer and information security professionals. These kinds of attackers have the potential to grow out of control, and with the aid of a shoddy security system, they have the power to bring down even major corporations. Watering hole websites, phishing scams, real-world baiting, whaling attacks, pretexting, and quid pro quo attacks are examples of social engineering attacks.

Deception is a key component of social engineering, and con artists are a common term used to describe those who carry out these attacks. The art of the con, as mentioned in "The Dark Art of Social Engineering," is one of the oldest forms of social engineering. Con artists essentially try to persuade users to perform, purchase, or sell things they would not normally do. They take advantage of their confidence in what they are predicting for their own personal gain. Most cons do not involve anything technological. On the other hand, a skilled con artist who is familiar with networks, computers, and security would be a highly threatening person. These hybrid con artists are commonly referred to as modern social engineers.

Social engineering is frequently used as the first step in a wider effort to enter a system or network and steal sensitive data or spread malware. Impersonation of the user's boss, supplier, IT team member, or delivery firm is one of the most prevalent social engineering attack techniques. The attackers frequently desire to gain money or sensitive information, regardless of who they are trying to harm. However, it may be additional reasons why attackers might utilize social engineering occasionally.

According to Purplesec's 2021 report, 98% of cyber-attacks rely on social engineering. If the social engineering attack can be stopped, it will be extremely helpful to the cyber security team in stopping other cyberattacks. As a result, social engineering is a critical cyber-attack that must be handled. Researchers and experts from various organizations are constantly proposing novel strategies to combat social engineering attacks. People's vulnerability to social engineering attacks may be somewhat reduced if they comprehend them. This is the major motivation behind this book's composition.

This chapter will cover the following topics:

- History of social engineering attacks
- Definition of social engineering attacks
- Attacker's preference for social engineering attack
- Motivation of attackers
- Impact of social engineering attacks.

1.1. History

Although social engineering attacks are a prominent security issue today, the concept of a social engineering attack is not new. Social engineering tactics can be located in ancient epics and novels. They used social engineering strategies even though they did not refer to it as a "social engineering attack." This section investigates the history of social engineering attacks as a result.

It is difficult to pinpoint when the social engineering attack was used. However, the ancient epic, *Odyssey,* contains the concept of social engineering. In this story, the attackers used the trojan horse as a weapon to deceive their enemies. The story was something like this: the trojans, who had been residing in Troy for about ten years, were under attack by the Greeks. It was challenging for the Greeks to enter Troy because of its excessively large wall. As a result, they attempted to enter the city using social engineering techniques.

The Greeks, under the leadership of Odysseus, constructed the enormous wooden horse that would later serve as Troy's emblem and placed it outside the city's walls. They then acted as though they were sailing away. The trojans considered the enormous wooden horse to be a peace offering to their gods and hence a symbol of their victory during a protracted siege. They moved a large wooden horse through the streets of the city.

The fascinating part is that the trojans were unaware that a small squad of Greek soldiers had been stowed away inside the horse by the Greeks. That night, after the trojans had gone to bed, the Greek soldiers in the horse were able to dismount and open the city's gates, allowing the remainder of the Greek army to enter after sailing back in the dark. The Greeks were finally able to take Troy by surprising the trojans in the middle of the night.

1.1.1. 1800 - 1900

The term "social engineering" was originally used in an easy book by Dutch businessman J.C. Van Marken in 1894 as *sociale ingenieurs* (also known as "social engineers"). The book contains several stories regarding social engineering attacks. The idea was that modern employers required specialists to assist them to deal with human difficulties just as they needed technical competence (traditional engineers) to deal with non-human challenges (materials, machines, processes).

As per the report of Carlson, 2005, the term "social engineering" first emerges in 1899 in a less shocking setting. A department shop in Boston was looking for someone to take care of its employee's requirements, and William Tolman, the League of Social Service's secretary, described the job as "essentially, that of a social engineer."

A small journal called *Social Engineering* was published in 1899; it was renamed *Social Service* in 1900. William H. Tolman, the journal's previous editor, used the term as the title of a book in 1909 (translated into French in 1910).

With the publication of *The Social-Engineer* by Social Gospel sociologist Edwin L. EARP during the "efficiency craze" of 1911 in the United States, a new usage of the term was launched that has since become standard: "Social engineering" came to refer to an approach of treating social relations as "machinery," to be dealt with in the manner of the technical engineer.

1.1.2. 1900 - 2000

Another fascinating social engineering example involves the France Eiffel Tower. In 1925, social engineering attacker Victor Lustig planned to sell the Eiffel Tower. At the time, the Eiffel Tower's fame was dwindling, with few visitors and scathing criticism. The financial problems of maintaining the edifice prompted suspicion that the monument would be sold. Victor Lustig regarded this as a wonderful opportunity to pull off a scam unlike any other. He created a fake access card to the Eiffel Tower and a letterhead from the mayor of Paris claiming ownership of the structure.

He then located the city's most influential scrap dealers and extended an invitation to a "secret meeting" at the Crillon hotel. He then increased his authority in their eyes by using his fake access card to lead the men to the tower. The offers started coming in, and one young dealer Victor had his eye on fell for the trick and purchased the tower from Victor due to his lack of experience. Arriving at the tower and claiming ownership from the confused guards, Lustig had already left the country. The victim never brought a complaint against Lustig because he felt so embarrassed.

As time went on, numerous fields started to employ social engineering attack techniques. Whereas social engineering attacks are common in the digital age, where attackers use these strategies to accomplish their goals. The following is a discussion of a few of the significant accidents related to social engineering tactics.

Phreaking, commonly referred to as phone phreaking, is the dishonest manipulation of phone signals to make free phone calls. It first appeared in the US in the late 1950s, listening to phone tones to determine the routing of calls. Joe Engressia, called Joybubbles, was a blind 7-year-old boy with perfect pitch and the improbable father of Phreaking.

Steve Jobs and Steve Wozniak in 1971, Steve Wozniak reads an article regarding Joybubbles and other phone phreaks, meets John "Captain Crunch" Draper, and discovers how to hack into phone systems. To break into phone networks, he builds a "blue box," device and he used social engineering strategies to pretend to be Henry Kissinger and place a hoax call to the Pope. The devices were put into mass production by him and his friend Steve Jobs, who then sold them to classmates.

As a joke in 1982, Skrenta developed the computer virus known as Elk Cloner. When Skrenta shared computer games and software with his companions, he frequently modified the floppy discs to cause the program to crash or display mocking on-screen messages. As a result, Skrenta acquired a reputation among his friends for playing practical jokes. Many of his friends simply stopped accepting floppy discs from him as a result of this reputation. Skrenta came up with ideas for ways to modify floppy discs without actually touching or damaging them. Skrenta learned how to have his Apple II computer's messages automatically launched when he was on Christmas break from Mt. Lebanon High School in Mt. Lebanon, Pennsylvania. He created a boot sector virus, which he started spreading among his high school friends and a nearby computer club in early 1982 through a gaming CD. Skrenta used social engineering strategies in this situation, and the victims thought it was just a game.

Scientist Joseph Popp created the AIDS Trojan and distributed 20,000 infected CDs to attendees of the AIDS conference held by the World Health Organization in 1989. The discs were marked "AIDS Information - Introductory Diskettes," and they came with leaflets that stated that the software would "Adversely affect other program applications" and that users would be responsible for any resulting costs as well as potential damages to PC Cyborg Corporation and that their microcomputer would cease to operate normally. The attackers exploited the use of a diskette with details on the AIDS virus to gain access to a computer system using social engineering techniques. A harmful program called a Cryptovirus, which ransomed users for cash by encrypting their system files, was generally present on the diskette.[1]

In 1988, Robert Morris is credited with developing the first Internet Worm. It affected thousands of systems and effectively shut down the Internet for over a day. The "Morris Worm," which took advantage of a few unpatched vulnerabilities on Vax and Sun computers, was possibly the first fully automated hacking tool.

Kevin Poulsen, a multi-talented hacker who went by the alias "Dark Dante," also dabbled in lock picking and forgeries. He narrowly evaded incarceration as a youngster, and after being hired by the research organization SRI International, he persisted in his criminal activities. In 1988, when a storage locker's unpaid fee led to the discovery of stacks of blank birth certificates, fake identifications, and a picture of Poulsen breaking into a telephone company trailer, his escapades came to light. When Poulsen ran away, a massive manhunt was launched. His most well-known hack occurred in June 1990 when he commanded the phone lines of a Los Angeles radio station that was luring the 102nd caller with the promise of a Porsche 944 S2. Later, after the phone lines for the show unexpectedly crashed, his case was covered on NBC's, *Unsolved Mysteries*. In April 1991, the infamous multi-hacker was finally caught.

Kevin Mitnick, a well-known hacker, broke into some of the most secure networks in the world, including those of Nokia and Motorola, using

[1] https://www.knowbe4.com/aids-trojan.

complex social engineering techniques. He then used the credentials to access internal computer systems. In the early months of 1970, this attack took place. In the late 1980s and early 1990s, Kevin was at the top of the FBI's Most Wanted list for hacking into a number of significant organizations only to test his strength. He was imprisoned in 1995, charged with stealing intellectual property, and found guilty of breaking into computer networks without authorization. After serving five years in prison, Mitnick now operates a security consulting business that offers security guidance to businesses.

Typosquatting is a form of social engineering attack in which the perpetrators seize control of an internet domain. In 1997, a typosquatter made millions of dollars from his website alone by creating the pornographic and political entertainment website (www.whitehouse.*com*), which was similar to the White House's official website (www.whitehouse.*gov*). Typosquatting, sometimes known as cybersquatting, is the practice of scammers purchasing domain names that are confusingly identical to those of legitimate websites. It was made popular by domain investor John Zuccarini. Users who enter the URL of a legitimate website incorrectly will be sent to a malicious or fake website.

A prominent instant messaging service offered by service provider America Online (AOL) experienced growing success in the same year. Hackers who pretended to be AOL workers used instant messaging to access users' passwords and take over their accounts. These cybercriminals identified themselves as Warez communicate and claimed to have created an algorithm that generated a random credit card number. Opening AOL accounts and sending spam to countless customers both used fake credit card numbers. The attack was classified as phishing by the Usenet newsgroup AOHell on January 2nd, 1996. The term "phishing" was first used and officially registered.

The game of the cyber world changed to that of cyber attackers once phishing was discovered. Phishing is a technique of social engineering that is widely used to obtain user information, including login credentials and credit card details. It takes place when an attacker assumes the identity of a reliable source and convinces the victim to open an email, instant message, or text message. The recipient is subsequently persuaded to open a malicious link, which may lead to the installation of malware, the freezing of the machine as part of a ransomware assault, or the leaking of private data.

1.1.3. 2000 - Present

The ILOVEYOU computer worm, which first appeared in 2000, spread via email attachments, and its victims were tricked into opening the attachment by using social engineering tactics when it was sent to them. The ILOVEYOU Worm made use of the fact that Windows' scripting engine was turned on by default and was developed in Microsoft Visual Basic Script (VBS). A variety of ILOVEYOU versions were produced with payloads that could overwrite data, alter files, download other malware, and send emails using Microsoft Outlook.

Tennis player and model Anna Kournikova was used by hackers to capture their attention and transmit malware. It is a method of social engineering designed to trick people into falling into a trap. The email attachment that contained the malware code was supposedly a photograph of tennis player Anna Kournikova. The attack was repeated in 2001 using the same Worm-generating script.

In the same year, emails were sent to E-Gold members to trick them into entering their login information into phishing websites. This was the first known phishing attempt against a financial institution. Despite the attack's lack of great potency, it did provide bank robbers a fresh angle to attack.

The popularity of commercial websites increased in 2003, and it is well-known that each website has a unique domain name. Attackers started registering domain names that were slight versions of legitimate e-commerce websites like PayPal and eBay. They then sent mass mailings to customers asking them to visit the websites, enter their passwords, and update their credit card information. The victims gave their credentials away via emails with phony domain names because they could not figure out the difference between those of real websites and those of scammers.

Attackers tricked victims into providing personal financial information such as credit card numbers, usernames and passwords for accounts, social security numbers, and other items in the following year by using a large number of fake emails and websites. According to data, the attacker can convince up to 5% of receivers to react to them by posing as well-known banks, online retailers, and credit card agencies.

Beginning this year, cyberattacks grew increasingly sophisticated. Identity theft, credit card fraud, and financial loss are issues that many people and organizations face. One of the biggest frauds in history was carried out between 2005 and 2007 by an American computer hacker and criminal, Albert Gonzalez. It was estimated that over 170 million credit cards and ATM numbers were stolen and resold. Gonzalez and his friends stole data from inside corporate networks by injecting malware into the databases of numerous business systems. Address Resolution Protocol (ARP) spoofing was used to carry out this attack. According to reports, he celebrated his birthday by throwing himself a $75k party and whined about having to hand count $340k after his currency counting machinery malfunctioned during his spree.

The first data breach occurred in the same year, exposing over one million records (DSW Shoe Warehouse). The Privacy Rights Clearinghouse received reports of 136 data breaches in 2005 alone, and more than 4,500 data breaches have subsequently been made public. Furthermore, up to 1.2 million federal employees, including some U.S. Senate members had their personal information on computer data cassettes lost by Bank of America Corp. A data breach occurs when information is stolen or removed from a system without the owner's knowledge or authority. An organization of any size may have a data breach. Examples of sensitive, proprietary, or confidential information that might be stolen include credit card numbers, customer information, trade secrets, and information related to national security. Social engineering techniques like phishing and pretexting are responsible for 93 percent of successful data breaches, according to Verizon's annual Data Breach Investigations report.

Social networking sites were found to be heavily used by people for communication in 2005. As a result, social networking sites were a popular phishing target because personal information on such sites can be used to commit identity theft. Samy is a cross-site scripting (XSS) worm that Samy Kamkar created with the intention of spreading throughout the social networking site MySpace. Samy was the fastest-spreading virus ever when it was released on October 4, 2005, since more than one million users had already run the payload in just 20 hours.

Attackers using social engineering in 2006 primarily targeted VoIP systems. A communications technology called voice-over-Internet-protocol (VoIP) enables users to communicate with one another via audio over an Internet connection as opposed to an analogue connection.

In 2007, a trojan-type malware known as Zeus was discovered and it was utilized to steal information from the US Department of Transportation. This malware is designed to perform malicious actions on the victim's computer and is compatible with different versions of Microsoft Windows. To steal banking records using form-grabbing and man-in-the-browser Keystroke tracking, the Zeus banking trojan was created A virus known as

"Koobface" targets Facebook's 120 million members who utilize the social network's chat system to infect PCs before attempting to collect sensitive data like credit card details. It was first discovered in December 2008, and a stronger version first surfaced in March 2009.

Anti-virus software is frequently used by people to protect themselves from malicious software that is unfamiliar to them. However, some antivirus programs have been created by criminals to distribute malware. In 2010, Google discovered 11,000 domains distributing fake antivirus software, which accounted for 50% of all malwares spread through web advertisements. Over 1.5 million websites worldwide have been compromised by the scareware distributed LizaMoon SQL injection attack since March 29, 2011. The credit and debit card information of over 10 million PlayStation Network and Sony Entertainment users was stolen in 2011, costing between $1 and $2 billion in losses, making it the costliest cyberattack in history.

More than 850 IT and security professionals from around the world responded to the global survey, which found that 86% of businesses view social engineering as a growing concern. The majority of respondents (51%) cited financial gain as the main reason behind attacks, followed by competitive advantage and retaliation. In the years following 2011, attackers of the current generation employed a number of strategies to carry out social engineering attacks. It will be challenging for anti-social engineering attack organizations to lessen the effects of this strike.

In an interview with SearchCloudSecurity, Frank Abagnale,[2] the world's most famous con man-turned-security consultant whose life and crimes were the inspiration for the film, *Catch Me If You Can*, said that while social engineering remains the same at its core, attackers are now employing different attack methods.

> Some have referred to me as the "Father of Social Engineering." That's because I learned everything I required to know when I was 16 years old - I knew who to call and what questions to ask - but I only had access to a phone. People are still doing the same things 50 years later, except they are using the phone, the mail system, the internet, email, and the cloud. There's a lot else going on, whereas they are still performing social engineering.

---

2 https://securityboulevard.com/2020/10/catch-me-if-you-can-how-to-protect-your-identity-in-the-modern-era/.

1.2. Defining the Term, "Social Engineering Attack"

The term, "social engineering" combines the words "social" and "engineering," where "social" refers to people's personal, professional, and daily life, and "engineering" describes the use of systematic methods to complete a task while attaining a given goal. It can be described as a collection of techniques and processes in one approach. The majority of the time, it is a non-technical intrusion in which someone is regularly persuaded to disregard the fundamental security regulations that have already been set at an organization. However, social engineering is a fairly prevalent cyber assault strategy in the digital age. Consequently, a wide range of definitions of social engineering attacks is being presented by numerous experts.

Social engineering employs influence and persuasion to fool people by convincing them that the social engineer is someone he is not, or through manipulation, Mitnick and Simon, 2003 wrote in their best-selling book, *The Art of Deception*. As a result, the social engineer can take advantage of people's willingness to share knowledge, whether they use technology.

According to the FBI, social engineering refers to the use of deception to target and influence people into disclosing sensitive information and then using that information fraudulently. Social engineering in the context of information security may also refer to psychologically persuading people to take actions that unintentionally provide enemies access to assets or protected information. Additionally, campaigns, voter groups, and others can be humiliated and embarrassed through social engineering.

For the purpose of distributing malicious code to the victim's machine, several attackers employed the social engineering approach. A social engineering attack is "a vast variety of malicious operations executed through human contacts," according to Imperva, a well-known cybersecurity company. It tricks people into giving sensitive information or committing security lapses by playing on their emotions. The attackers might trick an unsuspecting user into launching a malicious file or clicking on a link to a malicious website.

According to Chloe Pilette of NortonLifeLock, social engineering techniques, in contrast to traditional cyberattacks, focus on human weaknesses to gain access to illegal devices or networks.

It is also referred to as "human hacking" as a result. Cybercriminals that use social engineering to carry out their attacks have two goals in mind:

- The initial goal of the social engineering attack is to perplex the targets.
- Acquiring assets, such as money or valuable information, is the second goal.

According to Mouton et al., 2014, a social engineering attack has a social engineer, a target, a medium, a purpose, one or more compliance principles, and one or more strategies. It moreover uses direct or indirect communication. The following elements are included in this definition to explain the social engineering attack:

- *One social engineer*: An attacker could be a single person, a group of people, a robot, or another type of attacker, according to social engineers. The many categories of social engineers will be briefly outlined in the section afterward.
- *One target*: The term "target" refers to the intended victim of an attack, such as a person, group, or organization.
- *One or more compliance principles*: the principles used to lure people into the social engineering trap. Six principles of influence, including reciprocity, commitment, social proof, authority, liking, and scarcity, were proposed by Robert Cialdini.
- *One or more techniques*: the techniques employed in a social engineering attack to accomplish the desired results. Examples of social engineering attacks include phishing and smishing.
- *One medium*: To contact the victims, several mediums, including email, SMS, and phone, are used.
- *One goal*: the goals that encourage attackers to engage in social engineering attacks.

The conclusion drawn from all the descriptions is that social engineering may be described as a deception tactic that takes advantage of human error to gain access to, or assets from, a person or group of people. Additionally, social engineering attackers employ a variety of techniques and channels of communication.

1.3. Types of Attackers

The names of several social engineering attackers have been mentioned throughout the history of social engineering attacks. The individuals who launch social engineering attacks are usually referred to as attackers, con artists, cybercriminals, threat actors, bad actors, or hackers. An attacker can be divided into three categories: white-hat hacker, black-hat hacker, and grey-hat hacker.

- *Black-hat hackers* are also known as unethical hackers or security crackers. These people illegally hack into the system to steal money or further their own malicious goals.
- *White-hat hackers* also go by the term's ethical hackers and penetration testers. In order to secure the system from outsiders, they examine it and seek vulnerabilities.
- *Gray-hat hackers* combine elements of both white-hat and black-hat hackers.

The black-hat hacker will be covered in this section. Although the public is familiar with the attacker who has been named as a specific individual, it need not be an individual. A group or an organization might potentially be the attacker, according to the source of Wang et al., 2021. Currently, numerous organizations are in direct competition with one another over markets with comparable goals. It is unlikely that a single attacker from a competing company is responsible; rather, a team of attackers from competing companies is collaborating to pursue the same goal that is damaging to other companies.

Another misconception regarding the attackers is that they are actual people, however, this is untrue because it is possible that they are robots. In most cases, bots mimic or replace human user behavior. They work significantly faster than human users because they are automated. For instance, a computer program was created to simulate human-to-human communication via text or voice messages. The chatbot responds to commands or questions from users and carries out user-requested actions.

Artificial intelligence (AI) tools including Natural Language Processing (NLP), picture, audio, and video analysis are used by chatbots to replicate human discussions. One of a chatbot's most intriguing qualities is its ability to learn from its errors and previous encounters. This ability makes chatbots, also known as Smart Bots or AI Bots, clever and smarter over time. Chatbots are useful for both customers and organizations, but they moreover pose a number of security risks. A chatbot may be attacked by attackers and transformed into an evil bot. This evil bot might try to impersonate a real person in order to obtain another user's data through a bot that offers such services. According to speculation, chatbots will be used in future cyberattacks.

It is known that an attacker may be a real person or a bot, whereas the next concern is how an attacker could attack a company. There are essentially two ways: internal and external. A social engineering attack could thus be carried out by an internal or external attacker.

1.3.1. Internal Attackers

A person or group inside an organization launches an internal attack when they want to sabotage operations or take advantage of organizational resources. Internal attackers are able to easily breach any organization's security barrier, which results in significant financial loss for the company. Internal attackers occasionally steal sensitive data from the business and sell it to rivals or the black market.

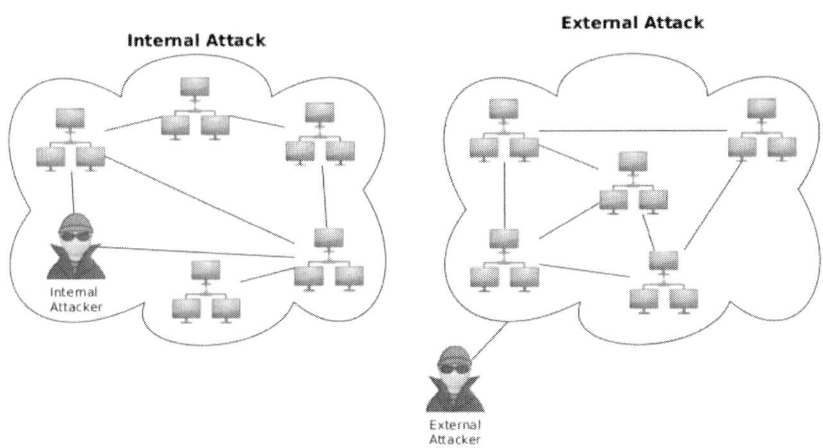

Figure 1.1. Internal and external attackers.

The case centers on Armstrong Teasdale, a company with headquarters in St. Louis that opened an office in Wilmington, Delaware. Four former partners of Elliott Greenleaf have a business with a Wilmington location. The four defendants—Shelly A. Kinsella, Jonathan M. Stemerman, Eric M. Sutty, and Rafael X. Zahraldin-are accused of plotting their leave from Elliott Greenleaf, copying and erasing company records, and then abruptly departing and joining Armstrong Teasdale. In addition to taking company information, they destroyed some paper records from their previous office.[3]

1.3.2. External Attackers

An external attacker attempts to wage an attack from the outside of an organization. They use various communication mediums to break down the walls of organizations and attempt to steal sensitive information. Phishing and smishing are examples of external attacks. The external attackers impersonate internal employees of a company and motivate them to disclose sensitive information.

Some outside attackers try to break into the organizations and physically steal the data. They might be dressed in cleaning attire, masquerade as delivery boys, or occasionally come to give critical messages. In certain circumstances, they design employee badges or generate an access code to enter the office. One of the most well-known techniques is tailgating, also known as piggybacking, in which an unauthorized person follows an authorized person into a secured area.

1.4. Why Social Engineering Might Be Used by Attackers

Social engineering strategies are increasingly being employed in cases of fraud and data breaches. Phishing, vishing, and impersonation are examples of social engineering techniques that are being utilized to make attacks more effective and unavoidable. According to Bassett et al., 2021, 93 percent of successful data breaches are caused by social engineering attacks.

A 2016 survey by Information Security Media Group found that 60% of businesses claimed they had been the targets of social engineering attacks the year before. 65 percent of the companies stated that the incidents resulted in

[3] https://digitalguardian.com/blog/suit-claims-attorneys-stole-destroyed-data-joining-rival-firm.

the compromise of employee credentials. Another 61 percent of firms cited spear-phishing as one of the most significant challenges. These assaults will not stop happening. Cybercriminals use social engineering and spear-phishing because they are successful.

It has been observed that social engineering attacks are expanding because social engineering attackers are intelligent, dedicated, and clever. After determining an objective, they conduct comprehensive research on the target such as search engines, social media, and the company's website, and collect information as much as possible. To be a successful social engineering attacker, it is optional for attackers to be skilled programmers or possess technical knowledge. As a result, many attackers choose to use social engineering. In addition to this, the following list contains some more factors that enable attackers to select social engineering attacks.

1.4.1. Humans Are the Weakest Link in the Security Chain

Social engineering is one of the most effective techniques because it deals with humans. It is found that technical defenses such as firewalls and overall software security have become substantially better at protecting against outside entities and adding extra security protection. However, humans are the weakest link in the chain of security. It is human nature for everyone to desire to assist others.

Furthermore, humans are prone to making mistakes because no apparent solution exists. As a result, people are unpredictable, they will commit the same error several times. At its core, individuals are the weakest link in the chain since they are unable to prevent themselves from repeating the same error. As a result, attackers can exploit this and obtain information. Staff found that 45% of respondents admitted to opening emails they considered suspicious and that the same number also admitted they did not report them to their IT or security staff.

Moreover, it comes up because of ignorance and lack of training to the personnel in the organization or any other mark. It is also easily accessible, as one just has to walk up and start the conversation. It is effective because it is intricate to detect. As a result, attackers employ social engineering tactics because they are effective. There is no patch for users who have not received adequate training. It may be possible that a security professional disregards what they know. DarkReading revealed that although 78 percent of

Americans claim to have received special awareness training, 60 percent still open potentially suspicious emails.

Attackers take advantage of staff members' arrogant confidence in their capacity to recognize threats. According to a poll by Webroot of 4,000 working professionals, 92 percent of employees predict they seek signs of social engineering tactics in email communications, but only 43 percent actually verify to observe if email links go to the correct places. Additionally, most employees are uneducated to recognize social engineering variations and frequently fall for emails that request credentials linked to the organization.

1.4.2. Social Engineering Is the Path of Least Resistance

In general, persuasion and manipulation of individuals require less effort and are very effective. On the other hand, other types of attacks take a long time to understand the essential design of the system and develop attack plans. Moreover, they require additional time to investigate the network or system for vulnerabilities. It is simple to hack organizations using the social engineering technique because it only requires the use of persuasion techniques and communication channels like email, phone, and text messages. Without using any digital communication channels, the attackers will occasionally make direct attempts at their targets via social engineering techniques. This could be accomplished by an attacker pretending to be a delivery person, construction worker, or tech assistant.

Lukas Yla penetrated some of the biggest Bay Area tech and advertising organizations in October 2016 by pretending to be a Postmates delivery boy. Although there was no malice intended, this impersonation shows how simple it is to enter places by merely dressing as the delivery boy (Gillett).

1.4.3. Social Engineering Methods Can Be Used to Spread Malicious Software

Malicious software (also known as malware) is any software that causes harm to other users' devices, websites, or networks, primarily for unethical goals such as data breaches, identity theft, espionage, and among other examples. Although many people are unaware of it, a significant percentage of malicious software requires user interaction to install or activate. One common method for convincing consumers to take such action is social engineering. As one of the most common social engineering attacks, phishing emails are thought to contain malicious file attachments. An attacker can convince a victim to open the malicious attachment by pretending to be an invoice or other crucial document. According to the Proofpoint, 2019 research, human factor, and social engineering techniques are used in 99% of cyberattacks to deceive people into installing malware. Some of the most common malicious software that spreads using social engineering emails are listed below (Bahgat, 2022):

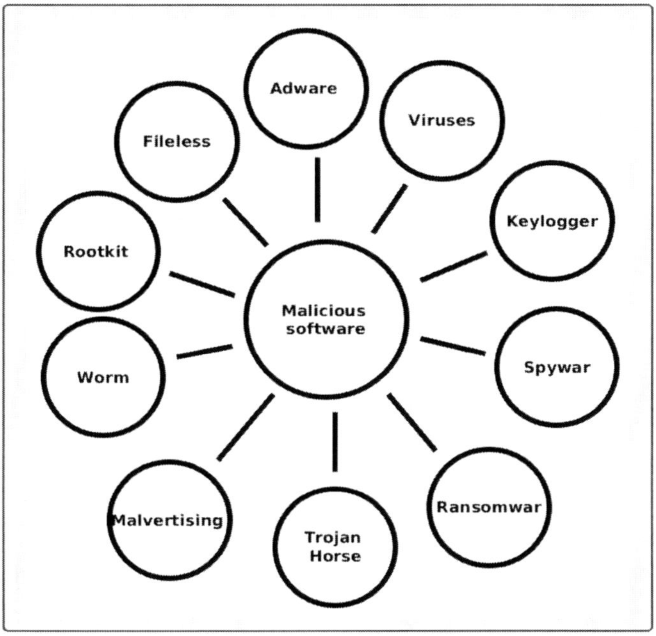

Figure 1.2. Types of malware.

1.4.3.1. Viruses

A virus spreads between computers and corrupts software and data. Viruses are a kind of malware or harmful software. Viruses can reproduce by themselves, whereas they require a human to spread and harm. The infectious code of computer viruses frequently executes when an executable host file they have attached is opened. Through networks, discs, file-sharing programs, infected email attachments, or other means, the code then spreads from the software or document to which it is attached. If a user's system is connected to a network, viruses may steal sensitive information or shut it down, in addition to altering data files. In addition to Distributed denial of service (DDoS) attacks and ransomware, viruses are also capable of launching other sorts of cyberattacks.

1.4.3.2. Ransomware

Ransomware is a sort of virus that stops or restricts users' access to their system, either by locking the system's screen or by encrypting the users' files until a ransom is paid. The fascinating part is that even if the user pays, it is unassured that the attackers will open the file. Infections with ransomware initially appeared in Russia between 2005 and 2006. Trend Micro reported in 2006 on a case involving a ransomware version that compressed specific file types before overwriting the original files, leaving only the password-protected zip files on the user's PC. Moreover, it generated a text file that served as the ransom note, alerting customers that the files could be recovered for US$300.

An example of a ransomware attack WannaCry ransomware which was a worldwide cyberattack carried out in May 2017 by the WannaCry ransomware CryptoWorm. It encrypted data and demanded Bitcoin ransom payments from computers running the Microsoft Windows operating system. The attackers initially sought $300 worth of Bitcoins, but eventually raised the ransom demand to $600. The WannaCry ransomware assault warned its victims that their files will be irreversibly wiped if they failed to pay the ransom within three days.[4]

1.4.3.3. Worms

A worm is similar to a virus in that it has the potential to self-replicate, but unlike a virus, it can spread across networks without the help of humans, files, or host applications. Mydoom, an internet worm that spread in 2004, created a backdoor that allowed its developers to take over an infected system. The worm is frequently used in this manner, acting as the thin end of the wedge that allows attackers to fully access the computers of their victims. Additionally, a worm has the ability to corrupt files, steal sensitive data, and cause other types of damage by taking advantage of security software flaws. Sometimes a worm's main objective is to repeatedly replicate itself in order to consume system resources like bandwidth or hard disc space.

---

[4] https://www.kaspersky.co.in/resource-center/threats/ransomware-wannacry.

1.4.3.4. Trojan Horse

A trojan horse is a type of malware that masquerades as genuine software to obtain access to a user's computer. It might even pretend to be an antivirus, warning customers that their device is infected and instructing them to run the software to remove it. trojans can even impersonate trustworthy websites or emails by including harmful links. Magic Lantern, WARRIOR PRIDE, FinFisher, Beast, Tiny Banker, Zeus, Netbus, Beast, and Shedun are some examples of trojans.

A trojan does not replicate itself, in contrast to a computer virus. Therefore, in order for it to function, a user must download it through email or SMS attachments and other sources, then install it on their system. Its objective is to give hackers and con artists a backdoor to receive sensitive data from victims, including passwords, IP addresses, and financial information. The trojan software will remain in the infected machine until it is executed by the victim.

1.4.3.5. Fileless

Fileless malware often referred to as a non-malware, zero-footprint, or macro attack, differs from traditional malware in that it does not require the installation of malicious software on the victim's computer in order to infect it. As an alternative, it exploits flaws already present on the victim's computer. It is present in the RAM of a computer and launches attacks by injecting malicious code into trusted and often secure processes like javaw.exe or iexplore.exe.

According to Zhang, 2018, it can be challenging to prevent, identify, and eliminate fileless malware because it does not require downloading any files. This is due to RAM's limited ability to retain data when the user's machine is off. The infection is no longer active once the user turns it off. However, attackers can still take advantage of that flaw to steal information from the victim's computer or even add additional malware to make it persistent. For instance, to carry out more attacks, attackers can configure scripts to launch whenever the machine restarts.

Fileless malware is becoming more prevalent. In 2017, 42 percent of businesses polled by the Ponemon Institute reported at least one fileless malware attack. Respondents also stated that roughly 30% of the attacks were fileless. In addition, 77% of all successful attacks were fileless.

1.4.3.6. Spyware

Spyware is a form of malware that is installed without the user's knowledge or permission. It enters the system through an app installation package, a malicious website, or a file attachment. Keystrokes, screen captures, and other tracking codes are used to monitor and collect data. Once information is stolen, it is given to the attackers of spyware to be utilized directly or sold to third parties. In 2005 research conducted by AOL and the National Cyber-Security Alliance, 61 percent of the surveyed users' PCs had spyware on them.

Pegasus is spyware that can be secretly installed on mobile phones (and other devices) running the majority of iOS and Android versions. It was created by the Israeli cyber-arms business NSO Group. Pegasus uses a zero-click attack to take advantage of iOS versions up to 14.6. By 2022, Pegasus may read texts, monitor calls, gather passwords, track locations, use the microphone and camera on the target device and gather data from apps.

1.4.3.7. Adware

The term "adware" is a combination of the phrases "advertising" and "software." Any software that shows advertising on a computer, whether intentionally harmful or not, is considered adware. It is advertising-supported software that causes computers and mobile devices to show full-screen auto-play advertising, flashing pop-up windows, large banner ads, and misleading advertisements. Adware targets both persons and businesses, whereas it primarily targets individuals by promoting new games, movies, or offers that end up being fake. The ability for third parties to monitor a user's browsing history and target them with particular adverts is a feature of adware, which is comparable to spyware. The user's contacts, passwords, browsing history, and even credit card information may be stolen by more nefarious varieties of spyware. According to research conducted by the security company Avast, adware currently makes up 72 percent of all Android smartphone infections. The remaining 28 percent of malware was made up of downloaders, lockers, fake applications, and banking trojans.

Malvertising is the practice of a cybercriminal concealing malware within a legitimate advertisement. In this example, the attacker purchases an advertisement to display on a legitimate website. When victims click the ad, the malware is either automatically installed on their systems or they are directed to a malicious website.

1.4.3.8. Keyloggers

Keyloggers are designed to record every keystroke that users enter on a computer or mobile keyboard, creating records of every action. These are employed to covertly monitor consumers' online activities while they regularly utilize their devices. Keyloggers are used for legitimate reasons, such as gathering user feedback for software development, whereas they can also be abused by criminals to steal user data. Cybercriminals frequently utilize Keyloggers as a Spyware tool to steal crucial company data, login credentials, and personally identifiable information.

PandaLabs has identified Punkeypos as a new variation of point-of-sale malware. The RAM Scraper and Keylogger malware software are the two types of malwares that this new point-of-sale malware introduces into the Point of Sale (POS) Systems. Similar to other POS malware, Punkeypos automatically and without the user's knowledge installs itself on the computer. The Keylogger monitors and captures Keystrokes made at POS terminals in retail establishments. It simply records information regarding credit cards. The POS terminals' system processes' memory is read by the RAM Scraper. The information from the magnetic strips on the cards is taken and stored in the POS terminal's memory before being encrypted and sent to the hacker's Control and Command Server (C&C). PandaLabs has stated that this new Punkeypos malware version has infected roughly 200 retail locations that use POS systems.

1.4.3.9. Rootkits

A group of tools or programs known as rootkits give an administrator-level user access to a computer or network. These rootkits are installed into the host computer by an attacker using Microsoft Word documents, executable harmful files, maliciously created PDF files, or email phishing campaigns. These rootkits conceal their presence by utilizing some of the low-level operating system components, rendering them almost invisible to conventional anti-malware software. The term "rootkit" is a composite of the words: "root" and "kit," which refer to the set of tools to be used to create the rootkit and the most privileged user of the computer, respectively.

User mode rootkits, kernel mode rootkits, bootloader rootkits, memory rootkits, and firmware rootkits are the five categories into which a rootkit can be subdivided.

- *User mode rootkits* affect the administrative functions of the operating system. They have access to the highest level necessary to modify the user's PC's security settings.
- *Memory rootkits* conceal themselves in the computer's RAM, or random-access memory, where they carry out their malicious operations.
- *Bootloader rootkits* load the user's operating system when the user turns on their machine. An operating system attack with a bootkit can take the place of a legitimate bootloader.
- *Firmware rootkits* can infect the portion of a user's machine that is unconnected to the operating system. They may impair their computer's hard disc or BIOS (Basic Input/Output System), which are frequently responsible for starting up their system.

1.4.4. Victims Might Not Have the Right Safeguards to Spot a Social Engineering Scam

Three countermeasures, including *policy*, *awareness*, and *technology*, are required to identify the social engineering attack. Therefore, a lack of awareness campaigns, outdated technology, and poor policy are the primary reasons why people fall prey to social engineering scams. Generally, many companies are not keeping their network-level security mechanisms, such as email filters, firewalls, and other defenses, up to date as they should be. Due to these vulnerabilities in their cyber defenses, hackers and internal threats like resentful ex-employees or contractors may take advantage of them. As a result, businesses are vulnerable to a number of risks, including social engineering.

1.5. Attackers' Motivations or Goals

Everyone who engages in online crime has a motive. There are valuable assets (financial or otherwise) that any company or person possesses, therefore attackers may attempt to take advantage of them. In the world of cyberspace, social engineering attackers have a wide range of objectives. Bryan Sartin of Verizon claims that while hacker tactics have not changed all that much over time, their targets, motives, and attack sites have. Businesses continue to struggle with convincing employees to accept and be eager to actively support and engage in security awareness training despite investing more money than ever before in security. Financial motivation is widely regarded as a driving force behind many cyberattacks, but other factors inspired the attackers as well. Attackers are motivated by a variety of factors to conduct social engineering attacks; the following are some of the more prevalent ones:

1.5.1. Financial Motivation

Financial gain is regarded as the major inspiration for attackers to commit social engineering attacks. Attackers attempt to gain money through a variety of social engineering approaches because they are in need of it. Almost all financial institutions have experienced a cyberattack in one form or another, and the number of attacks is simply increasing. It is simpler, quicker, less expensive, and less risky to engage in criminal activity online than it may have been in the past. Financial firms are 300 times more likely than other organizations to experience them, according to the Boston Consulting Group, 2019.

Victims are frequently duped into disclosing confidential information through a variety of social engineering approaches. If the attackers are successful in their attack, people will have their identities stolen, their bank accounts will be emptied, and money will be taken in their names. As a result, many companies have suffered significant financial losses, which can have a negative impact on their economy or even lead to bankruptcy. Furthermore, some businesses' reputations are tarnished among stakeholders, customers, and the public.

Social engineering attackers have recently been found to be concentrating their efforts on streaming media services. For instance, by pretending to be Netflix, Amazon Prime Video, and other firms, attackers can get victims to pay their membership fees. Other well-known scams include Bitcoin and love scams, in which people are targeted through bogus profiles on dating sites or prominent social media sites to form connections, with the fraudster then requesting money transactions while preying on the victim's emotions (Isabel Arkvik, 2021).

1.5.2. Emotional Motivation

Many attackers are primarily motivated by emotions such as love, anger, Fear, and so on rather than to support a financial or ideological goal. When attackers feel emotionally attacked, mistreated, or socially rejected, they may use social engineering tactics to exact revenge on others, causing harm to their personal lives or businesses. As an example, employees who are dissatisfied with their current or former employers then they attempt to earn money, data, or the opportunity to disrupt a company's system. More threatening possibilities include a healthcare worker who inappropriately reads celebrity medical records to observe what treatment they are receiving or a hacker who attacks a website primarily for the enjoyment of the lawlessness of the act (Casey, 2015).

During the COVID-19 pandemic, more people were spending their days at home. Many were dealing with stress, anger, Fear, sadness, and loneliness at the time, and this feeling pushed people to become cyberattacks and engage in cybercrime. Their participation in cyberattacks regularly gives them an overloaded and fulfilling existence. However, some people are actively involved in cyberattacks in order to gain more knowledge regarding them. Although many attackers lack coding skills, social engineering is a straightforward process for collecting passwords compared to other cyber operations.

1.5.3. Commercial Motivation

Commercial refers to commercial activity, such as profit-making business operations and every business has its own ideas to operate its business. This is a type of motivation that is utilized to obtain an advantage over a competitor. Many businesses hire attackers from the dark web to obtain property such as procedures or techniques, locations, customer information, pricing, sales, research, bids, or tactics. Theft of trade secrets, bribery, extortion, or surveillance are all possible scenarios. In some more threatening cases, the current employee may occasionally steal proprietary information from their own company to compete in the future.

Industrial espionage is a tactic whereby attackers steal a rival company's trade secrets in order to gain a competitive edge. It is frequently carried out by an insider or an employee who secures employment with the specific intent of spying and obtaining data for a rival. Instead of being carried out by governments for the sake of national security, industrial espionage is carried out by businesses for commercial motives.

In 2019, two General Electric employees committed industrial espionage by stealing trade secrets to advance their careers. General Electric subsequently suffered many tender losses to the other companies. The attackers were found guilty and punished after a lengthy investigation, and they will each pay General Electric $1.4 million in compensation. Investigations revealed that the GE employees had persuaded a system administrator to grant them access to data they were forbidden to have, which is how they were able to download the trade secret-containing files from the business servers.[5]

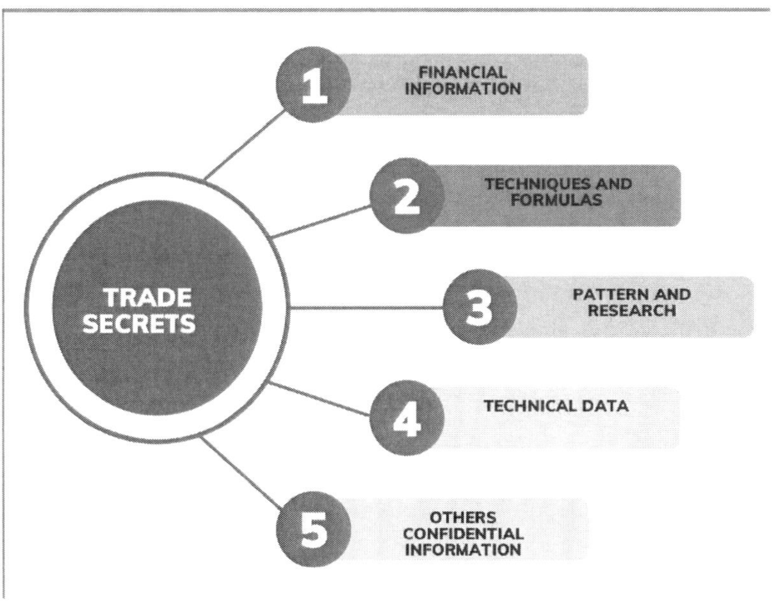

Figure 1.3. Trade secrets.

Another form of espionage is competitive intelligence, which looks at trade publications, websites, and patent filings to legally obtain information from public sources. Unlike industrial espionage, which is illegal, competitive intelligence is a moral activity that involves gathering information from a variety of sources. It helps companies understand the competitive landscape and any potential challenges.

[5] https://syspeace.com/internal-external-threats/.

1.5.4. Ideological Motivation

The term "ideological motive" describes a group of ideas as well as the idea of someone choosing an ideological stance to support the main idea, whether ethically or morally. Ideologically motivated criminal hackers, sometimes known as hacktivists, are criminal hackers that target people in order to draw attention to themselves or bring regarding the change. These attacks can result in high-profile operations. Hacktivism is primarily driven by an individual's or group's perception of what they consider to be "wrong" or "unjust," which motivates them to take action. Since the majority of modern nations rely heavily on their information infrastructure, governments take such attacks very seriously because they could have catastrophic results.

Some of the most significant hacktivist attacks in recent history have been perpetrated by Anonymous. Anonymous is a backdoor multinational activist and hacktivist group and movement most known for its numerous cyberattacks against various governments, government institutions and agencies, corporations, and the Church of Scientology. It takes on organizations and governmental bodies on behalf of the people. The Anonymous Hacking Group has a large following and is known for breaking into government websites and leaking private data.

In 2011, there was a noticeable increase in actions against the threat to internet transparency, as well as the group's success in breaching corporate and security agency servers, taking down government security sites, stealing sensitive data like credit card numbers, and defacing commercial websites. They committed these crimes to assist the larger cause of resisting internet control and government spying, not to profit themselves personally or monetarily.[6]

1.5.5. Recognition and Achievement

The sense of accomplishment that comes with breaking into a huge system motivates some hackers. Some people operate in groups or on their own, but they all desire to be recognized on some level. This is related to the fact that cyberattacks are competitive by nature and enjoy the challenge that their acts present. They frequently push each other to accomplish increasingly intricate hacks.

---

[6] https://www.checkpoint.com/cyber-hub/threat-prevention/what-is-hacktivism/.

Some of the most notable social engineers are listed below:

1.5.5.1. Kevin David Mitnick

Kevin David Mitnick is a computer security expert, author, and convicted hacker from the United States. He is best known for his high-profile arrest in 1995 and five years in prison for computer and communications-related offenses.

1.5.5.2. Frank William Abagnale Jr.

American author and convicted felon, Frank William Abagnale Jr. Abagnale preyed on individuals and small businesses, but in the late 1970s, he rose to fame by alleging a wide variety of victimless workplace frauds, many of which are now questioned. Abagnale co-wrote his autobiography, *Catch Me If You Can*, in 1980. The book developed a story around these alleged victimless frauds.

1.5.5.3. Susan Headley

Susan Headley was a phreaker and early computer hacker in the late 1970s and early 1980s. Headley, a member of the so-called Cyberpunks, specialized in social engineering, a type of hacking that involves pretexting and misrepresenting oneself in contact with targeted organizations in order to elicit information essential to hacking those companies.[7]

1.6. Impact of Social Engineering Attacks

Every year, thousands of businesses fall victim to some type of social engineering. The reason for the rise in social engineering is that human psychology remains unchanged. Social engineering attacks directly manipulate human psychology with the latest technologies. Victims make the same mistakes again and over again, making them an easy target for social engineering attacks. As a result, social engineering has a huge impact on business in the current generation as shown in Figure 1.4.

[7] https://wikimili.com/en/Psychological_subversion.

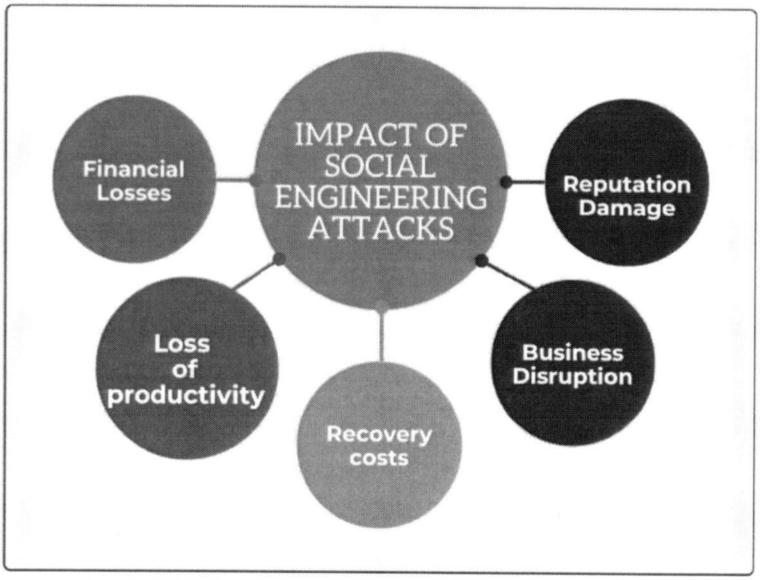

Figure 1.4. Impact of social engineering attacks.

The following are some of the consequences of social engineering:

1.6.1. Financial Losses

As was previously said, the attackers carry out the social engineering attack in order to profit financially. Social engineering's fatal effects on the company might include financial losses. The Federal Bureau of Investigation reports that from 2013 to 2017, businesses paid $1.6 billion as a result of social engineering attacks. Contrarily, Accenture published the 2017 Cost of Cyber Crime Study, which found that businesses spend an average of $11.7 million a year on cybersecurity and have 130 security breaches annually. The financial sector was the most commonly targeted by phishing attempts in the first quarter of 2022, accounting for 23.6 percent of all attacks, according to the APWG report.

1.6.2. Loss of Productivity

After a successful cyberattack, many people and businesses experience decreased productivity. The database containing employee records, workload, and other activities is damaged by a specific type of social engineering attack. As a result, top-level employees must put off other tasks in order to handle the attacks. Additionally, the employee requires to acquire training on how to stop similar attacks in the future. The largest steel companies in Iran were reportedly forced to suspend production as a result of a cyberattack, according to a report in The Hindu, 2022.

1.6.3. The Cost of Recovering after a Social Engineering Attack

Once the cyberattack has reached its intended target, the companies are severely damaged. As a result, businesses require funding to pay recovery costs from incidents like spear-phishing and ransomware attacks. For instance, if a corporation's database is breached by hackers, the company will create an incident response team, purchase software to stop such attacks from happening in the future and address the matter with consumers if their data was stolen.

The results of a global survey by Sophos, a leader in next-generation cybersecurity, titled "The State of Ransomware 2021," show that the average overall cost of recovering from a ransomware attack has more than doubled in a year, going from $761,106 in 2020 to $1.85 million in 2021. The typical ransom is $170,404. Only 8% of firms were able to recover all of their data after paying a ransom, according to global statistics, while 29% were only able to recover half of their data.

1.6.4. Cyberattacks Cause Business Disruptions

A successful cyberattack interrupts their typical business operations; they may incur disruption in product manufacture, shipping, or other operations. This can result in the organization losing customers or even suppliers. In addition, their insurance provider and the bank may wish to investigate their organization's cybersecurity measures following the attack.

1.6.5. Social Engineering Hacks Damage Reputations

If a consumer or a supplier of a firm suffers a severe cybersecurity breach, they will no longer trust that company. People do not want to jeopardize themselves or their information, so many firms lose a large number of clients and suppliers as a result of a security breach. According to an AON assessment, one of the UK's most high-profile cyber assaults in recent years targeted telecommunications provider TalkTalk, revealing that the personal information of over 150,000 consumers had been compromised. Aside from the immediate costs associated with the occurrence, the corporation lost over 100,000 consumers.

Summary

This chapter provided a basic overview of the social engineering attack, including its history, definition, and types of attackers. Furthermore, the attacker's motivations, why they prefer social engineering attacks, and the social engineering attack's outcome. The effects of social engineering on people or businesses are examined in the final section. The life cycle of a social engineering attack, or what steps attackers utilize to succeed at social engineering, will be covered in the subsequent chapter.

Chapter 2

A Social Engineering Life Cycle Model

Attacks using social engineering have many different life cycle models and taxonomies. A life cycle model depicts how different actions taken by attackers lead to the success of the social engineering attack. Attackers spend a significant amount of time researching their targets and creating attack plans. A social engineering attacker generally creates a model with multiple steps that are linked to one another. The attack's success depends on how effectively the attackers carry out each step. The social engineering life cycle model was initially created by Kevin Mitnick, and several researchers subsequently developed numerous versions.

This chapter covers the following topics:

- Mitnick's life cycle of social engineering
- Target identification
- Information gathering
- Attack preparation
- Relationship development
- Target exploitation.

2.1. Mitnick's Life Cycle

The most well-known model is the one Kevin Mitnick designed for his book, *The Art of Deception: Controlling the Human Element of Security*, which details the social engineering attack cycle. The four phases of Mitnick's attack strategy include research, developing rapport and trust, exploiting the trust, and utilizing information as shown in Figure 2.1.

Many experts, security teams, and companies mostly accept this model as a means of demonstrating how a social engineering attack works. This model works as follows:

- *Research*: In the first phase of the approach, the attackers select their targets and gather the information from a variety of online and offline sources, including social media, journals, blogs, websites, search engines, and occasionally Physical visits to the targets' organizations.

- *Develop rapport and trust*: Once the information has been acquired, the attackers try to win the victim's trust and rapport by using influential techniques like Robert Cialdini's six principles of influence. To get someone to do something that may or may not be in their best interests is the purpose of influencing them.
- *Exploit trust*: The attacker keeps attempting to gain the victim's trust for him to be believed. Once there is trust between the perpetrators and the victims, the attackers can begin to take advantage of it. The aim of the attackers is to obtain the victims to reveal private information.
- *Utilize information*: In this step, the attackers will make use of the sensitive data in a variety of methods, such as selling it on the dark web, creating false profiles for their victims, logging into legitimate websites in place of the victims, and more. Finally, cut all communication with the victims completely.

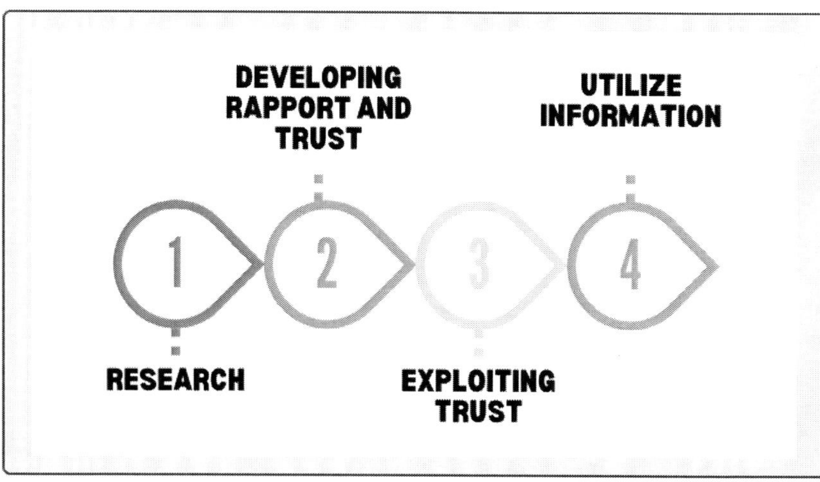

Figure 2.1. Kevin D. Mitnick's social engineering attack cycle.

A sequence of attacks is perhaps used by an attacker to get closer to their target because trying to reach the intended recipient directly is probably doomed to fail. Depending on the kind of attack and the target, the cycle could run through numerous repetitions. Possibly more than once will be performed on each stage. A privilege escalation attack is one that takes advantage of previously established familiarity or a reference from within the target company or information obtained from prior contacts.

On the basis of the Mitnick model, other researchers proposed numerous models in the succeeding study. The author Mouton, Leenen, and Venter modified Mitnick's attack model as depicted in this research paper, "Social engineering attack examples, templates, and scenarios," and added more components to the model. In order to understand the social engineering attack, this model presents six-core phases: *attack formulation*, *information gathering*, *preparation*, *developing relationships*, *exploiting relationships*, and *debriefing*. the workflow of the model is shown in Figure 2.2.

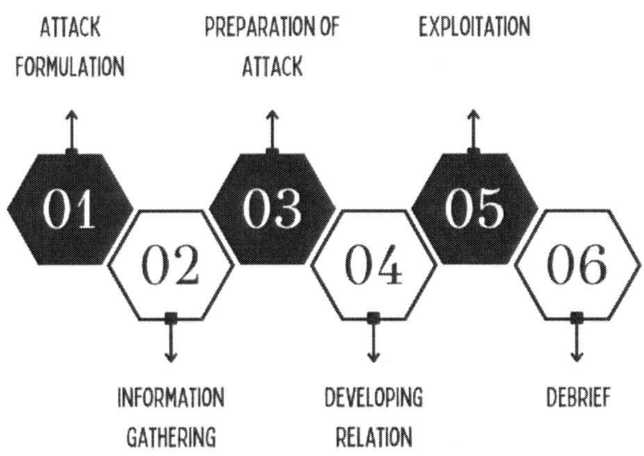

Figure 2.2. Social engineering attack life cycle.

Each element of the attacking model is explained below:

2.2. Attack Formulation

In this stage, the attackers determine their targets very carefully. Targets are primarily chosen depending on their position in the company and their line of work. Other considerations, though, can lead attackers to select a target. In the earlier chapters, a basic explanation of the social engineering attacker's motivation was provided. For example, monetary gain, access to business information, fun, and retribution are common motivates.

Social engineering attacks are a global problem that affects every area of the company. According to Statista Research Department, of the 688 recorded breaches in the first half of 2018, 309 affected businesses, while 181 affected institutions involved in medicine or healthcare. Financial, banking, and credit institutions made up the top three (84 breaches), and the government and military made up the remaining five top targets with 49 and 45 breaches, respectively. These sectors are the ones the attackers most frequently try to attack. It will be stated below whom the attackers will target out of the numerous people that work in these fields. These are a few of the targets that attackers attempt through social engineering attacks:

2.2.1. Ordinary People or Persons

It is a common misconception among us that attackers primarily target prominent users, but this is untrue. Since most people are unaware of social engineering attacks, attackers target common users or clients. For instance, students, farmers, senior citizens, the self-employed, and other users are involved on social networking sites, chatting, and conducting various online transactions. They maintain their information on many internet sites, which provides attackers access to their data through a back door. The attackers persuade the victims into disclosing their private credentials using this information. It can be estimated that half of the computer users have fallen victim to some sort of social engineering attack. The following people are highly targeted by attackers.

2.2.1.1. Senior Citizens

Senior citizens are one of the main social engineering targets. According to a business-standard report, Tsaaro's poll on privacy among senior citizens indicated that senior citizens are unable to protect their personal information online and have a limited understanding of privacy issues. Attackers might, for instance, phone a senior citizens person pretending to be their grandson and request financial assistance. The attackers requested the grandma not inform anyone once they collect the money. Numerous attackers target senior citizens who seek insurance, senior citizen, health benefits, and other benefits.

2.2.1.2. Students

Students are easily influenced by social engineering attackers because they are immature, unaware of cyberattacks, and uninformed. The Identity theft Resource Center (ITRC) claims that students are a prime target for social engineering attacks. For the following reasons, attackers choose to target students:[8]

- A student might or might not recall applying for a scholarship when they receive a call informing them that they have been selected. All the caller needs to deposit the money is the student's bank account details.
- Attackers may use alluring job offers to attempt to take the identities of unwary students. These thieves might target a student's financial resources, private information, or even physical security.
- A student can receive a call from someone posing as a school representative informing them that their tuition or other fees are past due. The victim receives a phone call demanding immediate payment or faces severe repercussions, such as being dismissed from all classes.
- False promises to pay off student loan debt and reduce monthly payments were used by the attackers to entice their victims.
- Criminals are aware of the possible needs of college students, such as a new apartment, textbooks, or moving services. They are also aware of the possibility of using attractive offers to entice students, requesting advance money, and then never actually delivering the goods or services.

2.2.1.3. Others

Farmers and the self-employed are currently the targets of social engineering attacks. Many attackers offer farmers various fraudulent schemes in an effort to get them to apply using their credentials. Loan, insurance, tax, health, and voter fraud are common examples of social engineering attacks.

---

[8] https://www.idwatchdog.com/education/9-college-student-identity-scams/.

2.2.2. Employees or Staff

A person who is employed to work for someone or a business, whether in the public or private sector, and who receives payment in return for their services is called an employee. In an organization, employees are divided into various levels based on their experience and skills including entry-level, intermediate, mid-level, and senior or executive level.

Attackers frequently target all staff levels inside a business using social engineering scams. Attackers require information regarding the businesses that employees are in charge of managing, despite the fact that money is the main motivation. Entry-level personnel maintain very little information, whereas senior or executive-level employees maintain very sensitive data.

2.2.2.1. Entry-Level Employees

Entry-level employment in a corporation often does not require experience, training, or a higher degree of education. It offers individuals the opportunity to study and develop experience and is frequently filled by recent graduates. Due to their lack of familiarity with the company's policies and procedures, this group of employees is a prime target for social engineering attacks. In addition, they have no special training in cyber security. The main issue is that because they are unaware of other employees, the attackers act like them and try to get information. To establish communication with the other employees and conduct the cyberattack, the attackers only require one person, and they generally attempt entry-level employees.

Attackers continuously research entry-level employees and collect publicly available information from different sources and attempt to attack. They can usually obtain the victim's name, contact information, and email address online, giving them a heightened sense of confidence that their messages will be read. These employees' credentials could be stolen, giving access to client lists and other data. As members of the accounting, management, and finance teams are likely to believe messages from entry-level employees, stealing their accounts will also open up a new social engineer attack vector for them. As a result of this, the organization can suffer a significant loss due to this entry-level employee.

2.2.2.2. Intermediate Employees

The intermediate employee has some experience in a particular organization. They also remain easy targets for social engineering schemes, even if they are somewhat aware of cyber risks. Many companies fail to recognize the importance of their personnel in addition to the technologies they use when defending themselves against cyberattacks. As explained above, attackers first aim for a single employee of the company; if they are successful, they then impersonate the employee and continue to be other members of the team. The systems of every employee are occasionally connected. A malicious software infection on one system will spread to other affected systems.

The Cybersecurity Breaches Survey found that 80 percent of businesses reported phishing attacks, while 28 percent noted instances in which someone impersonated a company online or via email, and 27 percent reported incidents involving viruses, Spyware, or malware, including ransomware attacks.

Lack of knowledge of security procedures is another factor contributing to employee prey falling victim to social engineering attacks. According to a survey by the Harvard Business Review, 20 out of every 30 work duties had an average failure-to-comply rate, with 67 percent of participants reporting failing to fully abide by cybersecurity standards at least once. The top three reasons given by participants when asked why they disregarded security restrictions were "to better achieve tasks for my job," "to obtain something I needed," and "to assist others to get their work done."

The following factors make intermediate employee's victims of social engineering attacks:

- Organizations lack adequate policies and procedures to protect themselves from attacks.
- Although some organizations have policies, they are weak, and no employees adhere to them.
- Employees are not receiving sufficient awareness training to defend themselves from social engineering attacks. An organization's weakest link is its workforce.
- Organizations lack effective safeguards against malevolent, phishing, and other types of social engineering attacks.

2.2.2.3. Mid-Level Employees

The mid-level employee is also known as the administrator of the organization. They have the experience and skills to run the employees. An administrator is an important part of an organization, serving as one of the crucial positions to ensure the smooth operation of workplace technology. An administrator manages and maintains the systems used in office environments, often assigned to perform day-to-day maintenance and installation of equipment throughout the office. While the employee is dealing with a hardware or server issue, the administrator is informed to resolve the issue and allow the employee to resume work.

The administrators are in control of the company's cybersecurity. However, such accounts can potentially put their company at risk for cyberattacks. For example, malware software has been installed on the company network by attackers in an effort to access all files and data there. In addition, attackers desire access to both regular and privileged accounts to create and destroy them and grant user accounts access permissions so that inside attackers can steal the information. According to Ekran, 2022, administrators can be divided into the following groups based on the nature and scale of the organization:

- *Database administrators*: Data, which can be both public and private, is the crucial element of every business. Public data is made available to the public, while private data is not. Any sensitive information that leaks could harm the company. Additionally, a database management system is used to store all kinds of data of the company. Therefore, it is the responsibility of database administrators to safeguard the main data assets of their companies. By acquiring the login information of the database administrator, many attackers try to breach database administration systems.
- *Network administrators*: Every device connected to the network, every application operating on those devices, and everything being passed across the network are all under the control of the network administrator. If malicious software is installed on the system, attackers can monitor the network and obtain details regarding secret communications. As a result, the network administrators ensure that the systems are safe from harmful attacks, that the installed software functions as intended, and that software appropriately interacts with one another and with other apps on the same system.
- *Security administrators*: A cybersecurity team's focal point is the security administrator. Installing, managing, and debugging security systems for a business are normally their duties. A company's first line of protection in spotting suspicious behavior, whether it originates from the local network or external internet traffic, is its

security administrators. Additionally, they create training manuals on security processes for colleagues as well as security policies.

- *Web administrators*: Websites are developed, maintained, and troubleshot by web administrators. The website would act strangely if the attackers installed malicious software utilizing cross-site scripting. Therefore, the web administrators address the problem before the client views the website. Failure to do so will allow hackers to steal the clients' data. Therefore, the most crucial guarantee is a secure and productive user experience. This could entail putting security measures in place, changing software, making backups, fixing software issues, upgrading material, and more. They perhaps design, develop, and monitor websites for a single business or a large number of clients.

Although administrators fall under many distinct categories, the company's policy will ultimately determine its position. One administrator may occasionally handle all the jobs simultaneously, or they possibly split up. Despite the widespread belief that system administrators are cybersecurity experts, they occasionally become targets of social engineering attacks. Generally, they occasionally create regulations regarding cyber-attacks, whereas they sometimes adhere to them.

2.2.3. Senior or Executive-Level

Senior or executive-level employees have critical information about the organization such as trading plans, finance reports, etc. A special kind of social engineering attack called a "whaling attack" targets prominent workers like the CEO or CFO in order to obtain confidential data from a business. Attackers may also use business email compromise (BEC) methods to persuade high-value victims, particularly CEOs, and other corporate officers, to authorize fraudulent wire transfers. In certain instances, the assailant poses as the CEO or another corporate executive to persuade staff members to make cash transfers.

Even though they acutely know the risks that technology presents, these senior professionals regrettably do not commonly adhere to the strictest cybersecurity regulations and procedures. The CEOs of their organizations, according to over 40% of IT leaders, have weak links in cybersecurity. In the same study, it was discovered that 76% of CEOs admitted to eschewing cybersecurity rules and processes to save time. Even though 84% of executives acknowledged being the subject of at least one assault in the preceding year, many still admit to eschewing security precautions.[9]

The attackers move on to the following phase after choosing their target, which is to determine the information that will be useful to them.

2.3. Information Gathering

The act of collecting information on a possible target is known as information gathering. The more information gathered regarding the target, the greater the probability of obtaining relevant results. Before beginning to gather data, the attackers determine what kind of information they will need to accomplish their objective. After making a decision, they employ a technique to gather data. Attackers should also consider how much time is available to complete the mission. Based on their motivations, attackers acquire the following categories of information.

2.3.1. Collecting Publicly Available Information

Attackers gather the information that is publicly available to support their attacks before targeting their victims. Anyone may read or access information that is made available to the general public. Blogs, forums, websites, and social media platforms are frequently used by internet users to publish their content. In order to be recognized in society, business, and community, people publish information. For illustration, employee information may comprise names, salaries, job titles, job descriptions, work locations, work phone numbers, honors and awards received, payroll time sheets, university e-mail addresses, and other information.

Attackers either manually or use technology to gather information. In the manual method, the attackers visit the user's profile in different sources such as search engines, social networking sites, organization websites, etc. In the technology method, the attackers apply several tools, like Nmap, Maltego, WhoIs, and others, to gather the information.

---

[9] https://carnegieendowment.org/specialprojects/fincyber/guides/ceo-level.

2.3.2. Authentication Credentials

Attackers mostly target authentication credentials, but they do not have easy access to this information. To figure out the authentication credentials, they look for hints. Authentication is the process of proving the veracity of a claim or the authenticity of a record. The typical method by which a user establishes their identity is by presenting their credentials, which are a shared secret between the user and the system. In general, users tend to utilize secure logins on financial websites but not secure logins on other websites. Attackers entice victims to sign bogus pages by offering them something of value. On a fictitious website that the attackers establish, the victims enter their information. Victims mistakenly assume that providing bogus information on a fraudulent website will not have any consequences. However, the attackers exploit this standard sign-out page to try and guess the strong credentials.

2.3.2.1. Username and Password-Based Information

The most common authentication method is username and password, which is also known as password authentication. Accessing a user account on a website or service provider, such as Facebook or Gmail, is a well-known example. Users must first authenticate their identity by providing the relevant login credentials, as shown in Figure 2.3.

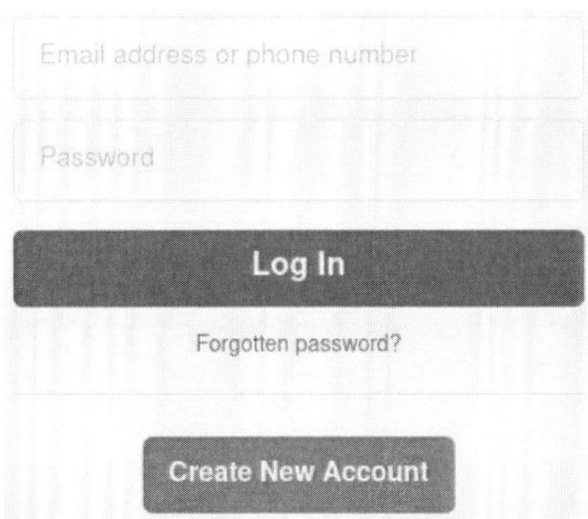

Figure 2.3. Username and password.

A screen containing a username and password is usually displayed while using a service. The data entered by the user is then compared to values previously saved in an internal repository. The service provider will enable users to proceed and provide them access to their account if they enter a valid combination of these credentials. This strategy relies heavily on online banking or financial services. The aim of major cyberattacks is to collect the username and password-based authentication. Furthermore, many victims use random passwords for irrelevant websites, yet attackers may guess these passwords from this hint.

Even though obtaining the username and password for financial institutions is challenging, obtaining information from other websites is simple. Attackers might, for instance, make false e-commerce, material, or blog sites, after which the victims can easily enter their details to access the site. Attackers use two different password-guessing techniques if they find any information regarding the password:

- *Brute force attack*: A sort of password-guessing attack known as a brute force attack is attempting every conceivable code, combination, or password up until the attackers discover the one that works. The duration of this kind of attack is perhaps considerable. A complicated password can lengthen the time it takes to crack it using brute force.
- *Dictionary attack*: Another kind of password-guessing attack is the dictionary attack, which examines the user's password using a dictionary of widely used words. Only the passwords on their list are susceptible to guessing by the attackers.

Once the attackers get the correct victims' usernames and passwords, they can log in with the victim's credentials and transfer their money to the attacker's account. Attackers use phishing techniques, such as building a fake website that impersonates a real website and requesting login information from users. The victims cannot distinguish the false website from the real one, so they enter their credentials, which are then stored in the attacker's database. To protect against this attack, several service providers offer multi-factor authentication, which allows the provider to verify their customer's identity multiple times.

2.3.2.2. Certificate-Based Authentication

Certificate-based authentication is a characteristic of the commonly used SSL/TLS protocol, but it is also present in a number of other internet security protocols. This is most noticeable in web browsers, which utilize certificates to authorize online transactions and warn users if they try to access an untrusted or unverified site.

Typically, the certificate authority (CA), which issues certificates to users and servers, is responsible for this authentication. Public and private keys are among the many details included in the certificate, but they are the most crucial. Now that the users wish to authenticate, they can provide the server with their Userld, and the server will then confirm their Userld. A random challenge (RC) will be sent to the users if the Userld is accurate. Using the private key contained in the certificate, the users generate the encrypted random challenge (ERC). Users send the server an encrypted random challenge, and the server maintains a database with a mapping between the Userld and the public key. Now, the server uses its public key to decrypt the encrypted random challenge and generate the decrypted random challenge (DRC). The user is authenticated if the RC and DRC are identical. If the attackers collect the information on the certificate, then they can communicate with the server as legal users.

In a social engineering attack, attackers can create a fake certificate by obtaining the CA's username and password and then approving the certificate signing request. The attackers can also construct their self-signing certificate and install the root certificate on the victim's workstation, causing the browser to display a padlock icon with HTTPS when the user visits the false website. In 2011, an attacker used the hacked networks of a trusted partner of SSL certificate issuer Comodo to create nine false SSL certificates.

2.3.3. Confidential Information

Confidential information is non-public information that users are expected to keep secret. It could be about the technology, business, funding, transactions, or other aspects of a company. It includes both commercially important information and personal data, such as trade secrets and company information. Many businesses engage social engineering attackers to obtain their competitor's information so that they can wager them. In general, three types of confidential information are highly hacked from the organization: employee information, client information, and business information.

2.3.3.1. Employee Information

The employee information is related to the personal identifying information such as an employee's Social Security number, home address or telephone number, e-mail address, Internet identification name or password, parent's surname before marriage, or driver's license number. The attacker uses one employee's personal information to attack other persons, or sometimes to steal the entire business information. This attack is also known as identity theft. The End-of-Year 2019 Data Breach report from Kleut reveals that there were 1,473 documented data breaches in 2019. This amounts to a 17 percent rise from 2018.

For attackers, personally identifying information is extremely valuable. They use this information to send phishing emails, make phony phone calls, and other examples. They occasionally use this information to create new credit cards or other lines of credit in the victim's name. They sometimes utilize the victim's current credit and debit cards to make unlawful purchases. Social engineering attackers frequently use the victim's Social Security number to file a tax return and collect the victim's refund. In most circumstances, the employer will fire the individual who is stealing.

2.3.3.2. Client Information

One organization keeps a lot of information about clients for business objectives. For example, financial organizations have clients' credentials, financial statements, and others. It is well-known that attackers attempt to steal sensitive information for their financial gain. Organizations use many technologies to protect this information. However, apart from the sensitive information, many other sector organizations retain clients' information for business growth. This information is used to find insight regarding clients such as what the customer or user thinks, what the customer or user feels, what the customer or user does, and others. Generally, this type of data is used to obtain more insight into consumer satisfaction and frustration, and to assist in determining whether or not a new type of product or service has a potential market, among other things.

For collecting this information, the organization may conduct many interviews, group discussions, online questionnaires, and other methods. An organization spends a lot of time collecting this information. Once the information is collected, the organization analyzes the information using various methods and generates business information like a trade secret. Some of the methods are widely used by many organizations to generate secret information. According to Kreimer, 2020, the top five techniques for increasing conversion rates come from client information:

- *Customer journey analysis*: a flowchart that shows the steps their customers take to interact with the company, whether it is through the purchase of a product, a retail encounter, an online experience, a service, or any mix of these.
- *A/B testing*: It is commonly referred to as split testing or bucket testing, which compares two iterations of a website or app to observe which one performs better. In a nutshell, A/B testing is an experiment in which consumers have randomly presented two or more variations of a website, and statistical analysis is utilized to ascertain which variation performs better for a specific conversion objective.
- *Usability testing*: it is a technique for assessing the usability of a website or product. User experience researchers can assess whether their actual users can use their product or website quickly and intuitively by testing its usability with a representative group of their users or customers.
- *Website personalization*: it is the process of giving website visitors unique experiences. With website personalization, businesses may provide users with distinctive experiences that cater to their requirements and preferences rather than offering a single, generic experience.
- *Cart abandonment*: Customers who add products to their shopping carts but depart before checking out are said to have abandoned their carts. Due to its significant correlation with customer conversion rates and revenue, the cart abandonment rate is a crucial business measure that retailers should keep an eye on. A high incidence of cart abandonment is a typical sign that there is difficulty with their checkout procedure or experience.

It has been seen that the client's information is crucial for business purposes. Therefore, the attackers try to obtain the client's information to comprehend the objective of their business. This kind of information is regarded as crucial information because it aids in the expansion of the company. Generally, client information is used to improve product design.

Data makes it far simpler for businesses to comprehend what customers desire from them, the exact goods and services that customers are looking for, and even the preferred methods of customer engagement.

2.3.3.3. Business Information

Business information is needed to target the business plan of the organization. Business information is referred to as "proprietary information" or "trade secrets" and this information is widely unrecognized and would normally be unavailable to rivals unless obtained illegally or improperly. Organizations generate this kind of information through a discussion with employees, clients, and experts. Organizations require many times to prepare this information. If the rivals get this information, then the entire efforts of the organization will go into the water. Therefore, they keep this information secret. However, attackers attempt to steal this information to understand the objective of the business. Every company needs to be aware of what its rivals are doing to stay ahead of them and maintain its market share and sales. A company should be able to evaluate the sales, marketing, and development efforts of competitors with the assistance of routine research and communication.

Many businesses use industrial espionage to obtain knowledge about their rivals. Industrial espionage is the secret, and occasionally illegal, technique of looking into rival companies to acquire a competitive advantage, as was described in the previous chapter. A trade secret, such as a formula or proprietary product specification, or data on corporate strategies could be the subject of an investigation. Industrial spies frequently just examine for information that their company may use to its benefit. An industrial spy could be an insider danger, such as a person who joined the company with the intent of spying or a dissatisfied worker who trades information for retaliation or personal benefit. Spies may also enter a building through social engineering techniques, such as deceiving a worker into revealing confidential information.

2.3.4. Hardware Information

Hardware information is required for attacking the hardware of the organization. Hardware information refers to computer system resources such as CPU, memory, disk, software programs, and most importantly data/information stored in the system. An adversary can learn more about the system and develop an attack strategy with the aid of system data or debugging information disclosure. Organizations engaged in criminal activity could be motivated to sell fake goods or steal confidential data for later sale. According to a 2019 report by Dell, 63% of organizations said they had experienced at least one data breach in the past year due to hardware security vulnerability. The following is a list of typical attack vectors that attackers use to compromise hardware.

Hardware cloning is a process of imitating information from one hardware to hardware. In a situation, one piece of hardware is damaged or lost then the hardware engineer makes hardware by imitating the previous hardware. However, the process is used by attackers. For example, access control systems that are tricked by clone attacks could endanger businesses by leaking information and costing them money. This kind of attack tries to trick a system by utilizing an unauthorized cloned card that is perhaps an exact replica of all the data on a card, merely some of the data, or perhaps just the identifying number.

Generally, attackers target hardware because of side-channel attacks.[10] The cryptographic security measures of a software program, which are based on mathematical problems deemed too difficult for people without the key to resolving, can be bypassed by side-channel attacks. Instead of deciphering their code, the attacker examines the hardware's operation by measuring its calculation time or power consumption while these algorithms are being run. In this case, the purpose is generally to retrieve information rather than to destroy a device.

Meltdown and Spectre flaws are hardware vulnerabilities that affect most computer chips manufactured in the past 20 years. Meltdown and Spectre make use of serious flaws in contemporary processors. These hardware flaws give programs the ability to steal data that the machine is already processing. While malevolent programs can make use of Meltdown and Spectre to access secrets kept in the memory of other running programs, programs are normally not allowed to read data from other programs. This may contain private images, emails, instant messaging, business-critical documents, and passwords kept in a password manager or browser.

[10] https://news.cnrs.fr/articles/when-cyber-attacks-target-hardware.

2.3.5. Network Information

Network information is needed to target the organization's network. The network information includes the domain name, internal domain names, IP addresses of the reachable systems, private or rogue websites that are part of the domain, access control mechanisms, protocols used, existing VPNs, analog and digital phone numbers, authentication mechanisms, and system enumeration. This type of information is extremely valuable to attackers to take control of the organization's network which leads to data loss, theft, and sabotage.

Attackers may use commands like "tasklist," "ver," "ipconfig," and "systeminfo," among others, to gather information regarding the network, processes, and OS in order to determine what kind of machine they were able to successfully infect. Attackers employ a variety of tools to gather network information and identify attackable security gaps. Nmap and maltego are the tools that many attackers employ for collecting network information. These tools will be discussed in Chapter 6.

2.4. Preparation of Attack

In this step, attackers must properly organize their attack before launching it. If the plan is insufficient, the targeted users will recognize the attacker's strategy and the attacker's objective will not be achieved. As a result, they accurately assess the target's information and set up the attack, and employ an offensive strategy based on their plan. Attackers employ a variety of attack strategies to carry out social engineering attacks. In general, the attackers used six different sorts of approaches: physical, social, reverse social engineering, technological, and socio-technical. Here is a quick overview of these approaches:

- *Physical approach*: The information is physically gathered by the attackers from the victims. An instance would be a dumpster diving attack.
- *Social approach*: To reveal their information, the attackers use psychological manipulation. Attacks like impersonation, for instance.

- *Reverse social engineering approach*: The attackers do not approach the targets to request information. The victim is tricked into communicating with the attacker on her own instead. Recommendations attack, as an illustration.
- *Technical approach*: The attackers use technologies to collect the information. Third-Party Applications, as an illustration.
- *Socio-technical approach*: The socio-technical approach combines the social approach and the technological method. Attacks like phishing are an example.

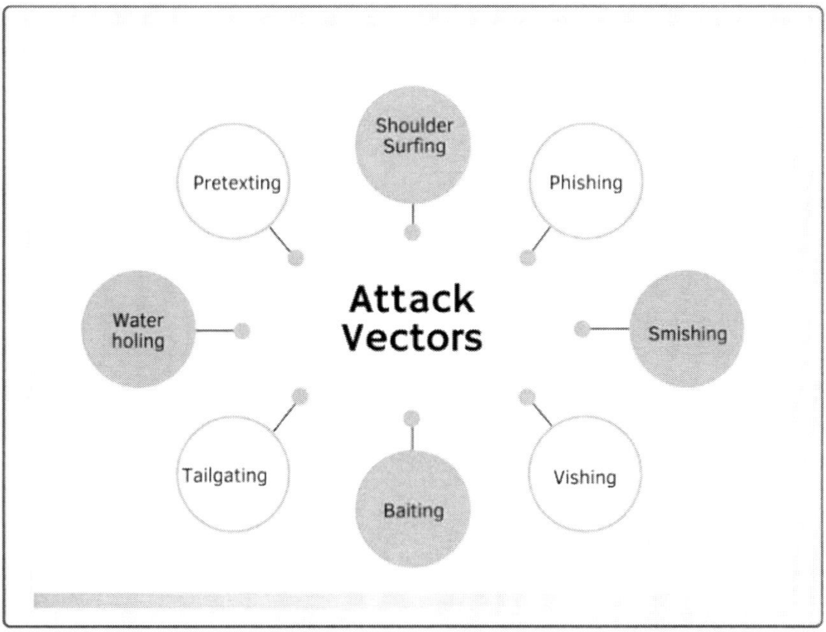

Figure 2.4. Attack vectors.

The attack vectors for these approaches as shown in Figure 2.4. As an example, let's look at a phishing attack that involves the use of a bogus website by attackers. Let's say that a bank employee is the target of the attackers and that he has an SBI bank account. The attackers then mimic the SBI website's design to create a fake website that looks like an authentic website. Apart from the URL, attackers imitate every piece of data from the bank website. The attackers in this scenario might employ the typosquatting approach. By using the typosquatting strategy, attackers can construct a domain that is only vaguely related to the real one, which many users will overlook. The attackers have finished creating the fake website and URL and are now ready to begin their attacks. However, they must first get in touch with the victims via emails, SMS, calls, social media, and any other relevant channels. Initial exchanges between the attackers and victims occur across communication channels.

Apart from digital communication, the attackers frequently try to physically enter the company in order to grab sensitive documents. They need to create fake employee identification cards, access keys, delivery boy costumes, housekeeping records, and other information for this purpose. Sometimes they wait at the organization's entrance, and when a real employee comes in, the assailant comes in behind him. Other times, they pretend to be there to deliver a crucial message. The next section will discuss how to communicate with the victims.

2.5. Developing Relations

Once the information has been obtained, the attackers can utilize it to establish a rapport with the target or another important person, which can aid in a successful attack. Attackers primarily use the six principles of influence from the book of Robert Cialdini. Professor Robert Cialdini claims in this book that certain triggers can almost automatically affect people's judgments. The six guiding concepts are scarcity, social proof, authority, likability, reciprocity, and consistency. The fact that individuals still make the same mistake in modern times while using technologies like the phone, email, the internet, and the cloud in place of the conventional communication system. Though human nature is unchanging, technology is progressing. However, the attackers are still employing social engineering while other activities are ongoing. In the digital world, a wide number of digital communication channels are used to communicate with each other. Therefore, this section will discuss the various communication channels that make it possible for attackers to understand their targets.

2.5.1. Emails

One of the most significant communication channels is considered email. Email is almost universally regarded as an authentic form of technology for sending messages, files, and other types of information. Email servers receive, deliver, forward, and store emails. Email is accessible across both local area networks and computer networks, primarily the Internet. Over a billion individuals use email on a daily basis across the world. Email has grown to be a significant vulnerability for individuals and companies as one of the most widely used services.

The negative side of emails is that emails are a major contributor to the majority of current cyberattacks, including phishing emails, spear-phishing, URL spoofing, the use of malicious attachments and scripts, trojan horses, and many others. Attackers use social engineering techniques to the contents of emails and attach dangerous software, leading recipients to believe they are legitimate communications. However, as soon as the victims open the attachment, the virus sneakily infects their computers and steals their data. Malicious malware can propagate over an organization's entire network if it infects just one system.

Recent analysis from Thomas indicates that since March 2020, email phishing assaults have increased in frequency for 81 percent of enterprises worldwide. According to Vidwans, over 15 billion spam emails are sent per day, with 45% of all emails being identified as spam. Another study revealed that 66% of malware is installed through phishing emails. However, the intriguing problem is that 97% of individuals are unable to identify phishing fraud.

2.5.2. Short Message Service

Short Message Service (SMS), also known as "text messaging," is a service that allows users to send short messages to mobile devices, such as smartphones and cellular phones, with a character limit of up to 160 (or 224 if utilizing a 5-bit format). 65 percent of the world's population, or 5 billion individuals, send and receive SMS texts. The countries with the highest SMS users are China and India, with China having 1,081 million users and India having 730 million. In North America, approximately 292 million text message users are counted, or 80% of the entire population. Russia has the greatest rate of mobile users, with 89 percent of the population sending and receiving texts (SlickText, 2022).

Text message recipients are tricked into divulging personal or financial information by the attacker through social engineering techniques. Malware and Spyware that can steal information and carry out other unwanted operations are also distributed through links or attachments in fake SMS messages. The attackers try to persuade the recipient to act right away by including some sort of urgency, threat, or warning in the messages. Cooke, 2022 states that more than 3.5 billion phone users worldwide receive spam text messages every day from any number. Smishing is part of a phishing attack in which the attackers send phishing activities through text messages.

Figure 2.5. SMS phishing (Smishing).

2.5.3. Telephone Calls

A telephone call is used by attackers to directly request credentials from the victims. For example, the victims receive a voicemail notification from an automated system informing them that their bank account has been suspended and that they must contact a number to reinstate it. An automated system picks up the call and starts questioning them with a series of personal queries in order to verify their identity. In truth, the attackers are only compiling all the victim's personal information in preparation for identity theft.

Calls made over the phone are frequently utilized in social engineering attacks for two reasons:

- There are fewer security systems that monitor phone calls and can identify and prevent an attack than there are for email.

- It is considerably simpler for criminals to convey emotion over the phone, increasing the likelihood that they will fraud their victims.

According to FirstOrion, 2020 Annual Scam Call report, attackers are becoming more adept at convincing victims to divulge their personal information. According to the survey, attackers became more effective in 2020, mostly leveraging the COVID-19 pandemic to acquire personal information from millions of victims. According to Truecaller, 2021, 59.4 million Americans have fallen victim to a phone scam in the past 12 months. Vishing and pretexting attacks are the most common attacks using a telephone call.

2.5.4. Social Networking Sites

Users of social networking sites can interact with individuals in their social network by exchanging ideas, posts, digital photos, videos, and details about their own and other people's activities and events both online and offline. Connecting people and organizations is the primary goal of social networking websites. Additionally, it has created numerous business potential for businesses and enterprises. The act of social networking involves increasing one's interaction with other people, usually through social media platforms like Facebook, Twitter, Instagram, LinkedIn, and many more. According to the Global social media attacks rate among businesses in 2019, one in 10 social media attacks was directed against 33% of global enterprises. Comparatively, just 4% of all organizations in the world were the targets of more than 100 BEC assaults throughout the study period.

Social networking's rapid growth has made it simpler for attackers to perpetrate online crimes. The social engineering techniques used by attackers to perpetrate cybercrime. For example, identity is misused when an attacker assumes another user's identity. Attackers access information from social networking sites by using applications that request authorization to access that information. If a user permits it, they will have access to all the data, and that data is perhaps used improperly without the user's awareness. The reverse social engineering approach is one of the most dominant types of social engineering attacks using social networking sites.

All the various games and apps request the user for permission before accessing personal information. A certain amount of access to the user's information is granted by the user to the app. As well as some of these programs that are running in the foreground can unintentionally download malware to the user's computer or phone. Through intrusive adverts, viruses, and malware frequently get access to the victim's computer.

2.5.5. Instant Messaging (IM)

Instant messaging is a group of communication technologies that enable text-based conversation between two (private messaging) or more (chat room) people via the Internet or other types of networks. Instant messaging is still quite popular today, and IM apps are the most frequently used smartphone apps, with over 1.3 billion monthly active users of Whatsapp, Facebook Messenger, and WeChat in 2018 alone. Instant messaging is now a widespread means of conversation, whether it is across the building or on the other side of the world. Attackers employ social engineering to cause Physical or mental harm using instant messaging applications. If a cybercriminal gains someone's trust through a chat platform, the victims may give personal information such as where they live, what they own, and even the hours they are at home.

According to Ferris Research, 500 million IM spam messages were delivered in 2003, more than doubling the number sent in 2002. Spammers prefer instant messaging. For one thing, the immediacy of IM makes users more likely to click links on the spur of the moment. Furthermore, because it avoids antivirus software and firewalls, IM is an easy way to spread not only commercial messages but also viruses and other malware.

2.5.6. Blogs

A blog is a frequently updated website or web page written in an informal or conversational style that is often operated by a person or small group. With blogs covering many topics and facets of life around the world, blogging has unquestionably grown to be a significant part of the internet world. The attackers are continuously targeting the blog because it has approximately 409 million users who observe more than 19.0 billion pages a month, and 53.6 million new articles are published each month, according to WordPress.

Attackers are sophisticated, and creative, and use a variety of social engineering tactics to attempt the blog. ZAHARIA, 2015 claims that the blog can be attacked with the techniques described below:

- Self-hosted blogs are susceptible to malware infection through the web hosting control panel. Users can manage their servers and hosted services through a web-based interface called a web hosting control panel, which is offered by web hosting companies. It primarily contains a web server, database, or file management that could become infected by malware.
- It has been observed that many blogs allow advertisers to promote their items. However, it is also conceivable that it may use the Malvertising mechanism to spread the malware. Malvertising, as defined in the previous chapter, is an attack in which criminals insert harmful code into trusted internet advertising networks.
- The administrator account's credentials have been hacked by certain skilled attackers, who then steal user data.
- The HTML of the blog may occasionally be attacked with malicious code. Anyone who visits the blog can thereby download the malware onto their computer.
- Additionally, it is feasible for malware to infect users' preferred blogging platforms through plugins and other third-party applications.

2.5.7. Forums

Forums are online discussion forums where users can post and comment on various topics. It operates in real-time, which means that when a comment or message is posted, it is immediately published for all to view. A blog and a forum are both online, but a blog contains posts and comments that its authors have written and is organized. On the other hand, in a forum, user-generated topics and comments are divided into a number of sub-forums. Like blogs, forums can also become infected with malware, except here, attackers publish malicious links and bogus websites. Furthermore, social engineering techniques are used in the comments to lure readers into the trap. The most popular forums include Reddit, Quora, and Stack Overflow.

Quora is a prominent Q&A website where anyone can pose a question and receive an answer. In 2018, Quora's security update revealed that one of its systems had been hacked, exposing around 100 million users' data to an unauthorized third party. The following information was disclosed for the 100 million users: 1. account information such as name, email address, encrypted password, and data imported from linked networks when approved by users, 2. Open content and behaviors like questions, replies, comments, and upvotes, and 3. private content and behaviors such as response requests, downvotes, and direct communications.[11]

2.6. Exploitation

Once the attackers are able to establish a friendship with the victims, they start to gather information about them in order to abuse them. Although this information is utilized for financial purposes, depending on the users' objectives, it perhaps used in a variety of ways:

- *Authentication information*: The attackers exploit the authentication information of victims to login into the genuine website in the place of the original person. If the website is a financial website, then they withdraw and transfer money to their own account.
- *Personal information*: Personal information is used to gain benefits at the victim's expense. Identity thieves possibly drain the victim's bank and investment accounts, open new credit lines, get utility services, steal the victim's tax refund, use the victim's insurance information to obtain medical treatments or give police the victim's name and address when they are arrested.
- *Commercial information*: This stolen information can be used to harm companies. Generally, the attackers possibly sell confidential information to a third party such as competitors with a huge amount. This information includes trade secrets, business information, or personal information.
- *System/network information*: Criminals can try to gain access to company networks to spy on them and infect them with malware.
- *Policy information*: Every organization has some kind of policy to operate effectively and successfully. It provides guidance, consistency, accountability, efficiency, and clarity on how an

[11] https://www.bleepingcomputer.com/news/security/quora-hacked-100-million-users-data-exposed/.

organization operates. In many cases, the attackers steal this information to sell the new startup organizations.

- *Media information*: Attackers can intercept personal media assets, including photographs, videos, and other files, and steal secret data in exchange for money to keep the material from being made public. Additionally, they have the ability to lock people out of their own devices or encrypt sensitive data, and then demand ransom in return for access.
- *Research information*: This category of information is used for research purposes. In the current generation, datasets, research papers, and others for research are crucial to evaluate their proposal model, and it is uneasily available to all people. Therefore, attackers possibly exploit the publishers and journals for stealing information without paying an amount for it.

2.7. Debriefing

The outcome of the social engineering attack will depend on this phrase. Due to this, two situations develop at the end of the social engineering attack. In the first instance, the attacker succeeds in making the victim feel good about themselves for assisting someone else, which increases the likelihood that future contact will occur. It is possible that the information the attackers have obtained from the victims is insufficient to carry out some fraudulent actions. In the second instance, an attack finishes before the intended victim asks what's going on. As a result, the attacker removes all traces of themselves online and makes sure nothing or no one is left behind. It is believed that the attackers were active only for 2 or 3 days.

Summary

Social engineering attack tactics were discussed in this chapter. There are various phases that can be used to carry out this attack, as has been observed. In the initial step of an attack formulation, the attackers must identify the targets they intend to assault. Information that will be utilized for fraud is gathered in the second step. Attacking vectors, such as social engineering tactics, are included in the third step of attack preparation. Establishing a relationship, which involves a channel of communication with the victims, is the fourth phase. Collecting sensitive data from victims in order to take advantage of them is the fifth phase. A pass-or-fail outcome determines whether social engineering was successful in its goal.

Chapter 3

Principles of Social Engineering

Although social engineering attackers may use various technologies, they still adhere to the same general principles. It is impossible for victims to predict where the next attack will come from. Six principles of influence were proposed by Robert Cialdini, a behavioral psychologist and author of the 1984 book, *Influence: The Psychology of Persuasion*. In this book, the author examines the factors that affect people's decisions, particularly when it comes to sales and purchases. On the other side, attackers employed their principles in a social engineering attack to influence and persuade people into the social engineering trap. People continue to fall prey to social engineering attacks despite the fact that they have been around for a century because these principles are so crucial to persuasion.

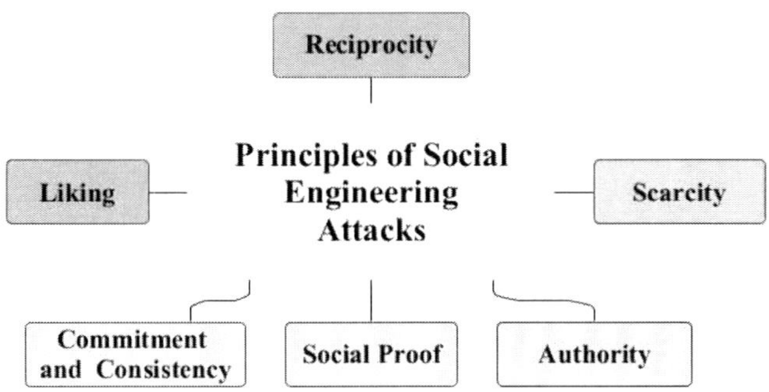

Figure 3.1. Six principles of influence.

This chapter will cover the following topics:

- Reciprocity principle
- Commitment and consistency principle
- Social proof principle
- Authority principle
- Liking principle
- Scarcity principle.

Greed, Curiosity, Urgency, Helpfulness, Fear, Sympathy/Empathy, Repetition.

3.1. Reciprocity: Give a Little Something in Exchange for Something in Return

According to Cialdini's first persuasion principle, people are naturally inclined to repay favors and debts and to treat others the same way that they have treated them. Psychology highlights that this is because people simply dislike feeling indebted to others. The Latin word *reciprocus* refers to giving and receiving and signifies going back and forth (retro-procus). In other words, the idea of equal giving and taking is not logically equivalent to the meaning that mutual exchange represents. Generally, reciprocity is a process of exchanging things with other people in order to gain a mutual benefit. According to the concept of reciprocity, people are compelled to give discounts or concessions to others if they have previously received benefits from those same individuals. Many mobile payment providers, like Google Pay, PhonePe, and Paytm offer coupons to customers who complete transactions through their applications. Customers may use these coupons for subsequent transactions to earn additional coupons, and so on.

3.1.1. Types of Reciprocity

Reciprocity is the exchange of goods and services with others for their mutual benefit, particularly when it comes to rights given to individuals, one group, or nation by another. Each reciprocal exchange is unique. Overall, three different types of reciprocity occur in human society all over the world, according to an anthropologist by the name of Sahlins, 2013, and they are generalized, balanced, and negative.

3.1.1.1. Generalized Reciprocity

This form of reciprocity is common with friends and family. Simply put, people help one another out of a sense of reciprocity. There is no requirement for a favor to be returned. Without expecting anything in return, parents assist their children with their financial needs for business, education, and other expenses. Generally, selflessness has a connection to this kind of reciprocity. For instance, if you purchase your friend a gift when you are out shopping, you might anticipate that he will give you one at a later date. However, if he insisted on purchasing you a gift at the same time that you bought him one, you would probably be highly annoyed. By doing so, he would be indicating that he is uninterested in engaging in an ongoing reciprocal interaction with you. It is a kind of rejection of your friendship gift.

3.1.1.2. Balanced Reciprocity

This type requires calculating the transaction's value and expecting a return favor within a set time period. Bihu presents, for instance, are frequently a form of roughly equal reciprocity in Assam (a state of India). There is a tradition that states that if you visit the homes of family members or close friends on Bihu and give them gifts, you will also expect to receive gifts from them. If you do not get them, you might assume that your family or friends are either not interested in you or made a social faux pas.

3.1.1.3. Negative Reciprocity

This type of reciprocity takes place when one side in the exchange tries to benefit more from it than the other person. One illustration of negative reciprocity is the sale of an essential item at an inflated price. For instance, one-person desires to relocate since they have a job offer in another place. Now when he wants to sell their furniture, his friend offers him $2000 instead of the $3000 he was hoping to get. He has no other choice, so he accepts the offer despite his reluctance. There was negative reciprocity because he exploited her predicament. Attacks involving social engineering heavily rely on this form of reciprocity. Attackers provide less for their victims and demand more of them.

3.1.2. Influence of Reciprocity on People

To determine how strong the reciprocity-related qualities are, an experiment was carried out by Regan, 1971. Numerous individuals pretended to be taking part in an art appreciation experiment with Joe, Regan's assistant, as their partner. The assistant left while the experiment was going on and brought the soda for the participants. Joe would encourage the participant to purchase raffle tickets from him once the first stage of the experiment was over. Participants were more inclined to purchase raffle tickets for Joe if they liked him more. Nevertheless, after Joe had given them a Soda pop and so made them obligated to repay him, it did not matter whether the participants liked Joe or not; the norm of reciprocity prevailed. Prior to making their request, participants have been seen to have given tiny gifts or favors they may not have particularly liked.

3.1.3. Attackers Frequently Adopt the Method of Reciprocity

Attackers who engage in social engineering make use of the reciprocity method to their advantage. They convince victims to give by promising something in exchange for their data. For instance, an attacker might send a user an email with a free voucher, Bitcoin, and other cryptocurrency or digital currency attached, followed by a request for account registration. Many non-reputable colleges offer financial aid to the hiring team in college placements so that they can choose students from their institution. Excellent placement encourages students to study at their colleges.

Pyramid schemes are one type of prevalent fraud. The attackers of this scam will claim to the victims that a modest investment will result in a significant payout or profit. It is also known as the Ponzi scam. However, the victims must also locate more investors. The "profit" that the victims receive is only the money that other investor invested. When the perpetrators run out of fresh investors or steal the entire investment and flee, the scheme is destroyed. Many individuals in India become victims of this con. Some attackers take note of this scam and invent a fictional company. They initially give clients some money to encourage them. After that, they kept extorting cash from customers while telling them that the users were their chosen partners. These new members then bring in even more new people. They themselves receive money from the participants at the following level as fees. The success rate of reciprocity is among the greatest of any persuasion strategies.

Another illustration of social engineering email is, "Your American Express account has been the subject of suspicious activity, according to our online security team. Please assist us in maintaining the security of your account by changing your password using the provided link" (Figure 3.2). Attackers create a fake American Express email and pose as a security team to encourage victims to believe what they are sending. Many victims believe that American Express is a trustworthy company, and they are trying to protect our account from suspicious activity. It is our responsibility to assist them by helping them reset their password using the link that the attackers offered. All of the information is saved in the attacker's repository after the users make an attempt to reset the password.

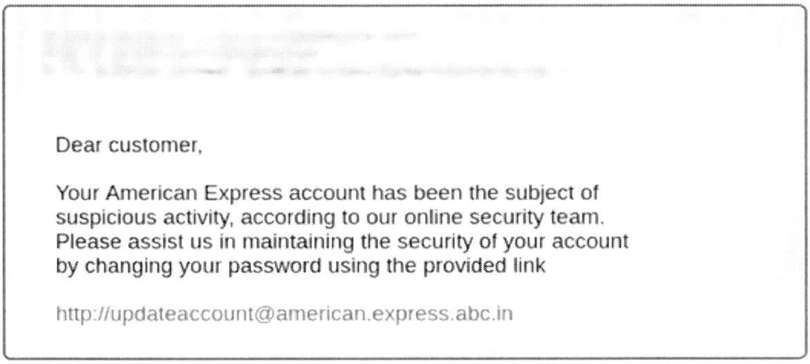
Dear customer,

Your American Express account has been the subject of suspicious activity, according to our online security team. Please assist us in maintaining the security of your account by changing your password using the provided link

http://updateaccount@american.express.abc.in

Figure 3.2. Reciprocity email.

3.2. Commitment and Consistency: People Want Their Actions to Be Consistent with Their Values

This principle explains how people want their thoughts and actions to be consistent with their values and conceptions of themselves. One of the most effective methods for employers to have an excellent impact on their workforce and improve the working environment for everyone is through the commitment and consistency principle. Any user who makes a commitment to something will naturally desire to appear to be consistent with that commitment. As a result of the initial commitment and consistency principle, psychologists have discovered that after we have made very little commitment to something, we are far more likely to make a greater commitment.

Thomas Moriarty, a psychologist, performed an experiment on a beach in New York City in 1972. A beach towel and a portable radio would be placed within 5 feet of a randomly selected person. The researcher would unwind on the towel while enjoying their radio before getting up and strolling down the beach after a short while. A second researcher would pass a little while later and take the radio before attempting to leave.

Only four out of twenty people tried to stop the theft when the first researcher did not attempt to encourage the person close to watch over their stuff. A simple request from the researcher to "watch my things" had a significant impact on the adjacent person's readiness to step in and stop the theft. Nineteen out of twenty people challenged the robber after he made this straightforward request.

Generally, due to concerns over their public image, many people strive to remain consistent in their profession. Higher levels of public trust can be attained through commitment and consistency. For example, many senior personnel in respected companies have a history of making promises and then regularly keeping them out of pride in who they are as people. People have more confidence in their decision after they commit to an action and are compelled to observe it through to completion. If they frequently cancel offers, customers will not believe them. Numerous firms experienced losses on both financial and other levels because of their commitment.

Another common example is numerous politicians making a lot of promises to the electorate before elections. While some politicians are able to address the public's concerns, many of them are not. Numerous factors, including insufficient funding and inadequate research, could be to blame for its failure. However, the main factor is the commitment's inconsistent nature. People will not vote for a politician again if they start to think that they are inconsistent in their commitment. As a result, the politicians lose the trust of the general public.

Many people conclude that they desire to keep their promises after thinking about this scenario of trust. This nature can occasionally cause severe losses, though, if they are identified by attackers. They attempt to persuade the victims into making a small-scale commitment initially and later on large on. In order to get the victims to look for a commitment, the attackers initially become friends with them and stay in touch with them. The attackers start using their weapons to harm the victims once the victims make some sort of commitment.

3.2.1. Commitment Used in Social Engineering Attacks

The fundamental reason social engineering attacks are still common is that people are still naive, irresponsible, and ignorant of them. In a social engineering attack, the perpetrators take advantage of people's need for consistency by asking for a small favor in the first email and a bigger favor in the follow-up message. People are more receptive to complying with larger requests if you start with a smaller one. Many victims are unable to cancel their agreements as a result, and they make mistakes. It could be more difficult for someone to decline a request for a bigger commitment once they are conversing with someone. A small error during a social engineering attack can lead to significant damage.

A typical illustration of commitment and consistency strategies is the con artist who starts by posing a question such as, "Do you want to save money?" Then, with a phrase like, "You mentioned you loved to save money," your reaction is reversed and reframed as a commitment to make a purchase. Attackers aim to lure their targets into a social engineering trap in this fashion.

The attacker must be constant in their demands. The attacker ought to begin slowly and gradually increase their information collection. Starting small and increasing with each new piece of information will make it seem natural to the victim and prevent them from seeing through it.[12]

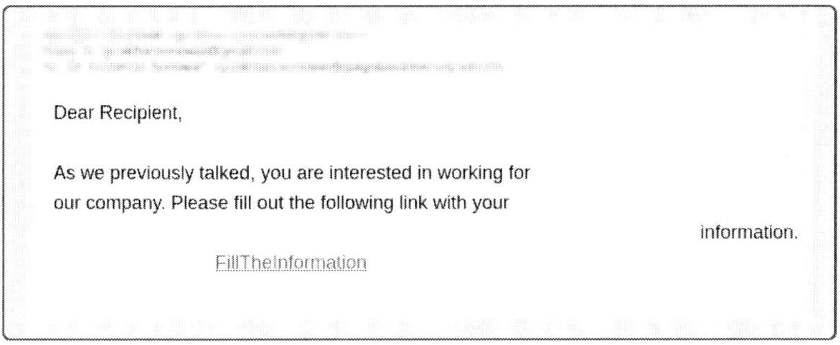

Figure 3.3. An example of the "commitment" principle.

3.3. Social Proof: The Sensation of Being Validated by Other People's Experiences

According to the concept of social proof, people will make decisions based on what other people perform. Most of the time, people make decisions based on what they observe around them. For instance, when people occasionally make purchases online, they first read other people's comments and product reviews. It is likely that people will not trust a company or product if it has a poor reputation or if their friends have expressed dissatisfaction with their purchases. Social proof is a strategy that is used by

[12] https://www.social-engineer.org/framework/influencing-others/influence-tactics/commit-ment-consistency/.

considerable groups as well as famous people. People, for instance, will purchase products that celebrities use because they believe these products to be currently popular in society. People primarily require social proof because of three reasons:

- An individual will follow the lead of others if he or she feels unsure.
- The person desires to do whatever other people are doing.
- People should not act in a certain way if others are not.

The social proof concept has a significant influence on the Fear of Missing Out (FOMO) strategy.

3.3.1. Fear of Missing Out (FOMO)

FOMO is a social-proof marketing tool that encourages customers to make purchases. It is an emotional reaction to the idea that other people have happier, more fulfilling lives than you do or that significant chances are being lost. 56% of users suffer from "Fear of Missing Out." Several FOMO techniques are as follows:

- It may display evidence of goods purchases by other customers.
- It might show a clock with the remaining time for the promotion.
- It may drive competition by indicating how many other people are considering the deal.
- It could promote experiences by displaying social proof of others liking the event or product.

Although the FOMO strategy works to get consumers to come more, it has a detrimental impact on customers by causing the melancholy and worries that FOMO causes.

3.3.2. Various Forms of Social Proof Have an Impact on People

People are prone to be persuaded by social proof to behave differently than they otherwise would have and to make different choices. Gui, 2019 identified the numerous types of entities, including persons and authoritative figures, that may provide different types of social proof:

- *Consumers*: Case studies or testimonials are examples of social evidence offered by current users or clients. For example, in a marketing environment, customer evaluations and product ratings assist potential customers in making decisions by allowing them to understand the experiences of current customers. Studies show that the degree of a person's influence over users grows with that degree of similarity. The cybersecurity team at SafetyDetectives discovered an open ElasticSearch database that revealed a planned false review fraud that was affecting Amazon.[13]
- *Celebrities*: Celebrities serve as role models for people. People will purchase any things advised by famous people. For product advertising, many large corporations use famous people like actors, athletes, and others. Due to celebrity influence, consumers frequently make aspirational purchases that reflect their ideal lifestyle rather than their actual ones. False celebrity profiles are abundant on Facebook, Twitter, and Instagram, created to mislead committed followers. The supporters of the real star are approached by con artists who desire money from them under various impressions.
- *Experts*: Companies will use a statement, review, or testimonial from an expert in their field to highlight the legitimacy of their brand. This works because when opinions are offered by experts in the field, people are even more likely to believe them. Experts may have positions of influence inside any organization. Attackers will pose as a bank, utility company, or other service provider and demand payment for an unpaid invoice. In some cases, they can compel users to download malware unintentionally, which mines their computer's files and sensitive data. The authority principles will go into more detail.
- *Crowds*: Humans naturally assume that something must be excellent if many people are doing it. When consumers download any software to their device, for instance, they look up the usage statistics. They consistently use software with more users. Another illustration is the fact that several restaurants increased sales of

[13] https://www.safetydetectives.com/blog/amazon-reviews-leak-report/.

particular dishes by 13-20 percent simply by designating them as "our most popular items."

- *Friends*: People accept recommendations from people they know, and trust much more seriously than they do other forms of advertising or promotions. A person will purchase a product if their friends or family members advise them to do so. 91% of people claim to consult friends and family members or online reviews before making a purchase. It occurs when an attacker places a real email address in the "From" line of an email to trick the recipient into believing it came from someone they know like a friend, someone they work with, or a business with which they would do business.
- *Certifications*: This kind of social proof occurs when an influential person in the industry endorses the products. For example, since 1955, India has used the ISI mark to identify industrial products as meeting standards. The mark testifies to a product's compliance with an Indian standard (IS) created by India's national standards organization, the Bureau of Indian Standards (BIS). Many restaurants display certificates on the walls that read "best restaurant by XYZ corporation" where the majority of the customers can observe them.

Even though these are just a few social proof approaches, many businesses use them. There are many other ways that people are using social proof to promote their products as technology advances. Similarly, social engineering attackers utilize these methods in their emails, SMS messages, and other communications to deceive recipients.

3.3.3. An Example of Social Proof

Bandura, Grusec, and Menlove, 1967 treated young children who were afraid of dogs using the social proof theory. The procedure was very easy. For twenty minutes a day, they simply observed a boy playing joyfully with a dog. 67 percent of the consumers began playing with a dog in a playpen after just four days.

Solomon Asch, a pioneer of social psychology conducted an experiment on social proof in 1951 (source: McLeod, 2018). In this experiment, 50 college-aged volunteers were informed that they would be taking a vision exam. The participants entered a room thinking it had other participants, but it included seven confederates, who were unknown to them. The next step was to display a target line alongside three lines (A, B, and C) and ask each participant to identify the line that was closest to the target line in length. The seven confederates would purposely choose the incorrect response even though the solution was usually pretty evident. The actual participant was the last to respond after hearing all the other responses. Asch discovered that throughout the course of 12 trials, participants conformed at least once 75% of the time, demonstrating how frequently people look to others for support and confirmation of the correct answer.

3.3.4. Social Proof in Social Engineering Attacks

Attackers often rely on social proof in their emails to trick their targets. They first gather data on their victims through official websites or social media platforms. Based on their knowledge, the attackers exploit social proof in the email's contents to increase the recipients' interest. Attackers may utilize outdated news as social proof by changing the date and informing victims that they must visit a malicious website to learn more about the topic. The attackers send the link to the victims, and many victims believe the information since the attackers employ a real organization signature.

Many people have fallen victim to a social engineering attack on an e-commerce website. The attackers create phishing websites by displaying products with more false reviews, comments, and so on. When victims observe the ratings and comments, they believe them and enter their credit card information on the website to purchase items. The attackers employ the Fear of missing out tactic with products like only one left, only a short while left, and others to support the message.

Many students are looking for colleges to pursue higher education. As a result, many fake colleges and universities solicit ratings from online users in exchange for money. Online users are unfamiliar with the real motive of the institutes and write only positive things about institutions or universities. Additionally, they promote these institutes through the use of experts, international cooperation, and other methods. Students who are being victimized read the review or observe the advertisements and register. They learned the truth about the situation after a few months at these universities, but they were powerless to act because at that point all reputable universities stopped accepting new students.

3.4. Authority: People Will Abide by the Rules

The authority principle describes a person's propensity to submit to those in positions of authority, such as legislators, law enforcement officers, physicians, attorneys, professors, and other persons who are regarded as experts in various subjects. In order to convey control in an organization, the authority is selected as one of the top individuals, and many of the workers in the organization follow the instructions that the authority offers.

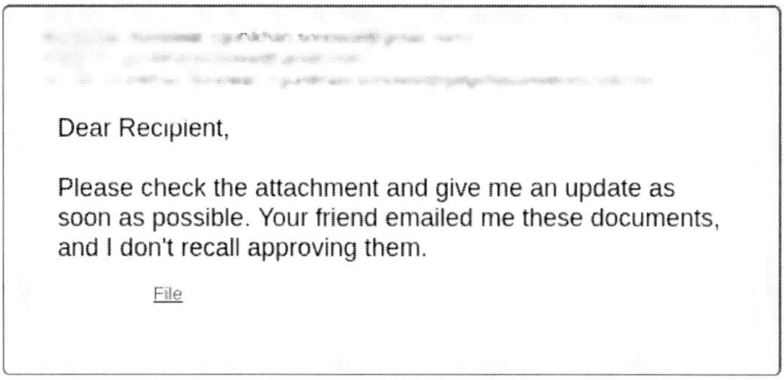
Dear Recipient,

Please check the attachment and give me an update as soon as possible. Your friend emailed me these documents, and I don't recall approving them.

File

Figure 3.4. An example of the "social proof" principle.

3.4.1. Types of Authority

Stanley Milgram, a psychologist, observed that subjects would go to tremendous lengths to obey an authority figure in a series of obedience experiments he carried out in the 1960s. According to Holland, the ability to influence others and persuade them to perform what users want or need them to do is known as authority. Although many different types of authority figures are selected, five have been chosen as having the greatest ability to persuade others.

3.4.1.1. Legal Authority

Things that are connected to the law are referred to as being legal. A person's capacity to influence others due to official position and power. Power is lost once the person in charge resigns from their formal post. Those in positions of leadership have the legal right to do so, and their followers respect this power. In the event that someone violates the law, the responsible party may serve legal notice on the recipient. In the digital world, legal notices can be sent by digital platforms. The legal notice includes the appropriate reference number, sender name with a legitimate domain, and other information.

3.4.1.2. Expert Authority

A person's capacity to persuade others through their knowledge and skills. People who are professionals and experts in a field have expert authority. These authorities typically solely focus on one or two areas. However, because of this, their peers highly appreciate their perspectives and thoughts. It has been observed that bank professionals, cyber security experts, and other experts offer their customers advice on how to protect their personal information. Although many clients disregard this kind of notification and become targets of a cyberattack.

Experts in medicine, including virologists, epidemiologists, public health researchers, and statisticians, have played a critical role in recommending strategies to stop the spread of COVID-19. To inform individuals about the COVID-19 pandemic, they are constantly sending emails, SMS messages, and phone calls.

3.4.1.3. Reverent Authority

The ability to influence others based on behavior, manner, and approach. People with reverent authority have acquired the respect of their peers through their interpersonal skills. It is founded on their regard for, sympathy for, and understanding of others. Those with this kind of power do not necessarily have to be subject-matter specialists. They instead have captivating personalities. As a result of their concern and consideration for all they do, people perceive them as authorities. Political spokespeople, religious leaders, priests, public speakers, and others are examples of this kind of authority. This type of authority sends emails or messages to their followers for charitable or helping purposes.

In many cases, an employee, sometimes not even a supervisor, leads only because others look to them to do so because they respect and believe in their skills and abilities. Many employees experience stress at work because they are unable to adjust to the organizational structure. These professionals have an easy time observing the system and aid others in making organizations run smoothly. As a result, they are regarded as having authority among the populace, and their words are respected.

3.4.1.4. Reward Authority

The ability to influence others by giving or withholding rewards. The ability to reward people for good deeds and behaviors belongs to those with reward authority. They might also have the power to punish. They can thus refuse rewards based on undesirable actions. Positive performance reports and pay raises are two examples of tangible benefits. For instance, teachers have a variety of ways to reward their students. These rewards are frequently used to affect student conduct. Reward authority could be used to describe this type of influence. They consist of grades, accolades, rewards, compliments, privileges, and everything else the teacher would logically infer that the students want and could bestow upon them. In businesses, rewards like compensation, promotions, or recognition are frequently used as rewards.

Many online industries on the digital platform, including e-commerce, UPI awards, and games, reward their clients if they reach their goals. For instance, an e-commerce site might reward users who purchase products over a particular period of time. When users make purchases using UPI apps, UPI occasionally provides cashback deals. Players who win the game receive rewards. This will motivate buyers to spend more money on their goods. Many users of their product only use it to earn rewards; if they are given a goal to reach, they make an effort to reach it. These kinds of rewards can occasionally be obtained via email, SMS, their website, or applications.

3.4.1.5. Punitive Authority

The ability to influence others by imposing a penalty for fault, offense, or violation. A person who has the power to impose punishment on others can do so when they violate the law. Legal and regulatory requirements are frequently used to determine who gets this power. When they leave their positions of authority, they might be taken away. Sports umpires and court judges are two examples. The outcomes of sessions falling under their purview can be managed by either of them using rules and legislation.

3.4.2. Authority Used in Social Engineering Attacks

Attackers take advantage of this by employing the social engineering strategy and posing as an authoritative figure, such as an expert, legal, reward, or Punitive authority in order to steal secret information from the business. The authority message typically scares victims, who then act without giving the message any thought. Examples of frequent notifications are, "Your insurance has been denied due to missing information. To submit your information, click here," or, "Your Internet access will be suspended because you downloaded files illegally unless you complete the required information in the form below." In order to make their fake emails appear more authentic, the attackers often mimic the logo and signature from the real emails.

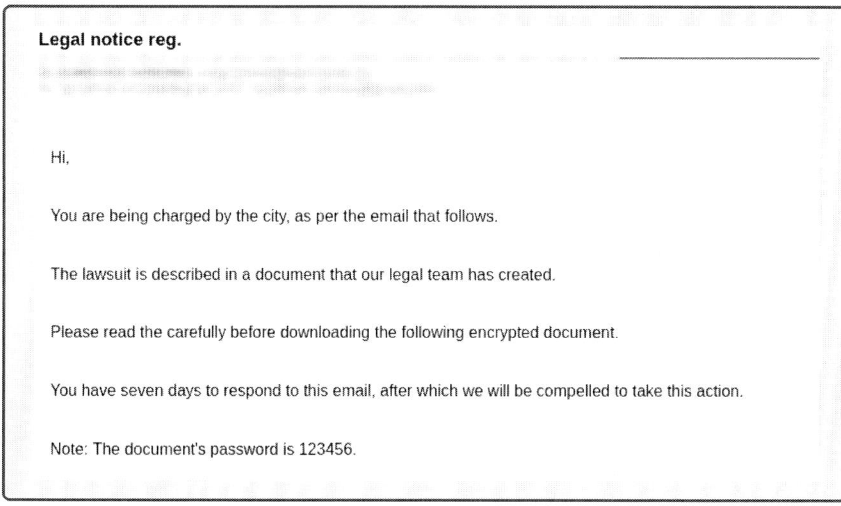
Legal notice reg.

Hi,

You are being charged by the city, as per the email that follows.

The lawsuit is described in a document that our legal team has created.

Please read the carefully before downloading the following encrypted document.

You have seven days to respond to this email, after which we will be compelled to take this action.

Note: The document's password is 123456.

Figure 3.5. An example of a fake legal notice.

Figure 3.5 shows the template of the fake legal notice sent by attackers. Over 100,000 corporate email accounts were inundated with bogus legal threats carrying malware, claims Krebs, 2019. Additionally, the majority of these false emails are produced using social engineering or phishing toolkits. The toolkits enable attackers to create emails with more ease and without having to know much about how to attack.

An HR scam is one of the dominant social engineering attacks because HR is considered one of the chief authority figures in a company. Many victims receive messages from HR, but the message is sent by attackers who impersonate HR. An attachment or link that when clicked may download harmful malware onto the victim's computer or device is frequently included in HR email scams. Encourage your coworkers to confirm the legitimacy of any requests for personal information by contacting the HR sender directly before sending.

3.5. Liking: People Are More Likely to Comply When Requests Are Made by Someone They Like

According to the liking principle, people are more likely to be persuaded by someone they like and aspire to be like. People frequently take a shortcut when deciding whether or not to trust someone by presuming that someone who is either similar to them or who is similar to someone, they already know will be trustworthy. For illustration, companies use Celebrities as brand ambassadors, which is why major brands employ influencers and micro-influencers to assist market their goods and services.

3.5.1. Liking Elements

Things that make people like one another are referred to as liking elements. Although numerous researchers list a variety of elements, Cialdini outlines five components that make up the liking principle in his book influence. These elements are widely employed in many different industries, such as marketing, political campaigns, and social engineering attacks. The five elements are explained in the following:

- *Physical attractiveness*: good looks convey positive qualities like trustworthiness. It depends on factors including the body's fragrance, color, and facial features. Many nations choose movie stars based on their attractive appearance, and they are referred to as celebrities. These celebrities are hired by marketing firms to promote their goods. Most people desire to be attractive or handsome, so they purchase these products in an effort to resemble famous people.
- *Similarity*: People naturally trust those with whom they have similar values, attitudes, and ways of reasoning, understanding, and making decisions. The phrase "birds of a feather flock together" perfectly describes similarity-attraction studies. In order to promote their product, the marketing team portrays personas that customers find appealing. Encyclopedia research has shown that people are more possible to like and be attracted to others who share their socioeconomic position, religious beliefs, social habits, such as how

frequently they attend parties, bad habits, such as drinking and smoking, ethnicity, and level of intelligence.

- *Compliments*: People feel great after receiving compliments. According to research, receiving a genuine compliment has a similar good effect to receiving money. It is commonly known that receiving compliments has advantages for one's happiness and health (Sugawara et al., 2012). Some individuals compliment others when they need assistance. People cannot just disregard helping if they receive compliments because it makes them feel pleased to work. On the plus side, Sarah DiGiulio, 2019 has shown that receiving a compliment actually activates the same brain regions as receiving a monetary incentive. Compliments and praise may be beneficial when it comes to acquiring new motor abilities and behaviors, according to additional research.
- *Contact and cooperation*: Persons like people who have similar goals to their own, aside from physical likeness. In an organization, team members who are working on the same project frequently stick together since they have the same objective or benefits. Generally, they are not aware of what they are creating. They simply know that working together is necessary to complete the task. They decide to sit down and discuss rather than engage in physical combat or run away from the potential collision of their starkly divergent worldviews. For instance, cyber security researchers collaborate to reduce cyber-attacks despite having various ideologies, religious beliefs, physical characteristics, etc.
- *Conditioning and association*: People immediately follow the connections they have created in their minds after mentally connecting various items. Making connections between things is a crucial aspect of how human minds operate. For example, the Aston Martin does not seem like just another vehicle when people observe James Bond standing next to it. It picks up characteristics of the mysterious international man, making it a "sexy," "masculine," and "cool" ride. The foundation of conditioning is the association principle, according to which pairing an artificial (conditioned) stimulus with a natural (unconditioned) stimulus can make the artificial stimulus just as efficient as the natural stimulus at eliciting the same reaction.

3.5.2. The Liking Principle in Social Engineering Attacks

Some of the brands that people are familiar with, like, and trust also fall under the "liking" principle. By falsely using well-known brand identification, such as Google, Microsoft, Netflix, or Amazon, attackers can quickly win over potential victims. In order to lure victims, criminals create phishing websites that imitate well-known legitimate websites. Many victims only focus on how the website looks, and if they recognize it, they are quickly persuaded to consider it to be trustworthy without even looking at the website's URL.

"Romance" fraudsters pose as potential partners on dating websites and mobile applications, or they get in touch with their victims through well-known social media platforms like Instagram, Facebook, or Google Hangouts. In order to gain their trust, the con artists develop relationships with their victims, sometimes communicating with them many times every day. They then fabricate a story to demand payment.

People are loyal to their friends and family, so the fraudster may call the victims pretending to be one of them, and urgently request money. A common defense is that they were involved in an automobile accident and needed money to pay injured parties or avoid going to jail because of security concerns. In other situations, victims could need to leave a foreign nation due to an epidemic or pay for medical care or college tuition in order to escape penalties. Attackers will act quickly to try to steal your money before victims realize it is a fraud.[14]

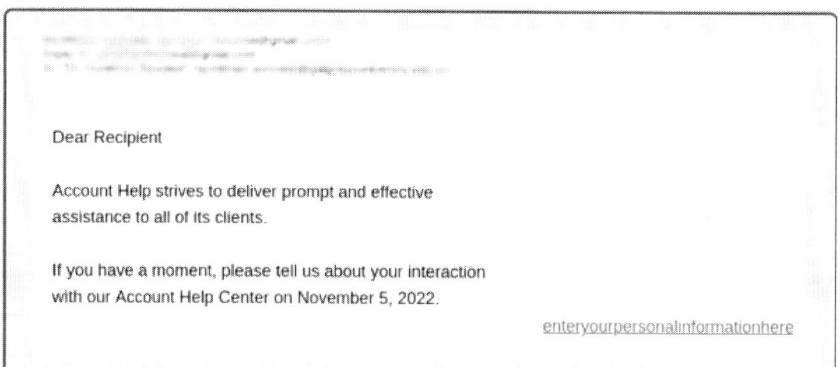

Figure 3.6. An example of the "liking" principle.

[14] https://resources.infosecinstitute.com/topic/phishing-technique-message-from-a-friend-relative/.

Affinity fraud is a kind of investment fraud in which attackers attempt to defraud members of a group that has come together because of a shared trait, such as age, race, or religion. Attackers pose as group members in an effort to gain the trust of the organization's leader and participants. If the group leader invests, the attackers believe that others will follow suit.

3.6. Scarcity: Victims Tend to Want Things More When They Think There Is a Shortage of Them

Scarcity is a term used to describe limitations, such as a shortage of specific abilities or resources like time, money, or services. Scarcity is the perception that products are more attractive when their availability is limited. For instance, Apple makes use of this to its advantage in its marketing materials. In order to capitalize on the concept of scarcity, Apple stores only keep a limited number of current products, such as iPhones or iPads, on hand on launch day. Long lines of customers wait to purchase the product, and numerous news outlets reported this circumstance to highlight their product.

3.6.1. Strategies for the Scarcity Principle

Many markets leveraged the scarcity principle to promote the product. Similar strategies are used in social engineering attacks to persuade victims to fall for the scam as explained in the next section. Although many tactics are used for the scarcity principle, below is a list of some of the strategies explained by the Indeed Editorial Team, 2021:

3.6.1.1. The Product Is Almost Sold Out

An online store can utilize scarcity marketing by displaying the fact that a product is nearly sold out or has low stock. On their company's website or e-commerce sites, marketers can use software to display real-time alerts of low supply so that customers can always know when there is not much of a product left to purchase. This may convince hesitant customers to purchase the goods before they sell out, which is advantageous for those customers who typically wait to purchase and end up forgetting about them as they move about their day.

3.6.1.2. Early Bird Discounts

Early bird discounts are typically limited time offers on product pre-orders or special promotions for dedicated customers to obtain a product ahead of time. These discounts encourage buyers to purchase a product before the discount ends and other people may obtain it, which could cause it to run out of stock more quickly. Sending emails to current customers with information about the promotion and posting a banner with the date the discount expires on the company store's website or in-person location are both effective ways to employ early access discounts.

3.6.1.3. Limited Time Bonus Items

During the holiday season or when they have a lot of smaller items to sell, marketers may employ this tactic to entice customers to spend a certain amount of money. For a limited time, customers who spend a certain amount at their store can obtain extra items. Most often, when people go shopping, they end up purchasing multiple goods. A strategy like this helps the sellers in selling more goods by utilizing inexpensive or overstocked items that do not cause a loss for their firm. This is especially useful during the holiday season when people exchange gifts because consumers might desire to purchase more items.

3.6.1.4. Items That Are Limited Edition

Many companies use this tactic to demonstrate the product's limited supply and high demand. Even though the business has the capacity to produce a wide range of goods, it uses scarcity to encourage buyers to buy its products immediately. Apple adopted these strategies, as demonstrated by the example presented above. To develop distinctive items that appeal to a variety of customers and expand their potential market, it is possible to consider collaborating with other companies or well-known people. If companies wish to use limited edition products to their advantage, they must establish an expectation for their release in advance to ensure that when these products are made available, as many individuals as possible are informed about them.

3.6.1.5. Platform-Exclusive Deals

Platform-exclusive offers are promotions that consumers can only access through particular platforms, such as discounts for purchases made through an app or sales available only on a website. These deals focus on how long a discount lasts and how customers can get it, rather than limiting the number of items that can be bought. A strategy like this could help a company's business gain more consumers across different platforms, which is advantageous for mobile apps because it gives people convenient access to their store wherever they are.

3.6.1.6. Seasonal Products

Selling limited-season products can assist businesses in increasing sales during particular times of the year and generating excitement for each season when they release new products or the same high-demand products from the previous year. People may sell seasonal products like food and drink, apparel and accessories, or useful objects, depending on the type of business they work for, to entice customers who need or prefer these distinctive items at times of the year. Many times, buyers who are enthused by seasonal goods also inform their friends about them, so expanding the customer base for the firms.

3.6.1.7. Popular or High-Demand Products

Another strategy for using scarcity marketing to increase sales is to include a feature that shows the number of consumers interested in a product in online product descriptions. This is one approach to represent the number of website users who have viewed the item, put it in their cart, or loved it. Even while companies might not be limited to the actual amount of goods available any more than usual, customers may want the product more because they know they might someday run out of it.

3.6.2. Scarcity in Social Engineering Attacks

In social engineering attack, the attackers applied tactics to manipulate the victims to disclose their credentials. It frequently works well with malware software and phishing assaults. People make snap judgments without giving them much thought. For example, the attackers alert the victims to the presence of the fake product, after which they are informed that there is a limited quantity or provide discounts and others. However, visit the fraudulent website right away and purchase the item. The webpage, where customers enter their information, is a fake version of the real business website. In the context of phishing emails, if the sender threatens to suspend, deactivate, or limit our account if users do not comply with his or her request, users may be tempted to comply out of fear that users will not be able to use our account once more, or until it is scarce or limited.

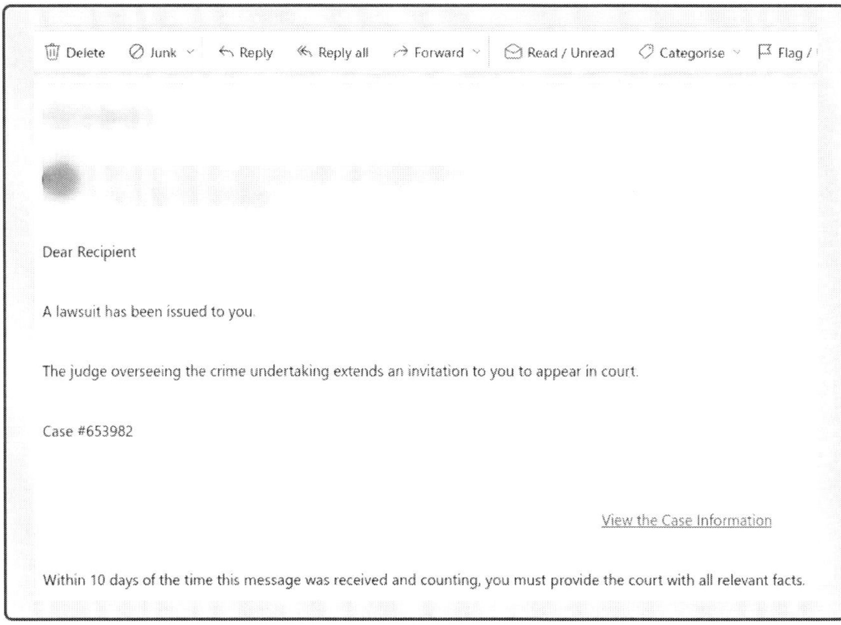

Figure 3.7. An example of the "scarcity" principle.

3.7. People Are Influenced by Other Persuasive Factors

It depicts people's motivations, feelings, and approaches or avoidance techniques. Sometimes people do not do things, but their emotions spur them to action. It is used in a variety of industries, including marketing and political campaigns, among others. These emotional manipulation techniques are also employed by attackers in social engineering attacks on their targets. Some of the techniques employed by attackers in social engineering attacks are listed below.

3.7.1. Greed

Greed is the biggest weakness in human psychology, and successful social engineering tactics are built on exploiting the victim's weakness. Many people fall victim to the psychology of greed every day, for example, many affluent people lend borrowers excessive amounts of money, so they can foreclose on the home and profit. People utilize a variety of strategies to take advantage of greed, and this strategy is used to influence the victims. Lotteries, gift baskets, monetary prizes, and other items all have a considerable impact on people. As an illustration, attackers may assume the identity of bank staff and trick the victim into believing they are used to interacting with them. They may be using a banking shirt and fake documents about the bank. As a result, they are supporting the victims with this payment, or the victim is chosen as the prize winner in a lottery. The attackers then request the account number and internet login information using some fake bank form.

3.7.2. Curiosity

A condition of active interest or a sincere desire to learn more about something is called curiosity. Attackers prey on human interest by promising fascinating things or illegal content. Attackers present the victims with a portion of a message and inform them that the complete message would be displayed when they provide their login information or payment. The victim is driven by curiosity to provide money or credentials to understand more about the message. Curiosity is a state of active interest or a desire to learn more about something. Attackers first conduct research on the victims' interests before designing a message. Once the attackers are aware of the victim's interests, they create messages that contain curiosities in an effort to stimulate the victim's interest and dupe them. By gathering information on the victim, for instance, the attackers can determine that the victim is concerned about their health. The message is then designed by the attackers to say something like, "Recently, researchers discovered a new drug that can treat this type of condition." Simply provide credentials to learn more about it.

3.7.3. Urgency

Urgency is a time-based concept that motivates the victims to take rapid action. It is one of the most frequent psychological manipulation techniques is to create a panic situation for the victim. A message that demands an immediate response from the recipient is considered urgent. The similarity in the last chapter is that scarcity was covered which is defined as a psychological trigger to encourage quick action. Users may get a message from a high-ranking official requiring them to do a task right away or face punishment. For example, "This is to inform you that your tax information is out-of-date, and you need to provide the information to update. We are from the tax department." Sometimes, attackers employ this tactic to pose as victims' friends and family members and request urgent assistance from victims. For instance, the victim forgot to bring his purse and is now dealing with a medical emergency. He, therefore, asks his friend to make a direct payment to the doctor on the following account. The attackers cut off the connection as soon as they got the money.

3.7.4. Helpfulness

Most people are willing to help, which is part of human psychology. People are trained to trust based on their own beliefs and morals; thus, it can be difficult to grasp that not everyone is acting with the same level of integrity all the time. As a result, using this strategy can easily lead to the manipulation of others. One of the most common scams is the charity scam, in which the attackers solicit money in person, over the phone, through the mail, over e-mail, or online. They could appeal for contributions on behalf of a group or an individual. The attackers utilize false banners, posters, or websites that mimic historical disasters to persuade the victims.

3.7.5. Fear

Everyone has some familiarity with the primal and natural sense of fear. It warns people when threats are nearby, whether they are genuine or imagined. The majority of people aim to be good, therefore when even the most logical among them receive an email informing them of a billing issue or the fact that they have unpaid taxes due, their fear response is triggered. Attackers exploit fear to deceive victims into paying for unneeded technical support services to purportedly cure software or device problems that do not exist. This problem affects the entire industry. The attacker's best effort is to persuade the victims to pay them to "repair" a false issue with their hardware or software. If the victims allow them to remote into their computer to carry out this "repair," the attacker will frequently install malware, ransomware, or other undesirable programs that can steal the victim's information or harm their data or device.

3.7.6. Sympathy/Empathy

Sympathy is the emotional condition experienced by people who are able to comprehend the thoughts or feelings of another person without actually experiencing those same feelings themselves. Empathy is the emotional condition of a person who can relate to another person's mental or emotional state because they have experienced the same thing themselves. Attackers frequently use it to their advantage to obtain what they desire from their target.

3.7.7. Repetition

People will eventually be convinced if something occurs frequently enough. People's brains are brilliant at matching patterns, and they get rewarded for exploiting this extremely practical ability. Repetition establishes a pattern, which logically and instinctively draws attention and then fosters a sense of familiarity. Some people simply need to try something out multiple times before deciding. Before they are persuaded, many people need to hear something repeated numerous times.

For example, Hitler's method of propaganda was called the "Big Lie." In order to get people to believe a major lie, you have to keep repeating it against any opposition or evidence. In *Mein Kampf*, the Nazi leader's autobiographical manifesto from 1925, Hitler described his "Big Lie" strategy: A certain amount of believability is frequently present in the "Big Lie." Minds are more susceptible to large-scale deception than small-scale deception because they frequently inform themselves of small lies in trivial situations but would feel guilty to use large-scale deception. People will eventually start to believe a falsehood if it is told often and in detail. (Camenker, 2015)

Repetition techniques are often utilized in social engineering attacks. Attackers used repeated messages to get victims to trust what they were saying. In general, the first two messages merely serve the purpose of establishing friendship; they do not contain any information about credentials. Once the target audience has been won over, the attackers will start asking for credentials.

Summary

The six principles of influence put out by Robert Cialdini were covered in this chapter. Despite being proposed in 1984, these principles are still effective in social engineering attacks because human nature never changes. These ideas are employed in marketing efforts, but attackers can also use them to manipulate people through social engineering. The attackers are using cutting-edge technologies with the same basic idea to target the victims.

Chapter 4

Types of Social Engineering Attacks

Social engineering is an umbrella term for any security exploit, and the strategies used to carry out a social engineering attack vary based on the attacker's point of view. It has been observed that many cyber attackers have a direct or indirect connection to social engineering strategies. Although technologies are constantly changing, attackers still employ similar tactics in social engineering attacks that are human feelings, which are still relevant today. Attackers use both technical and non-technical means to control human emotion. As indicated in Figure 4.1, the attackers use five different sorts of techniques based on their attack strategies.

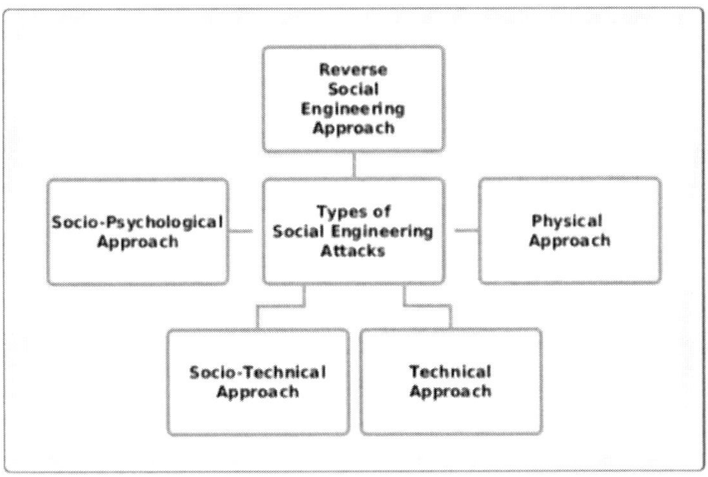

Figure 4.1. Types of social engineering attacks.

This chapter will cover the following topics:

- Physical approach
- Social approach
- Reverse social engineering approach
- Technical approach
- Socio-technical approach.

4.1. Physical Approaches

An attacker might take somewhat physical activity to learn more about the victim. The one thing these methods have in common is that they cannot be done from a remote location which implies that the attackers physically present a particular location to collect information. Sometimes, it needs little equipment or technology knowledge about the organizations. It is sometimes called a low-tech cyber-attack. As an illustration, the attackers might enter the target firm using a fake employee ID or by using technology to open the security lock.

4.1.1. Dumpster Diving

Dumpster diving is the practice of searching through other people's garbage for hidden treasure. Many people are unaware that items they discard could still contain private information. A social engineering attack may be possible if such information is recovered. Attackers can find bank statements, official documents, medical bills, resumes, and the like by looking through the victim's trash. Once in possession, the data is utilized to construct identity profiles, increasing the likelihood that social engineering will be successful. In a situation where an attacker obtains a receipt for a vending machine replenishment service, they may attack on the same day and at the same time as an anticipated delivery while wearing name badges to represent service providers.

According to the report of Ameet Sachdev and Tribune staff reporter, 2001, Procter & Gamble Co. admitted in 2001 that it had searched through the trash to learn more about rival Unilever's hair care division. A Unilever representative verified that the trash diving occurred in front of the company's 325 N. Wells in downtown Chicago hair care headquarters. Some of the most common sources for dumpster diving techniques.

- *CDs/DVDs*: The crucial source for gathering information is CDs and DVDs. Information is stored there to be Physically shared without the usage of the internet. Although flash drives are another tool for transferring information, many organizations avoid using them due to security concerns. Once people copy information from a CD or DVD, they do not dispose of the CD or DVD securely, which causes information to leak.

- *Personal computer/hard drive*: Attackers employ information diving to recover technical data from trashed materials, sometimes including proprietary or secret information. Recently, this has mostly come from data storage components in abandoned computers, particularly recoverable data still present on hard drives. Most of the time, those responsible for disposing of computers forget to wipe the hard drive. In these situations, installed software like word processors, operating systems, video games, etc. are frequently copied by information divers. There might also be other information available, such as credit card data that was saved on the device.
- *Random profile on the internet*: Online users frequently create profiles and then forget about them. They only keep the profiles that are often utilized. These kinds of profiles are occasionally also utilized by attackers to construct phony accounts they can use to hack victims. It has been observed that many websites allow users to build profiles before signing up. People believe that these profiles are treated as garbage, yet it will be helpful for the attacker to contribute a portion to victim impersonation.
- *Paper documents*: Attacks involving dumpster diving are typically vast. To save user profiles, phone numbers, or emails, people utilize sticky notes, phone books, and plain paper. After using the documents, they discard them in the trash or another unintentional location. These kinds of documents are gathered by the attackers, who then examine the victims. For instance, in an organization, if someone has a fever, they will ask their friend to keep working. In response to his friend's request for passwords to continue the work, he provided the password. Strong passwords were used, making it impossible for the friend to remember, so he wrote them down on paper. The friend simply kept the paper table after opening his profile. His paper was kept in the trash as the cleaning crew cleaned the space. However, once his paper was discovered by the attackers, he logged into his profile and gathered all the data. In many cases, business plans that are written on paper are frequently used.

Users are at risk if potential attackers have easy access to discarded materials, including hardware or storage media that contain sensitive data as well as paper documents and electronic data. Attackers may use the data they have gathered from trash diving for a number of purposes. They could use any network or security information directly in a hacking attempt. For instance, if a user wrote down their new password in a planner and then tossed it away at the end of the year, attackers may use that information to directly access the network.

4.1.2. Shoulder Surfing

Shoulder surfing is a method of social engineering that involves peering over the shoulder of the victim to gather information like personal identification numbers (PINs), passwords, and other private information. In crowded areas, standing next to someone and watching them complete a form, enter a PIN at an ATM, or use a credit card to make a purchase is a good approach to obtaining information.

As implied by the name, it can therefore just involve peering over the victim's shoulder. According to some hacker base analysis, attackers will use binoculars, stealthy video cameras, or other optical technology-based devices in the current day to spy on their targets. Therefore, it is an easy method to gather information, including usernames/IDs, passwords, personally beneficial or sensitive information, and credit card numbers, with the intention of utilizing it for financial gain. As a result, shoulder surfing is a type of social engineering that aims to gather personal information through interpersonal contact. According to Ionos, 2020, Shoulder surfing includes two types.

- *Direct observation attacks*: This is when someone watches the victim closely as they enter data, such as their PIN at a checkout terminal, and glances straight over their shoulder to observe what they are doing. For instance, a victim working on a laptop at lunch in a crowded cafe might not even be aware that the attacker sitting at the table behind them has a transparent view of their screen. In that situation, the victim would not be aware of the attackers were watching them attentively as they entered their passwords for their internet accounts.
- *Recording attacks*: The victim's activities during this attack were first captured on video. Criminals can later thoroughly examine these videos to gather the required data. Even if the display is hidden in the video, it is now possible to use video recordings to figure out the PIN for unlocking mobile devices. The access code

can be ascertained by the user's finger motions alone. For instance, the hidden camera enables the attacker to record the victim's entire login process and other sensitive information.

Shoulder surfing can hurt not only private persons but also businesses in a significant way. Anyone who uses their tools, server logins, or email accounts inaccurately while working in the public is inviting crooks in and endangering the privacy of clients, coworkers, and employees.

4.1.3. Eavesdropping

Although it is a form of shoulder surfing, it is used to monitor other people's conversations. Eavesdropping is the act of listening in on private communication such as a phone call, instant message, video conference, or fax transmission without the knowledge of the intended receiver. The act of standing under a house's eaves and listening to conversations inside is considered eavesdropping, according to Audin. With advanced technology, attackers use continuously new methods to attack the victims. Digital communication is highly vulnerable because attackers inject malicious software into their systems and record their conversions. Therefore, the eavesdropping attack is used following methods:

4.1.3.1. Direct Listening

It is a traditional technique used in the old days. It is the simple act of listening to other people talk without them knowing it. In a crowded place, people are discussing with each other through direct conversation, phone calls, and other communication mediums. The attackers listen to their conversion and then remember or record in paper or digital sticky notes. Something, the attackers directly use their confidential information on their website without delay. In many organizations, attackers come as guests, delivery boys, and technical supporters and listen to their conversion. Sometimes, the attackers use the wiretapping technique for listening in on a regular telephone connection.

4.1.3.2. Data Sniffing

In modern technology, attackers use this method very widely. It is easily done on a local network that uses a HUB since all communications are sent to all the ports of the network. This is also known as a passive sniffer, and it is operated at the data link layer of the network. Another form of the sniffer is the active sniffer where the attackers use the sniffing method through the switch. A device used in point-to-point networks is a switch. The switch actively monitors each port's MAC address to control the data flow between its ports, ensuring that only the intended target receives data. Sniffer devices must actively inject traffic into the LAN in order to enable sniffing of the traffic to capture it between the targets.

4.1.3.3. Voice-Over-IP Calls

It is an internet-based digital telephone system that allows users to place and receive calls rather than using the conventional Public Switched Telephone Network that is wired (PSTN). In a social engineering attack, the attackers can alter the Caller ID information, enabling the caller to masquerade as a relative, coworker, or member of the victim's family in order to obtain information, resources, or advantages from the target. This method is referred to as caller ID spoofing.

The attackers can continuously annoy their victims from many lines by using the infinite extensions offered by VOIP PBX capabilities. Automating the procedure is simple, and it can send numerous notifications to the target's voicemail. The caller can call frequently enough to prevent the target from receiving crucial incoming calls. When not employed for marketing purposes, this technique might be expensive for the caller.

4.1.4. Physical Access Control System

Managing a property's physical access levels is a crucial component of a company's overall security plan. Businesses must now be able to monitor and keep track of who has access to what resources or information when within their organization. Protecting any company's data centers, server rooms, and other high-value regions can be greatly improved by ensuring the right access levels. As a result of this, having dependable security solutions is essential in today's society.

4.1.4.1. Tailgating Attacks

Attackers can reach a password-protected or otherwise restricted physical location by using a simple social engineering technique known as tailgating. When entering a zone with limited access, one is said to be tailgating. For instance, as a typical employee opens a heavy door, a tailgating social engineer may seize the door just as it is about to close, waltzing right into the targeted physical system. The second and most typical instance of this type involves an attacker following a legitimate individual into a target area. An attacker may breach an organization's network and gain access to private papers after tailgating and breaking into an office. These documents might then be used to target and carry out a serious cyberattack on the company, one that could cost millions of dollars. Once inside, a perpetrator may use a device to access the company's network, steal confidential data, or even infect an unlocked computer with malware.

4.1.4.2. The Difference between Piggybacking and Tailgating

A tailgating attack is sometimes called a piggybacking attack. Tailgating and piggybacking are both in-person social engineering techniques used by unauthorized persons to enter restricted physical areas that are secured by electronic devices intended to prevent access. Despite the fact that both attacks were carried out in person, tailgating is not the same as piggybacking tactics, claims Karen Cohen, 2022.

Tailgating is the act of entering a restricted area without the consent of the person granted access. In other words, a worker swipes in with their badge while the criminal enters covertly behind them.

As mentioned in the example of technique supporters, piggybacking occurs when the person who has permission to enter the premises is aware that they have permitted someone in but believes they have permission to be there. From the firm website, the offender frequently has access to an employee's name, department, and occasionally even phone number.

Another instance of piggybacking is when an offender tries to enter a large corporation by striking up a conversation with a worker who is entering the building in the hopes that the worker would keep the door open. The offender might even go so far as to "admit" that they lost their badge or that they were meeting with a certain employee.

4.1.4.3. Methods Used in Tailgating or Piggybacking Attacks

Although numerous instances of tailgating or piggybacking attacks have already been discussed, some popular techniques are still employed by attackers to gain access to restricted areas. Below is a discussion of these techniques:

- *Follow staff members who are opening doors*: Social engineers observe opportunities to track employees who are opening doors. An employee might unintentionally allow a non-authorized individual with malevolent intentions into the building because it is common politeness to leave a door open for others behind us.

- *Masquerade as a courier*: In order to enter and move about freely inside a building, social engineers may pose as couriers or other delivery workers. If a worker or receptionist does not question them thoroughly enough, they might allow them into an office or floor where they're supposed to have a delivery.
- *Claim that their hands are full and are unable to open the door*: Social engineers may also be allowed entry if they approach doors while holding a number of items in their hands. Employees can be considerate and helpful by opening a door for intruders, much like when they leave doors open behind them.
- *Make the excuse that they forgot their ID*: Some social engineers might create the convincing claim that they forgot their access ID or that they left it at home in an effort to pass as an employee. They would do this in the hopes that they would be given a temporary pass or that someone would kindly open a door for them.
- *Pretend to have received an invitation from someone*: Social engineers will make the excuse that they were invited as a guest of an employee if all else fails or looks tough to pull off. They could even have a person's name and contact information ready to use as leverage to get access. Other social engineering approaches, including eavesdropping, can be used to obtain such information.

4.1.4.3. Access Card System

Organizations are providing access cards or key access to their employees to grant physical access to particular areas of a building. These access cards are verified by a security guide or device while trying to enter the location. Koorsen Fire & Security addresses the various types of access control key cards as follows:

- *RFID key cards*: In some firms, employees utilize key cards with radio frequency identification (RFID). The data recorded in the microchip of this sort of access key card is read and transmitted using radio frequency to open doors. Since RFID is encrypted, it is more secure and effective than conventional keys, which are mechanical keys that are simple to steal or copy. RFID also offers users a degree of freedom that is impossible with traditional locks and keys. For instance, to prevent illegal access, a business's IT team can design and customize the cards such that only a select few doors within that organization are opened by the employees. In addition, the IT team can quickly disable the cards from the control center if they suspect a breach, theft, or loss.

- *Smart cards*: Smart cards are employed in companies that require an additional level of security and protection. As a result, RFID cards do not have mutual authentication, they are usually more secure. To open a door with an RFID card, for example, all users need to do is stand within range of the card reader and swipe their card. A smart card system, on the other hand, uses microcontrollers rather than the RFID interface. They may be able to manage sophisticated functions such as data management, storage, encryption, and secure access. Data may be read from up to 10 centimeters (about 3.94 in) away, and it incorporates mutual authentication to prevent data theft. The data contained within it is also encrypted, making access to the information more difficult.
- *Wiegand key cards*: The Wiegand effect, magnetic phenomena, is utilized by these cards. To store unique numbers on cards that can be read by a Wiegand reader, the cards make use of some basic magnetic science principles. Due to their simplicity and usability, these cards are well-liked. Due to the cards' difficulty in duplicating or cloning, they also provide a respectable level of security. In comparison to RFID cards, they also have a longer lifespan. They can only hold a certain amount of data, though. The Wiegand protocol is also unencrypted. Any Wiegand card reader within range may therefore simply read the cards.

Although the physical access control system significantly increases corporate security, attackers still attempt to enter the facility without authorization by exploiting system flaws and causing harm. The attackers primarily use social engineering tactics to impersonate a fake card by copying the information of the original card. This is also known as a clone attack. A cloning Attack is a kind of attack that tries to trick a system by utilizing a fraudulently copied card that may be an exact duplicate of all the data on the card, merely some of the data, or possibly only the identifying number. This kind of attack is carried out by reading the essential information from a valid access control card to copy the information onto a new card or to simulate the copied information using a tool.

4.1.4.4. Biometric System

Many firms today utilize the biometric system to distinguish between real users and imposters. Allowing access to the resource depends on whether the biometric is accurate. A biometric system is a device that accepts data from a person's biological or behavioral traits in order to identify them. A biometric system is vulnerable to a variety of malicious assaults, which can be carried out by a variety of threats. Attacks on a biometric machine that are malicious are a security risk and damage the system's performance. Spoof attacks, noisy sensor data, interclass differences, interclass similarities, and other constraints exist in biometric systems. The social engineering attack is one of the most common in the biometric system. Ratha, Connell, and Bolle, 2001 identified eight places in the generic biometric system of Figure 4.2 where attacks may occur:

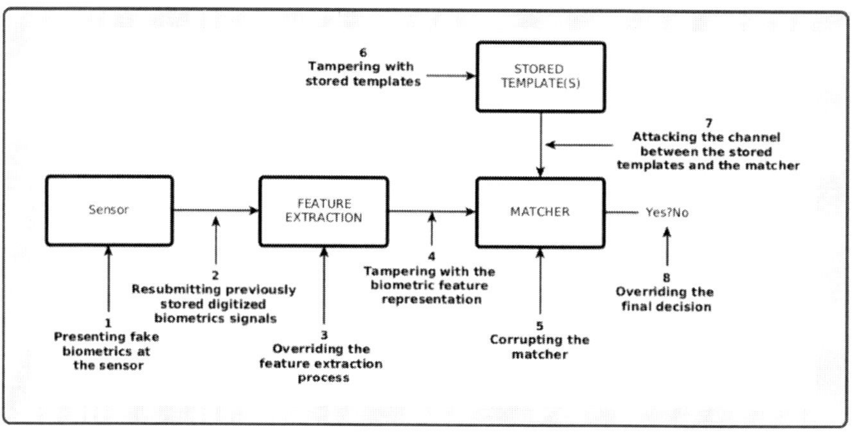

Figure 4.2. Biometric attacks.

1) *Presenting fake biometrics at the sensor*: Numerous organizations employ a variety of sensors, including sound, face, and finger sensors, to identify real people. If the sensor recognizes their biometrics, then they are allowed to access the organizations. The user data is gathered and sent to the server using this sensor. The server already has a template for biometric data that it compares to and ensures is accurate. However, the attackers modify it in an effort to gain access to the private area.
   - *Fake finger*: It can be made from a variety of materials, including gelatine, silicone, latex, and even wood glue, and is

typically generated by putting an originally stored fingerprint on a fake finger. The attackers use a variety of extraction techniques to gather the print left on a glass surface, and they then use one of the materials to shape the print into an object to show to a biometric scanner. The attacker would then use the fake finger to try to get access to the reader and collect sensitive information.

- *Facial*: It is possible to achieve this whether the method is iris, palm, facial, or vein recognition. Similar to the fake fingerprint technique, this can be done whether or not the person whose biometric data is saved agrees to it. In the case of Photographs and Masks then the deception involves presenting a reader with images and masks that impersonate an individual whose biometric data is saved and recognized. Although this approach is a little less sophisticated than other social engineering attacks, it can still fool some biometric facial recognition systems.
- *Voice playback*: An attacker might easily use a recording of an authorized person speaking when using speech recognition systems. A laptop or phone could be used for this. Similar to how facial morphing software may be used to make transcriptions that can be recognized by readers, voice morphing software can be used to alter the voice of a live person to sound like someone who is recognized by the biometric system.

2) *Resubmitting previously stored digitized biometrics signals*: Attackers intercept the signal and transmit the signal to its feature extraction location while posing as the original sender. The signal sent by the attacker is seen by the location as an authorized signal. Following the initial signal is received by the location. Due to the fact that the signal is received twice, this attack is also known as a replay attack.
3) *Overriding the feature extraction process*: A malicious program is installed to target the feature extractor, causing it to output feature sets that have been chosen by the attackers.
4) *Tampering with the biometric feature representation*: This technique is often referred to as a feature set spoofing attack. Spoofing of data refers to the replacement of the feature set with false or modified features. These kinds of spoofing attacks are frequently used to

infiltrate different networks, disseminate malware, and steal sensitive data.

5) *Corrupting the matcher*: Attackers compromise the matcher such that it generates bogus feature match scores that they provide.
6) *Tampering with stored templates*: A template is a set of distinguishing features that captures the essence of a person's biometric signal. Whatever image is submitted to the system, the templates can be altered to achieve a high verification score. The templates that are kept in the database are susceptible to replacement, theft, and even modification. Consequently, the system will suffer as the score for real users will be low. The methods for creating templates have been thought of as one-way algorithms.
7) *Attacking the channel between the stored templates and the matcher*: The matcher receives the saved templates over a communication connection. It might be possible to intercept and alter the data passing across this channel.
8) *Overriding the final decision*: The authentication mechanism has been compromised if the final match result is susceptible to the attacker's intervention. Despite having good performance features, the overriding of the match result has rendered the real pattern recognition framework meaningless.

It is highly challenging for enterprises to stop the attackers since they constantly employ novel techniques to access restricted regions. Many firms use biometric techniques to authenticate their employees, however, attackers steal the employees' biometric data and pretend to be the real employee. In other words, if the area is to be made safer, it takes a long time to verify the people, which can be annoying at times such as during airport checking.

4.2. Social Approaches

This attack is based on social psychological methods such as Cialdini's principles of persuasion to manipulate their victims as explained previously in Chapter 3. An individual's personality can be significantly influenced by socio-psychological factors, which combine social aspects like family, society, wealth, and religion with psychological factors like feelings, ideas, and beliefs. The attacker preys on the victims using social psychological techniques such as mimicking the victims' friends or family members or social activities to appeal to emotions like greed, urgency, helpfulness, or curiosity. It was briefly stated in the previous chapter how attackers target their victims using Cialdini's principles.

Some attackers assume the role of researchers from an institute or research facility and gather data for their research project. Utilizing persuasive techniques of helpfulness, they persuaded the victims that if they assisted them, they would improve society. They collect information using many methods like interviews, questionnaires, and others. Once the data has been gathered, it is sold on the black market or used in future attacks. The following list includes some of the more popular social psychological approaches:

4.2.1. Impersonation

The goal of the social engineer is to deceive users into granting access to their office, their information, or their information systems by impersonating or acting as someone they are inclined to trust or obey. This kind of social engineering takes advantage of people's innate propensities to trust those they meet and comply with orders when given by someone in a position of authority. It entails the deliberate manipulation of a victim to collect information without the victim being aware that a security breach is taking place.

Compared to other types of social engineering, impersonation is more difficult to pull off and takes much planning. Users frequently communicate with strangers, which explains why these tactics work. Humans have a tendency to believe that a badge or uniform is authentic, however, this is not always the case. Despite knowing that anyone can wear a uniform, users still trust them. Furthermore, visitors often determine a website's legitimacy when they visit it based on how professional it looks, disregarding the fact that anyone may copy and paste visuals. Users also tend to immediately trust people in positions of power. Infosightinc (a cyber security incorporated company), provides a list that includes a few social engineering roles:

- Adopting the identity of a different worker.
- Pretending to be a representative from a partner company, a supplier, or an auditor.
- Pretending to be a new employee and asking for help.

- Requesting access to local email while posing as an employee of a remote office.
- Pretending to be a higher-ranking individual.
- Posing as a system vendor to advertise a patch or system update.

4.2.2. Foot-In-The-Door (FITD)

The foot-in-the-door (FITD) technique is a compliance strategy used to persuade someone to agree to a major request by getting them to consent to a smaller one first. This technique mostly uses reciprocity, commitment, and consistency. Stanford University researchers Freedman and Fraser, 1966 first proposed the Foot in the Door Technique and undertook a study to test the hypothesis that approving lesser requests can lead to consenting to larger ones. Their findings corroborated what they had already thought to be true.

A group of women was asked to respond to various questions on their use of soap-related items (a small request). Following their responses, a more substantial request was made they were to allow a group of men to enter their home and make an inventory of the goods they had. The bigger request was made to one group, but not the smaller request to do the soap survey. According to research by Jonathan Freedman and Scott Fraser, participants in the foot-in-the-door technique group who had been given the modest request were much more likely to consent to the more demanding inventory request than participants in the group who had only been given the final inquiry.

A friend of a student who missed class requested him to provide a one-day lecture. Without saying anything, the student gave the lecture. It was quite difficult for the student to decline his friend's request after a few days when his friend once more requested the entire notebook.

4.2.3. Persuasion

Persuasion is the process through which communications from other people successfully change a person's opinions or behavior without using force. Many people employ persuasion as a means of controlling others to perform their tasks. This strategy takes advantage of the Liking, reciprocation, reciprocation, social proof, consistency, and authority principles to promote a specific behavior. Attacks using social engineering rely on the attacker being persuasive. As a result of research into the persuasion tactics used by attackers, various sets of persuasion principles have been developed. According to the Greek philosopher, physicist, and rhetorician Aristotle, three types of persuasions are highly used:

- *Ethos* is a technique for persuading readers of their writing's trustworthiness.
- *Pathos* is an emotional appeal made to an audience to generate feelings.
- *Logos* seek to convince an audience by using logic and reason.

4.2.4. Pretexting

One of the earliest forms of social engineering was pretexting. The term "pretexting" was first introduced by the FBI in 1974, and it was frequently applied to aid their inquiries. Pretexting is a form of social engineering in which an attacker creates a situation or pretext to lure victims into disclosing sensitive information that they otherwise would not. Pretexting in this stage involved the attacker calling the victim and asking for information only. Persuasion techniques are typically used in pretexting attacks. Unlike most scams, this one uses a pretext, or story, to deceive the intended victim into disclosing personal information and bank account details. Pretexting is a more focused attack where the attacker spends time getting to comprehend the victim and creating a believable cover story. Pretexting attacks are consequently significantly harder to identify and counter.

Pretexting transformed after this initial stage of social engineering's evolution (1974-1983), going from being a persuasion tool to a deception tactic. Pretexting techniques evolved in tandem with technological advancement. Due to the development of social media, hackers soon gained access to a larger audience of potential victims. According to a report by Stouffer, Hewlett-Packard employed private detectives in 2006 to verify onboard members' potential news leaks. The PIs did this by impersonating the board members and obtaining access to phone providers' call logs.

Pretexting, or creating a false pretense to obtain information, is frequently prohibited. Private investigators will occasionally employ pretexting to obtain phone records or other sensitive information. In these cases, the investigator will pretend to be someone in authority, such as a member of the police, a colleague, a bank employee, a tax official, an insurance investigator, etc.

Kaplan, 2006 reported that at the request of HP chairperson Patricia Dunn, Hewlett-general Packard's counsel had hired a group of impartial security specialists to investigate board members and a number of journalists in order to find the source of a data leak. Then, those security professionals hired private detectives who employed the spying method of pretexting. In order to get their phone data, investigators pretended to be nine journalists, including reporters for CNET, the New York Times, the Wall Street Journal, and HP board members. The details of the leak, which concerned HP's long-term strategy, were made public in January 2006 as part of a story on CNET.

4.2.5. Quid Pro Quo

Attackers entice victims to disclose information in exchange for something. Cyber actors offer people something in return rather than attempting to trick someone into falling for anything out of their own curiosity or fear. It basically comes down to "a favor for a favor," which is what the Latin term implies. The last chapter covers a wide range of topics, including reciprocity, which is widely applied in various industries, but quid pro quo is particularly useful in social engineering attacks. Social engineering attacks that demand an exchange of anything of value are known as "quid pro quo" attacks, which set them apart from other forms of social engineering.

The goal of other social engineering attacks, such as phishing ones, is to trick the target into exposing sensitive information or granting access to systems or data rather than engaging in exchange. An illustration would be if an attacker called the victim's phone purporting to be a technical support agent from one of their service providers. The attackers will attempt to assist the victims, but this will only be successful if the victims are having some difficulties. This attack is also known as a tech support scam. Therefore, the most typical type of quid pro quo assault happens when attackers pose as employees of an IT department or other technical support provider. Some of the real-time examples of quid pro quo in social engineering:

- A free download of a new software product in exchange for the victim's contact details. Many clients simply want to use the software and register using their login information instead of purchasing the product. However, they are unaware that their credentials are more crucial or that the product they plan to use to exchange their credentials occasionally is insufficient.

- Many victims seek discounts when purchasing any item. Attackers design websites that advertise several coupons for discounts, but the users must register in order to access the coupons. In most cases, the coupon does not apply to the product, and the users lose their data.
- Today, attackers rely heavily on emails to convey any kind of harmful material. To obtain the victim's email address, the attackers use a complimentary gift.

Once the attackers had all of the victims' information, they might have sold it on the black market or used it to plan another attack. By obtaining the victims' regular credentials, some attackers are able to guess crucial credentials like bank passwords.

4.3. Reverse Social Engineering (RSE)

In a traditional social engineering attack, the attackers contact the victims and use various persuasion techniques to get them to provide their credentials. However, in a reverse social engineering (RSE) attack, the attacker does not approach the victims. Instead, the victim is misled into getting in touch with the perpetrator on her own. As a result, since the victim was the one who first developed the relationship with the attacker, a high level of trust has been built between them. For example, legal issues are another technique to make the victims fear. Posting content that is offensive to any individual or community or country. There are legal risks associated with the use of social networking sites like leaking confidential information on sites or invading someone's privacy.

The initial stage of the attack involves "baiting" in some way to attract the victim's interest. Once the victim's interest has been stimulated, the attacker moves on to stage two, where they wait for the victim to initiate contact and make the first move. In order to carry out an RSE attack, the attacker typically needs to develop a profile that appeals to the victim and encourages them to make contact. Three potential reverse social engineering assault combinations are presented in the context of online social networks (Irani et al., 2011).

4.3.1. RSE Based on Recommendations

Users are given recommendations depending on their interests. Users' internet profiles, social networks, and other sources are used to gather information about their interests. For instance, when people watch videos on YouTube, they are often recommended other videos with comparable subjects. Many attackers include contact information on posters in public places so that people can contact them. Numerous recommendations on human issues are made in the poster. Once the victims get in touch with the attackers, they initially make an effort to become friends before requesting money to solve the issue. Social networking platforms are now frequently used to highlight the aim of their recommendations. These recommendations can be seen by online users who are frequently active on social media sites, and they can become victims of this trap.

According to Figure 4.3, the attacker first devises a recommended system using some social engineering techniques and then disseminates it over an online or offline platform. Many people receive this information, but some of them contact the attackers and end up being victims.

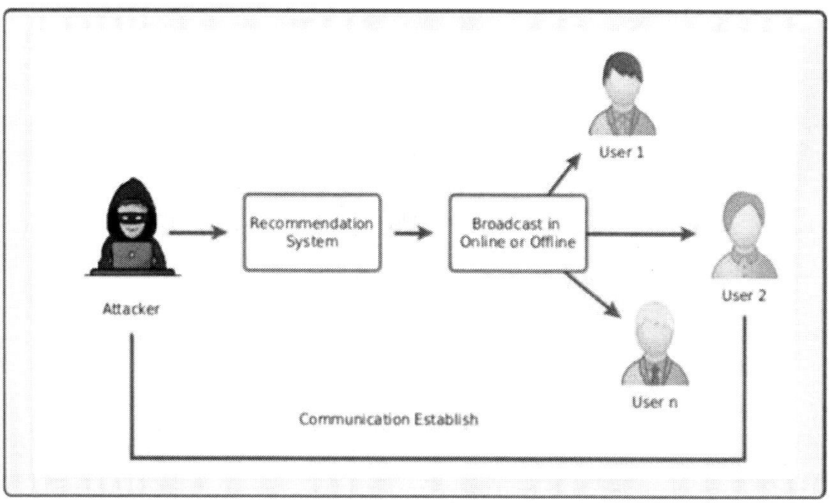

Figure 4.3. Reverse social engineering based on recommendation.

4.3.2. RSE Based on Demographics

People favor others who belong to the same age group, share their beliefs, or reside in the same area. A profile or a number of profiles that are likely to appeal to particular users are simply created by the attacker as part of the attack, and they are then left empty while they wait for victims to make contact. A general discussion of what people like or who they attract was covered in the previous chapter. Similar tactics are used by the attackers to Become friends and steal their passwords. Once the attackers observe this kind of profile, the victims instinctively approach them and become the target.

One of the most common types of cybercrime is the romance scam, in which an attacker creates a false online persona in an effort to win the victim's love and trust. After that, the assailants manipulate and/or steal from the victim by creating the appearance of a loving or close relationship.

Numerous attackers use false identities to sign up for matrimonial websites. They first make friends with any users they catch in the trap and then they become more like family. The attackers then demonstrate family health crises or other problems and demand money. The victim pays because he believes that his future wife is requesting money. Once they have money, the attackers cut the line.

4.3.3. RSE Based on Visitor Tracking

Members of several social networks, including Xing and Friendster, have the option to use a feature called visitor monitoring to observe who has accessed their online accounts. In this case, the attack benefits from the user's desire to view their profile page. The user might be interested in the notification that the page has been viewed, which would tempt them to read the attacker's profile and perhaps take action. The victims visit the page because it appeals to them in some way. The attackers then look for the victims on other websites to learn what their objectives are. Once the attackers identify their purpose, they can start communicating with their victims and manipulating them.

Attackers use the social media platforms listed below to contact their victims. People have access to all social media platforms in general based on their objectives. Instagram is a site for sharing photos, while LinkedIn is one for jobs or research, among others.

4.3.3.1. Social Media Sites

Reversed social engineering, as was previously mentioned, makes considerable use of social media platforms, where attackers employ the baiting tactic to get victims to call them. Social networking websites are the most useful weapon for attackers to obtain information from their victims. Additionally, attackers try to gather sensitive information from victims by using social media platforms. Although multiple social media sites are in every area of the internet, some examples of these websites are listed below:

- *Social networking sites*: Social networking websites like Facebook, Twitter, and LinkedIn are well-known to the majority of people. People can connect with friends, family, and brands through these channels. They promote knowledge exchange and emphasize close, one-on-one communication. A social networking site can accomplish everything. Users can engage in vibrant debates, curate information, submit photographs and videos, form groups based on interests, and share their ideas. They are designed with the user, their priorities, and their social networks in mind. Additionally, they aid in the measurement of social media ROI, which AIDS in the development of powerful marketing plans. Users share their information on social networking sites which can cause privacy breaches unless proper security measures are applied. For example, everyone can observe the information of a user if the user's default setting is 'public'. Each day, thousands of cyberattacks are launched against users of social media platforms like Facebook, Twitter, and LinkedIn. According to Time magazine, a Twitter phishing attack in March 2017 used "expertly customized messages" to target 10,000 employees at the U.S. Department of Defense.[15]
- *Sharing economy networks*: The popular locations to discover low-cost vacation homes or a specific service are websites like Rover and Airbnb. Networks in the sharing economy connect those with a need with others who have something to share. These communities create opportunities that would not be possible otherwise by combining resources in ways that are technologically impossible. According to cybersecurity firm Redscan, consumers of Airbnb are the target of a phishing scam that aims to take advantage of the General Data Protection Regulation (GDPR) when it becomes

---

[15] https://time.com/4783932/inside-russia-social-media-war-america/.

effective in 2018. Attackers are taking advantage of organizations actively seeking new user permission before the May 25 GDPR implementation date by impersonating a reputable company in email conversations. In order to continue using Airbnb services, the email instructs consumers to update their personal information by clicking a malicious link.[16]

- *Online forum sites*: Online forums like Reddit and Quora are created explicitly to start a discussion. Users can register with these forums and then go through the answers to various queries that have been published by others or self-answer the questions. Users tend to disclose less personally identifying information than on Facebook and Instagram, though. According to a report from the well-known question-and-answer website Quora, 100 million of its users may have had their account information hacked. It is thought that the hack exposed usernames, email addresses, encrypted passwords, any information users may have permitted Quora to import from other platforms, and any material they may have published, including questions, answers, comments, and upvotes. The intrusion is also thought to have affected user downvotes, direct messages, and other nonpublic content actions.[17]
- *Community blogs*: Shared blogging platforms like Medium and Tumblr offer a space to express one's views and a way to interact with readers. These community blog platforms provide an audience with a lot of options for customization and self-expression. The Tumblr phishing attempt, which was initially discovered by researchers at GFI Labs in mid-June and is intensifying this week, uses all the standard social engineering techniques to convince users to provide login information that gives attackers access to their accounts. According to GFI Labs researchers, numerous domains, including tumblriq.com, tumblrlogin.com, and tumblrsecurity.com, were the source of the phishing assault data, which was spread across 304 pages of Microsoft Word and had 8,200 lines of text.

[16] https://techmonitor.ai/technology/cybersecurity/airbnb-customers-target.
[17] https://www.nytimes.com/2018/12/04/technology/quora-hack-data-breach.html.

- *Video hosting sites*: YouTube transformed how people consume, produce, and approach video. The medium became more approachable as a result. The video has advanced further gratitude to recent advancements in technology and connection. Creators may put together material and publish it on a platform designed for streaming appreciation to sites like YouTube and Vimeo that host videos. Video is a very essential medium because of its accessibility. The phishing assault targeting YouTube content creators was noticed by Google's threat analysis team, who also uncovered the YouTube scam. Google had to recover 4000 impacted accounts and blacklisted 2400 harmful files in addition to 62000 phishing pages.
- *Image sharing sites*: The purpose of social media sites like Instagram, Imgur, and Snapchat is to increase the impact of image sharing. Users produce, collect, and share distinctive images that provoke thought and stand on their own. For a business, a picture might be worth a thousand words. As per the report of Statista Research Department, 2022b, the vast majority of Instagram mega-influencers with more than a million followers took part in fraudulent actions to artificially increase their engagement and fan base. In 2020, 66.77 percent of mega-influencers engaged in fraud, and nearly 62.8 percent in 2021. In 2021, 49.23% of influencers were on average involved in fraud.
- *Social review sites*: Sites like Yelp and TripAdvisor display reviews from locals for various destinations and experiences. By doing this, a lot of the guesswork involved in making a restaurant or hotel reservation is removed. According to the report of Hart, 2021b, more than 2 million reviews on TripAdvisor were denied or deleted as a result of attackers' frequent use of social review sites for social engineering attacks. 8.6 percent of the total for a number of factors, including fraud or bias 39.7 percent, and others.

4.3.4. Traditional Social Engineering vs. Reverse Social Engineering

The goal of traditional social engineering assaults is to acquire access to systems, data, money, or physical areas by tricking the target into providing sensitive information. Attacks using Reverse social engineering have a similar appearance, but a different methodology as shown in Table 4.1.

Table 4.1. Traditional social engineering vs. reverse social engineering

Traditional Social Engineering	Reverse Social Engineering
The attacker approaches victims to initiate communication	Victims initiate communication with attackers
The level of trust between the attackers and victims is low or medium	A high level of trust has been built between the attacker and the victims
Especially using email, SMS, and other forms of communications	Attackers often employ social networking sites

4.4. Technical Approaches

Technical methods are primarily conducted online or in applications. This strategy requires technical expertise aside from traditional social engineering approaches. The last chapter provides a general discussion of the many forms of information that attackers utilize to carry out social engineering attacks. Most individuals are unaware of the fact that they freely give up numerous personal information, which is useful to the attackers. Additionally, a variety of tools are built to collect data from the victims. Some of the tools or software where attackers primarily attempt to collect information from the victims are:

4.4.1. Search Engine Tools

A search engine is a software program that enables internet users to look for content on the World Wide Web (WWW). When a user types of keywords or key phrases into a search engine, a list of web content results such as the website's link, photos, videos, or other online data that semantically match the search query is returned. Currently, everyone uses a search engine to locate information related to their search. However, it also provides a back door for attackers, who can now utilize search engines to ascertain information about their intended victims.

The attacker recognizes the target individual initially, as was stated in the previous chapter. Following that, they use the search engine to find more data, such as the target person's profile in various sources. They attempt a social engineering attack after gathering all the required data. More information collection suggests their attack has an improved probability of succeeding.

Spamdexing is another type of often-used attack (or Search Engine Poisoning). In this attack, a search engine is tricked into placing a malicious website at the top of the results. It works well because many users believe the top search results to be the most relevant and are therefore more willing to visit them. As a result, it assumes consumers would consider the websites at the top of search results to be the most relevant, it takes advantage of the Conviction factor.

Some of the search engines are employed by attackers to gather details about connected devices, private information on users in a more curated way than traditional search engines, compromised passwords, and more.[18] An example of these search engines is Shodan. The primary function of Shodan is to search for Internet of Things (IoT) devices like security cameras, medical equipment, and more. There are currently about 31 billion of these devices, many of which are viewed as having little computing power. This search engine is used by attackers to discover weak systems on unprotected, publicly accessible devices. It can also be used by attackers to locate recently connected internet-linked devices. Another search engine is Censys which is a payment tool that allows attackers to view in real-time the attacks that various computer systems and applications are experiencing. Additionally, Censys offers a free domain search engine where intruders can access and view various details about the domains, including the protocols and ports they employ as well as the validity of their certificates. Furthermore, it contains a certificate search engine that allows attackers to verify whether a certificate is valid and to determine which key was the last one to remain so.

4.4.2. Social Engineering Toolkits

Currently, attackers use several tools for collecting information. A social engineering toolkit is a set of scripts/programs that allows an attacker to automatically set up various kinds of social engineering attacks such as phishing, spear phishing, website attack, mass mailer attack, and others. In addition, this toolkit includes graphics such as images and logos so that it looks like it is coming from genuine parties. The social engineering toolkits are created by teams or individuals and are available for purchase on the black market. These advanced kits are often challenging to come by, very pricey, and more likely to be bought and deployed by well-coordinated

[18] https://aofirs.org/articles/hacker-search-engines.

attack groups than by ordinary users. The attackers employed various toolkits to collect the information. This toolkit is explained in Chapter 6.

4.4.3. Third Party Applications

Every operating system, including Apple and Android, has applications that only work on that system. However, these third-party applications request the user's consent before they can access personal data from any of the different games or applications. The third-party application was made by a third party to carry out a certain task. For example, WPS Office, also known as Writer, Presentation, and Spreadsheets (WPS), is an office suite created by Chinese software company Kingsoft, based in Zhuhai, for Microsoft Windows, macOS, Linux, iOS, Android, and HarmonyOS. Many users use this kind of application for a specific purpose.

The attackers also create fake applications that mimic real ones and request people to install their platforms. This application contains malicious code designed to steal the victim's data. When users install these applications, they request authorization to access internal data. The user gives the application a particular amount of access to the user's data. The information is then stolen by these applications and sent to the attackers often without the user's knowledge. This category of application is highly vulnerable to mobile users.

4.4.4. Watering Hole Attacks

The phrase, "watering hole attack," refers to a situation in which predators in the wild wait near a watering hole before attacking their target. Popular consumer websites can be compromised by cybercriminals to further their objectives of conducting opportunistic Watering hole attacks for financial gain or to expand their botnet. Figure 4.4 illustrates the watering hole attack.

Attackers first locate a website with high traffic, which indicates that many users are visiting the site. The websites with lower security that are also more popular with clients can be targeted, regardless of the ability of all websites to do so. The attackers then identify a method to embed a malicious code payload into the website using JavaScript or HyperText Markup Language (HTML). The payload is activated when the victim accesses the hacked website, and an exploit chain is started to infect the victim's system.

The attack may result in a fake popup urging the user to perform an additional action that would download malicious code, or the payload may be automatic. The exploit chain could be a well-known, pre-existing exploit or one that the attacker independently developed.

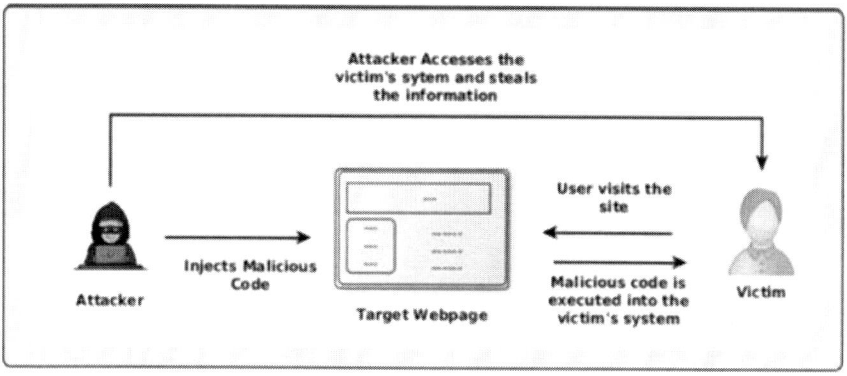

Figure 4.4. Watering hole attack.

Once the victim's computer has been compromised by the payload, the attacker can utilize that machine to perform a pivot attack in order to accomplish other objectives by gaining access to other network resources. The objectives could be to learn more about the victim, use the victim's computer in a botnet, or try to take advantage of other machines connected to the victim.

On December 4, 2019, Ivan Kwiatkowski and Delcher, 2019 identified exploited watering hole websites that were used to selectively launch a drive-by download assault while displaying fictitious alerts for an Adobe Flash update, as shown in Figure 4.5. Targeting religious and ethnic minorities in Asia, this campaign has been going on at least since May 2019.

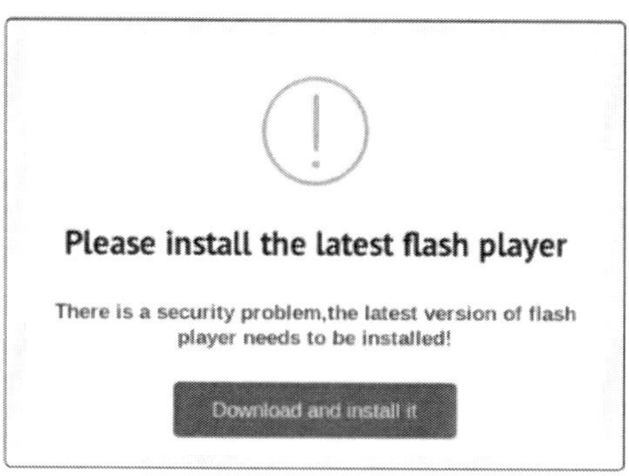

Figure 4.5. Holy water targeting attack.

4.4.5. Likejacking

A transparent layer, such as a transparent inline frame (iframe), is inserted on a legitimate webpage during this attack in order for the target to really click on the transparent layer, which directs them to the attacker's website. When a user sees the "like" button on a Facebook post, there is a transparent layer over it that the user cannot see. In likejacking, the user may click on the page and be taken to a malicious website. Two well-known and distinctive likejacking frauds spread like wildfire on Facebook in October 2011. The first scam offered Canadian Facebook users a gift certificate to Tim Hortons, a well-known coffee and donut store, as payment. Facebook users were urged by the scam to click a link and "Like" the resulting page. To obtain the gift card, they were then asked for their email address and other details. A day later, the identical scam was carried out, this time providing a $50 Starbucks gift card.[19] Two major hazards for victims were identified by Sophos, a global network of Internet security specialists, after investigating the scam:

- Victims were instructed to copy and paste an unidentified JavaScript script into the browser's address bar. Unknown JavaScript should never be executed since it can infect the user's computer with malware.
- A victim's name, address, and email address were requested as personally identifying data. A user's Facebook, email, or other accounts could be compromised if the hackers have access to sufficient information from this to do so.

4.4.6. Tabnabbing

This attack tries to trick the victim into visiting a malicious website that impersonates a valid website, requests the victim to log in, and then sends the victim's login information to the legitimate website while the victim believes the malicious website is the legitimate website. It frequently makes use of the browser's same origin policy, which allows a second page to access scripts from a third website as long as both pages share the same origin. It makes an attempt to steal private information such as login

[19] https://www.techopedia.com/definition/27758/likejacking.

credentials. It takes advantage of forgetfulness since the victim believes that a previously visited website is requesting login information once more.

4.4.6.1. Man-In-The-Middle Attacks (MITM)

A man-in-the-middle attack involves attackers intercepting traffic between the victim's network and external websites or from within their own network. Insecure communication protocols make it possible to steal transmitted data, obtain user credentials, and take over user sessions. In MITM, two methods are highly used for achieving it:

- *Passive attacks*: Attackers monitor networks without authorization, log on, and steal confidential information
- *Active attacks*: Attackers make an effort to corrupt, encrypt, or alter data while it is on the target or being transported to the target.

4.4.6.2. Code and SQL Injection Attacks

Many websites take user inputs without validating or cleaning them up. The attacker can then submit a form or conduct an API call while sending malicious code rather than the desired data values. The server runs the code, which enables attackers to take control of it. The British telecommunications operator TalkTalk's servers were compromised in October 2015 by a SQL injection attack that took advantage of a flaw in an old web interface and stole the personal information of 156,959 users.

4.5. Socio-Technical Approaches

The social approach and the technical method are combined to form the socio-technical approach. The technical approach is the technological medium used to interact with the victims, while the social approach is influenced by social factors, which combine social aspects like family, society, wealth, and religion with psychological factors like feelings, ideas, and beliefs. Currently, this approach is most widely used since people are using digital equipment to complete most of their daily work like online transactions, chatting, video calling, etc.

4.5.1. Phishing Email

Phishing is a type of social engineering attack that uses emails as a communication medium to manipulate the victims. Currently, email is used as one of the most crucial communication channels for organizations, and individuals, and it is regarded as genuine communication in place of offline letters as previously explained in Chapter 2. Email allows users to send website or file links, images, documents, and others along with the contents of the emails. It is possible to claim that phishing attacks are the modern counterpart of social engineering attacks. APWG recorded a total of 1,025,968 phishing assaults in the first quarter of 2022. Another study by Symantec revealed that in 2020, 1 in every 4,200 emails will be phishing scams. Therefore, phishing is a social engineering attack carried out by an email with no specific target, often known as spray-and-pray phishing. The attackers send out as many emails as possible in the hope that someone will fall for their scam.

Phishing is the art of creating a fake website that is similar to a genuine website and sending the link to the website through emails. Phishing websites have features like being identical to the real website and having one input field for credentials. The attacking strategies for phishing attacks are explained in Figure 4.6.

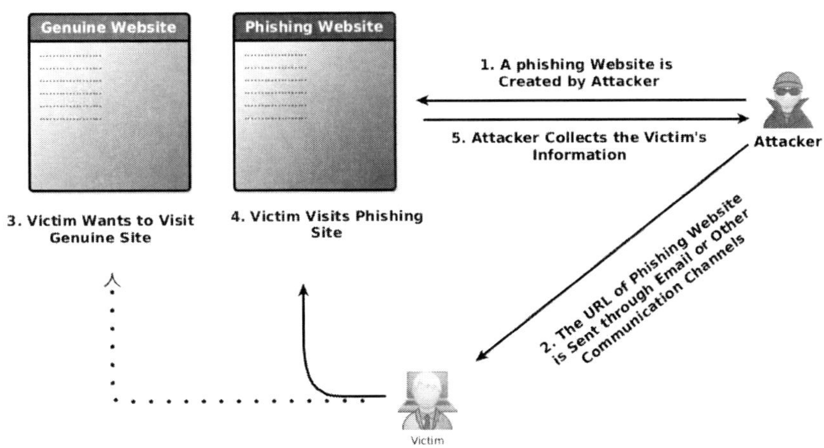

Figure 4.6. Phishing strategies.

To begin with, the attackers build a phishing website and send emails with its URL. The website's link is also created to look like the URL of an original website in order to encourage users to believe it. The attackers in this circumstance use the typosquatting technique to change the domain's appearance to present it with a more authentic appearance.

Another sort of cyberattack is called a typosquatting approach, in which the attackers generate a domain that is only marginally different from the original domain of the URL. As an illustration, the attacker may create the domain paypa1.com by replacing the letter "l" with the number "1" of the original domain paypal.com. It is also known as domain imitation, sting sites, fake URLs, and URL hijacking.

The difficulty with phishing attacks is getting to the target by clicking the link. The email's contents contain social engineering strategies employed by the attackers to stimulate the victim's emotions and persuade them to click the link. Users who click the link are directed to a phishing website where their credentials are required. If users enter their credentials on the website, the attacker's repository is where they are stored. The attackers then utilize credentials to a legitimate website to commit fraud. For example, the victim receives an email from PayPal stating that their account has been compromised and will be canceled until they confirm their credit card information. The victim is taken to a fake PayPal website by the phishing email's link, where their credit card information is stolen and used to commit more crimes.

4.5.2. Spear Phishing

Phishing emails are distributed to a relatively wide number of recipients, mostly at random, with the hope that very few people will reply. Spear phishing emails are specifically created to elicit a response from a single target. Through the use of social media and other publicly available information, criminals identify a specific target within an organization and create a fake email specifically for that person. Figure 4.7 shows an illustration of a targeted spear phishing attack. In this instance, the attacker is pretending to be the target's coworker. According to Symantec's 2019 Internet Security Threat report, nearly two-thirds (65%) of all known entities conducting targeted cyberattacks exploit spear phishing emails. Additionally, according to the research, 96% of targeted attacks have an intelligence-gathering objective.

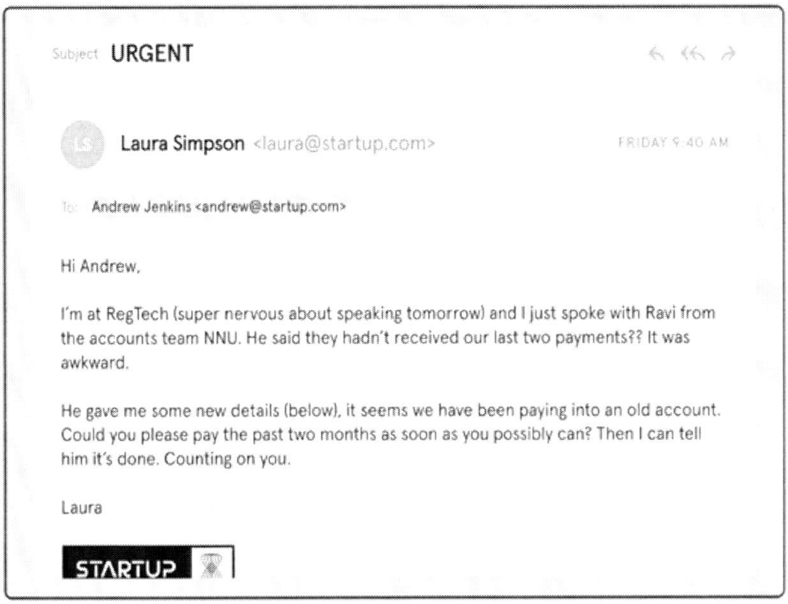

Figure 4.7. An example of the spear phishing attack.

The types of spear phishing attacks are listed below:

4.5.2.1. Whaling

As mentioned above, spear phishing targets specific people or groups of people, including employees, regular people, and high-level individuals, whereas whaling only targets high-profile employees, such as the chief executive officer (CEO) or chief financial officer (CFO).

4.5.2.2. Business Email Compromise

The term "business email compromise" (BEC) refers to an exploit when an attacker gains access to a company email account and mimics the identity of the owner in order to defraud the business, its staff, clients, or partners.

4.5.2.3. CEO Fraud

An attempt at spear phishing in which the fraudster poses as the CEO of the target organization and selects a different employee as the victim. According to Barracuda, a type of spear-phishing email assault called CEO Fraud involves the attacker posing as the CEO of an organization. The attacker typically attempts to dupe you into paying money to a bank account they own, submitting critical HR information, or divulging other sensitive information. In order to avoid suspicion and examination, a bogus email typically portrays a critical scenario. Generally, two methods are used to start a CEO fraud email. The first is called name spoofing, where the attacker uses the CEO's name but a different email address.

Sometimes (but not usually), the attacker will use an email address that is nearly identical to the company's domain but differs by a few letters (e.g., acrne.com instead of acme.com). The attacker uses name spoofing in the hope that the receiver would quickly respond and not detect the false sender address. It can be difficult to recognize this assault because many email clients, particularly those for mobile devices, do not by default display the sender's address. In the second type of spoofing, the CEO's name and the right sender address are both used by the attacker. To ensure that their response to your email will reach them, the attacker in this type of attack often chooses a reply-to address that is distinct from the sender's address.

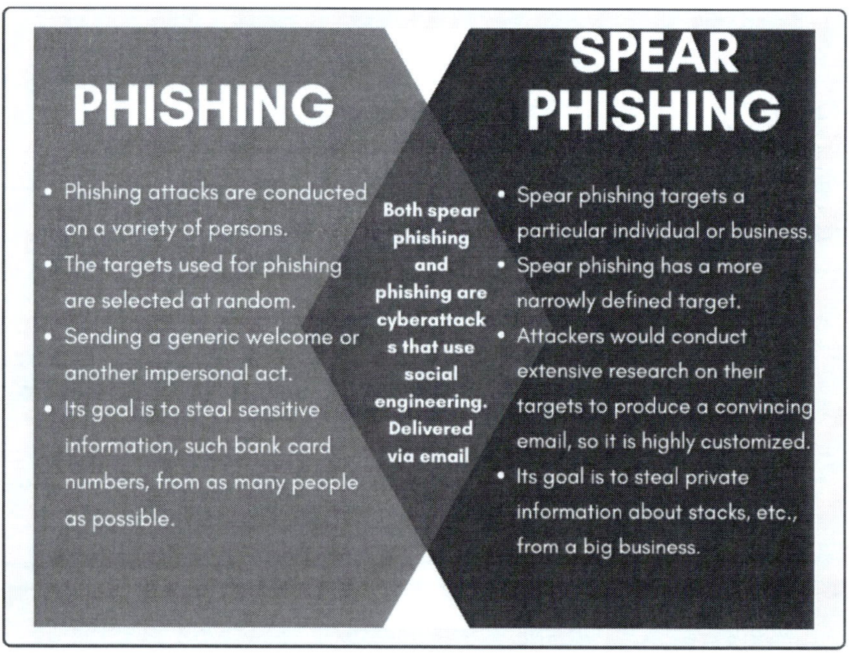

Figure 4.8. Differences between spear phishing and phishing.

4.5.2.4. Double Barrel Phishing

Two emails must be sent to a victim in order to build their trust and convince them that the emails are real. Nothing is incorrect with the first email. Therefore, it is merely a ruse. It does not have any malicious attachments or links, and the recipient is not asked to reply. Fraudsters may use similar signatures and email addresses to appear to be someone close to victims, giving the con more of a personal touch.

The objective of this email is to win the victim's trust by using a plausible narrative. Sadly, what comes next is a lot worse. To make the scenario seem more genuine, phishers will briefly postpone sending their next email. In contrast to the first communication, this one's attachment or link will expose you to fraudulent websites and carry malware. This is when the attack actually begins.

4.5.3. Angler Phishing

This attack lurks among user comments posted on social media sites like Yelp, looking for any comments that may need to be handled. For example, an attacker might come across a customer's grievance on a purchase or a bank transaction. The attacker then poses as a customer service representative for that company and requests the victim for specific information in order to address the victim's problem. A consumer may give personal information while unaware that they have been phished in the hope that the problem would be resolved. This attack takes advantage of the victims' susceptibility since they are in need of help and have faith in the suppliers.

4.5.4. Vishing

Vishing, also known as voicemail phishing, is the practice of using fraudulent voicemail to attempt to receive personal information. Vishing, which is similar to phishing, is when attackers pretend to be a reliable company or reputable individual via a voicemail message in order to acquire credit card numbers or other sensitive information. Vishing tricks email users into disclosing personal or financial information by using social engineering techniques. For instance, around the holidays, victims may receive a voicemail purporting to be from a reputable merchant warning them to call back and confirm their billing information immediately or else their product will not be delivered in time for the holidays. The only issue is that the false voicemail gives victims a bogus phone number to call back, and that number will use the information provided by the victims to commit fraud, identity theft, and other crimes. Similar frauds involve phony messages sent by online criminals posing as representatives of well-known computer manufacturers, the IRS, or just about any other reliable source they can find.

4.5.5. Smishing

Short messaging service, or SMS, or text messages more generally, is used in smashing (SMS + phishing) attacks. People are more inclined to believe a message they receive through a messaging app on their phone than a message they receive via email, which has led to the rise in the popularity of this type of attack. Any numeric combination that is equal in length to a phone number can be sent messages by the hacker. No harm, no foul - they are liberated to attempt any and all digit combinations. Users read 98 percent of texts and only respond to 45 percent of them, according to Pemberton, 2016 from Gartner. This makes the text a highly obvious attack channel for hackers, especially given that only 6% of the emails get replies.

Although many organizations provide two-factor authentication, some attackers overcome this technique. A wonderful illustration of how two-factor authentication could be circumvented by a scammer using pretexting can be seen on the KnowBe4 blog. While they were updating this information, the con artists called the victims, posing as his bank to check the odd charges and ask them to read the codes the bank was providing them, saying they needed to validate their identification. If the victim ever attempted to change his username and password, his bank would text him a six-digit confirmation code. They had those codes, and they had no trouble breaking into his account.[20]

4.5.6. Imishing Attack

Imishing is a form of phishing that is employed via instant messaging (instant messaging + phishing). The attackers use several social media

[20] https://www.csoonline.com/article/3546299/what-is-pretexting-definition-examples-and-prevention.html.

platforms or other sources to gather phone numbers before sending phishing messages via an instant messaging network. Conversations through instant messaging occur in real-time, unlike those over email or SMS (hence "instant"). Using information gathered from the internet, the attackers quickly make friends with the victims before asking them for crucial information. Without a phone number, the attackers can contact the victims on several instant messaging platforms by recognizing their registered ID names and initiating communication.

According to a survey from The Hindu Business Line, 2021, Whatsapp, Telegram, and Viber are the most popular communication apps among phishing scammers." Between December 2020 and May 2021, Whatsapp accounted for 89.6% of all fraudulent connections that were discovered, with Telegram coming in second (5.6 percent). Hangouts have less than 1% market share, while Viber came in third with 4.7%. To easily manipulate the victims, phishing attacks via instant messaging apps are on the rise. It resembles direct communication between attackers and victims. When a victim asks a question, the attackers immediately respond because they have already done their research on the victim through multiple platforms.

4.5.7. Evil Twin Phishing

Evil twin attack attracts consumers to connect to a fake Wi-Fi access point by imitating a reliable network. Attackers have access to everything once a person connects to an "evil twin" network, including their network traffic and secret login information.

Suppose a user chooses to join a public Wi-Fi network at an Airpot. Users trust that access point to be reliable and secure because they frequently go to other locations through the airport and have connected to it in the past. The difference this time is that attackers set up an evil twin network with the exact same SSID name (A wireless local area network's service set identifier (SSID) is a string of characters used to identify it (WLAN)) and a stronger signal than the genuine access point. Despite the fact that it is marked as "unsecured," the user connects to it.

Summary

Social engineering attack types were explored in this chapter. The five forms of social engineering attacks are classified according to the attacker's methods and include the physical approach, social approach, reverse social engineering approach, technical approach, and socio-technical approach. Targeting with a physical approach requires user input. The social approach makes use of social psychology methods used by users. Reverse social engineering techniques lure the victims into communicating with the attackers. In order to attempt the victims, the technical approach needs technical expertise, and the socio-technical strategy combines both the technological and social approaches.

Chapter 5

Identity Theft: Exploit the User's Information

In a social engineering attack, an attacker will use human interaction to deceive a victim into providing information. People have a natural tendency to be trusting. Social engineering attacks attempt to use this inclination to obtain personal information. The data could be stolen and then used to commit fraud or identity theft. Once an attacker impersonates the identity of another user, the identity is misappropriated. Attackers use software to request authorization to access information offered by Social Networking Sites. When a user gives permission, they receive access to all information, which can be misused without the user's knowledge.

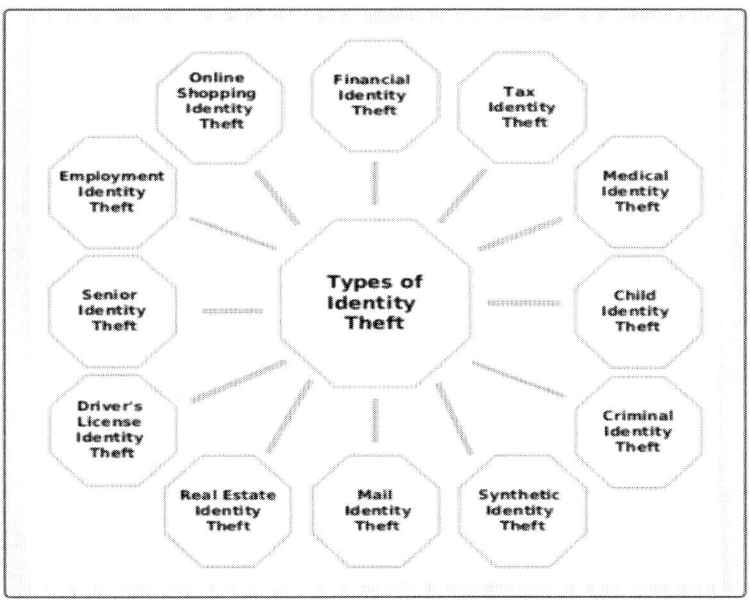

Figure 5.1. Types of identity theft.

According to the definition of identity theft in the National Crime Victimization Survey (NCVS), identity theft includes any one or more of the following three categories of incidents:

- Unauthorized use of, or attempt to utilize, an already existing account
- Unauthorized use of, or attempt to exploit, personal data to create a new account
- Misuse of personal data for deceptive purposes.

This chapter will cover the following topics:

- Financial identity theft
- Tax identity theft
- Medical identity theft
- Child identity theft
- Criminal identity theft
- Synthetic identity theft
- Mail identity theft
- Real estate identity theft
- Driver's license identity theft
- Senior identity theft
- Employment identity theft
- Online shopping identity theft

5.1. Financial Identity Theft

The use of another person's information for financial benefit is the most prevalent type of identity theft. As an illustration, an attacker may utilize a victim's bank account or credit card information to steal money or make transactions, or they may use the user's social security number to start a new credit account. A variety of scams involve financial identities:

5.1.1. Banking Identity Theft

The term banking identity theft refers to the use of deception to steal money or other assets from a bank, financial institution, or a bank's depositors. The most common cause of bank scams is financial identity theft. To steal money from the bank, attackers utilize information from the bank, modify the information, or pose as someone else.

Berry Law, 2022 mentioned some of the types of bank fraud:

- *Bank impersonation*: It takes place when someone sets up a fake financial institution or designs a website to entice customers to deposit money. For instance, a fraudster may pose as a bank employee and inform a customer that their account is in danger and that they need to move money to a safe account or set up automatic withdrawals to halt the funds.
- *Stolen checks*: A paper check is stolen by the attacker, who also imitates the signature. A check may be printed and used from a stolen account number in some instances by the attackers. It is commonly referred to as counterfeiting when a thief prints checks. If the bank recognizes the problem, the account is closed, the fraudster is eliminated, the bank is left with bad checks, and the victim of identity theft must cope with the consequences of having their data compromised.
- *Internet bank fraud*: These days, internet banking is frequently used to verify account information, make purchases, pay bills, transfer money, print statements, and more. The attackers typically use emails that seem to come from reliable sources to drive victims to bogus websites. The victims are then duped into disclosing private information, including bank account information.
- *Skimming attacks*: It is the act of reading a credit card or debit card's magnetic strip in order to get private information. The personal information of the cardholder is obtained by fraudsters by reading the magnetic strip on the back of a credit/debit/ATM card. It will be covered in the part after this one.

5.1.2. Credit and Debit Card Scams

Once attackers get hold of a victim's credit card details, they can use them to make purchases, carry out other transactions, or start new accounts. This is known as credit card fraud. The use of cloned cards, new account fraud, account takeover fraud, and cards-not-present schemes are a few instances of credit card fraud. According to a 2021 annual survey, more than one in three people who own credit or debit cards have been the victim of fraud more than once. Around 50% of all Americans have had fraudulent charges on their cards. This translates to 127 million Americans who have experienced credit card theft at least once.

5.1.3. Fraudulent Loans

It comprises utilizing a false identity or filing a loan application with false information to obtain funding. The information of the victim or falsified information may be used by the attacker to open a mortgage or loan. Another scenario involves lenders marketing mortgages or loans using false information, dishonest business methods, and other high-pressure sales techniques.

Loan fraud is seen as a sort of financial identity theft because it necessitates the stealing and exploitation of the victim's personal information. Loan or lease fraud will be ranked as the fourth most frequent identity theft in 2020. During the loaning process, many lending organizations simply request a small quantity of information. This means that to obtain a loan, identity thieves only require a few pieces of information, such as a social security number (SSN) or bank account number.

5.1.4. Investment Fraud

Investment fraud occurs when attackers attempt to deceive victims into making investments. This type includes selling investments or securities with false, misleading information on the legitimate investigation. It could be false promises, hiding facts, and insider trading tips. They could encourage their victims to make investments in securities such as stocks, bonds, notes, commodities, money, or even real estate. Investing fraudsters may pose as telemarketers or financial counselors by showing their identities. They come off as intelligent, affable, and appealing. They can claim that a potential investment opportunity is urgent. They work to gain the victim's trust so that they will hand them money as soon as feasible and without prodding.

5.2. Tax Identity Theft

The attackers steal the personal information of victims and then use it to file a tax return and obtain the victim's refund. The taxpayer then filed a tax return but was informed that it had been filed twice as shown in Figure 5.2.

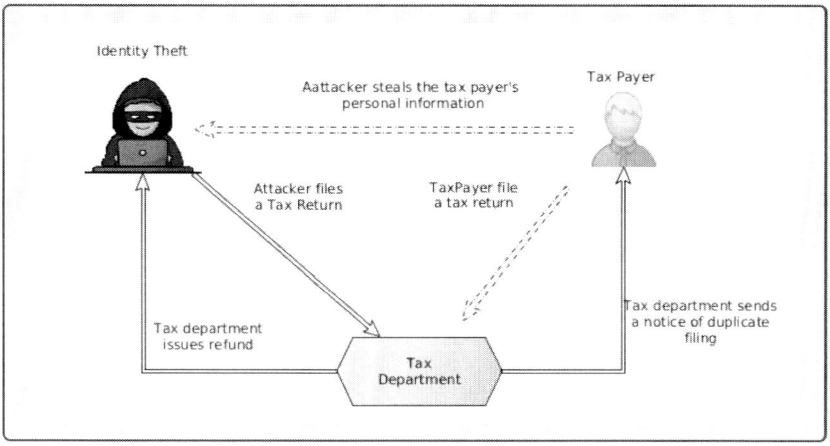

Figure 5.2. Tax identity theft.

The majority of people are unaware that they are victims of tax identity theft until the Tax Department rejects their tax filings. Over the past three years, the Federal Trade Commission (FTC) has received more reports of tax identity theft than any other type of identity theft. In 2010, more than 15% of identity theft accusations were related to tax or wage-related fraud. This percentage increased to 24% in 2011, and 43% in 2012. Consumer Protection Division, 2022 mentioned that identity theft related to income taxes contains two main forms:

- The first happens when the tax department receives income that does not belong to the victim and assesses the victim for more taxes than the victim owes. In this case, the victim will be responsible for paying someone else's taxes.
- The second takes place when attackers request the victim's tax refund. In this case, the victim might not get their withholdings as they were paid more than the taxes the victim owes.

5.2.1. Consequences

The following consequences occur when a victim is lured into a tax identity theft fraud:

- The victim's e-filed return is rejected by the tax department because their tax ID has previously been used to file a tax return.

- If the victims are failed to do anything, the tax department sends them a tax transcript, or they get a notification that an online account has been set up, accessed, or disabled.
- The tax department notifies victims that they owe taxes, that their refund has been offset, or that collection measures are being taken against them as a result of a tax return from a year in which the victims failed to submit.
- A letter asking the victims to confirm their identity and that the tax return they received is accurate may be sent to them if the tax department suspects that the victim's identity has been stolen.

Although the tax department attempts to assist the customers, the attackers may also pose as tax officials and either demand money from their victims or request their data.

5.3. Medical Identity Theft

An attacker who commits medical identity theft will utilize the victim's personal information to obtain medical treatment in the victim's name. Hackers target medical records frequently because, according to the FBI, medical identities are worth 20 to 50 times more on the black market than financial identities. According to Ann Patterson, senior vice president of the Medical Identity Fraud Alliance (MIFA), a coalition of several dozen healthcare institutions and businesses working to lessen the crime and its detrimental effects, about 20% of victims have reported that they received the incorrect diagnosis or treatment or that their care was delayed because there was uncertainty about what was true in their records as a result of the identity theft.

Types of medical identity theft:[21]

5.3.1. Financial Medical Identity Theft

Financial medical identity theft happens when someone uses the victim's name and/or insurance information to obtain medical treatment. In these cases, a doctor bills the victims or their insurance provider for services

[21] https://consumer.georgia.gov/consumer-topics/identity-theft-medical-identity-theft.

rendered to someone else. Healthcare fraud is thought to result in annual financial losses in the tens of billions of dollars, according to the National Health Care Anti-Fraud Association (NHCAA). A conservative estimate puts the loss at 3 percent of overall health care spending, but some government and law enforcement organizations put it as high as 10 percent, or more than $300 billion.

5.3.2. Criminal Medical Identity Theft

Criminal medical identity theft occurs when victims are held accountable for another person's illegal behavior. Using the victim's details, a criminal who has used drugs might verify into a hospital, for instance, causing this to happen. In such circumstances, the hospital could inform the police that they believe the victims have committed a crime. As one of the penalties, the victims can be arrested. In general, it is difficult to imagine that an identity theft victim may be jailed for the crime, yet it occurs almost daily. In Consumer reports expose, a stolen purse resulted in a woman's misplaced detention when a burglar obtained prescription medications using her health insurance card. When a pregnant lady used her identity at a hospital and gave birth to an infant with drugs in her system, another woman had a run-in with CPS (Andrews, 2016).

5.3.3. Government Benefits Fraud

The misuse of a victim's government-provided medical benefits is known as government benefits fraud. The victims are notified that the benefits have been used after the attackers have taken use of them. Free medical care was provided to many government employees, and it will continue after they retire. governments in many nations provide women, children, BPL families, and Senior citizens with free medical care. The medical officers only verify government-issued identification documents for things like age and nationality. The attackers are quite clever; they create fake paperwork, display several health issues, and take advantage of free medications and treatments.

5.3.4. Obtaining Medical Equipment

An attacker could exploit the victim's insurance benefits to purchase pricey medical equipment, then sell it on the black market. In the medical field, insurance fraud is very widespread. The attackers steal patient data such as diagnosis codes, billing information, policy numbers, and birth dates and use it to submit fictitious claims to insurers to receive payment for treatments that were never rendered. Additionally, it may be used to create fake identifications that can be used to purchase medical supplies that will be sold again or illicit pharmaceuticals for personal consumption. Community Health Systems revealed in 2014 that 4.5 million people's patient data had been taken by Chinese hackers. To steal patient data and sell it at a premium to third parties who might use it to perpetrate insurance fraud, sophisticated criminal groups from China target health systems like CHS.[22]

5.3.5. Impersonating a Health Care Professional

Attackers adopt the persona of medical professionals by researching medical material from many online sources, including social media and search engines. The attackers provide false information, such as fake medical degrees or names impersonating real medical professionals, among other things. Once they had gathered all the required data, they began rendering or billing for medical services and supplies without a license. Many people pay a premium price for the service without realizing they are targeted and end up being victims. This is also referred to as quack. A fraudulent or uninformed pretender to medical skill is defined as a person who falsely represents themselves professionally or publicly as possessing a skill, knowledge, certification, or credentials.

For instance, 18-year-old Malachi Love-Robinson of South Florida was detained when police claimed he was running an unlicensed medical practice while pretending to be a doctor. According to STAT News, he is also suspected of stealing three checks totaling $2,800 from a patient and over $3,500 from an elderly woman he allegedly treated for stomach problems.

[22] https://resources.infosecinstitute.com/topic/the-5-most-visible-cyber-attacks-on-hospitals/.

5.4. Child Identity Theft

Child identity theft occurs when someone tries to commit fraud using or attempting to utilize a minor's personal information, usually for financial gain. An identity thief might use the minor's information to apply for a job, register for government benefits, access medical care, request a loan, or open a credit account. A fraudster can open credit accounts in young people's names without being caught because the majority of them do not have credit records until they turn 16 years old. Some children who have been victims of identity theft might not be aware of the crime until they apply for student loans or a job. According to the 2021 Child Identity Fraud Study, revealed by Javelin Strategy & Research, 2021, a member of the Escalent family, more than 1.25 million children in the United States were victims of identity theft and fraud in the previous year, costing the average affected household more than $1,100. Johansen, 2021 highlighted various distinctive and alluring motives for child identity theft, including the following:

5.4.1. Children Are Easy Targets for Identity Thieves

In any situation, the attackers impersonate high authority people and collect information from schools, colleges, and others. Generally, children often have clean credit files and are unaware their identity has been stolen until many years later. Children are typically assigned social security numbers early in life, frequently at birth. An identity thief pursuing an adult has a good probability of obtaining private information that they cannot use because the credit is already ruined. Their opportunities improve if they select a child who has not yet established poor credit history.

5.4.2. Relatives Are Usually the Attackers

The most prevalent offenders of child identity theft are family members. Parents have used their children's identities to open bank accounts, secure automobile loans, and obtain credit cards. One mother, for example, allegedly exploited her son's name while he was serving in Iraq to pay for medical and other living needs, as well as to play video poker. Individuals unrelated to the child may also perpetrate child identity theft.

Another example is a parent or relative who is having trouble paying bills and may use a child's identity and social security number to get the water or cable switched on with a new account rather than paying off the previous one that is heavily in debt. They could even use their child's identity and social security number to obtain credit to fuel an otherwise expensive shopping, gambling, or narcotic habit.

5.4.3. The Duration of Child Identity Theft Is Longer Than That of Other Varieties

The crime of child identity theft may persist longer than other forms of identity theft because young children are less likely to utilize credit or take precautions to secure their identities.

5.4.4. Foster Children May Be Particularly at Risk

Children in foster care may be especially at risk for identity theft because their correct addresses are missing and because their personal information is frequently shared with numerous individuals and organizations. Another possibility is that they do not have an adult looking out for their financial interests.

5.5. Criminal Identity Theft

Although all forms of identity theft are illegal, this particular one involves the arrest of a suspect who then gives police the victim's personal information. In this case, the victims would not be aware of it until it had an impact, such as when a judge issued a bench warrant for their arrest after a speeding ticket was unpaid. The attacker of criminal identity theft may use real or fake photo identification, as well as information such as a name, Aadhaar card, driver's license number, or social security number.

Fernando Neave-Ceniceros, a 42-year-old Mexican national, admitted to using another person's social security number fraudulently to conceal his identity and lack of legal status in the United States in 2016. According to The Associated Press, Neave-Ceniceros used a bogus identity when he was arrested and fingerprinted by officials as a teenager. Marcus Calvillo, the victim in that long-ago tragedy, was incorrectly linked to Neave-Ceniceros (Weisman, 2016).

5.5.1. Consequences of Criminal Identity Theft

Identity theft is an extremely severe problem that could harm innocent people's reputations. People squander time trying to reclaim cases once they are issued. If the true identity of the criminal cannot be determined, clearing the record can take even more time. This kind of fraud can be challenging to identify until the effects, such as:

- *A court summons is sent to the victims*: A summons might be issued by the court, for instance, if a criminal uses their ID to pay for outstanding parking tickets.
- *A bench warrant is issued for their arrest*: A court may issue a bench warrant for unresolved issues such as unpaid parking fines. The victims might then be detained at any time, possibly even during a routine traffic stop.
- *An investigation is conducted*: Police will occasionally record an identity theft victim in their database as an alias for the real criminal. As a result of this, a fake criminal record can appear on their background check. Potential employers and landlords may have issues as a result.

Although it is by no means the most frequent form of identity theft, criminal identity theft is one of the more serious ones. It is quite challenging for the victims to prove their innocence once they have been drawn into this theft.

5.6. Synthetic Identity Theft

Synthetic identity theft, which involves constructing false identities using actual people's information, is one of the most rapidly expanding categories of financial crime worldwide. Fraudsters may use information from genuine people's profiles, such as birthdates, addresses, and Social Security numbers, to construct a false profile. They can then apply for loans or credit cards or engage in other financial crimes using this character. Since they rarely utilize their SSNs, children, and senior persons are frequently the targets of this type of fraud. The film, *Shawshank Redemption* (1994), provides a good demonstration of synthetic identity theft. In the movie, Andy (Tim Robbins) used the fake identity of Randall Stephens. He'd opened a number of bank accounts using Randall Stephens as the name on them. A few banks visited Andy on his first day of freedom in order to remove all the money from the fictitious accounts. Under Randall Stephens' name, the monies were designated for the warden.

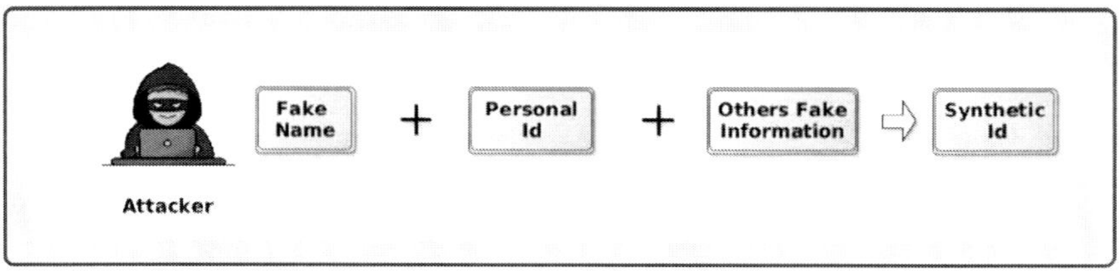

Figure 5.3. Synthetic identity theft.

As per reported by Jacoby, 2022, Financial institutions suffered $20 billion in losses in 2020 due to Synthetic identity fraud. Fake auto loan applications, Buy-Now-Pay-Later (BNPL) fraud, and refund fraud are all current issues; in 2020, the number of false auto loan applications surged alarmingly by 260 percent. Beyond these instances, there are several activities for using fake identities created in part using stolen data to defraud businesses and hurt the victims whose data was taken. The following are a few justifications given by Chauncey Crail, 2021, for why someone may use this more complex ruse to create identities:

- Synthetic fraud is a technique used by criminals to steal money, avoid being caught by authorities or financial institutions, or aid in the trafficking of people or drugs.
- Unauthorized immigrants may gain access to legitimate SSNs and use false personal information to live, work, and access benefits like healthcare in many countries such as the United States.
- Some people who find themselves in difficulty decide to adopt a false identity to avoid being persecuted or attacked by a dangerous person.

- Synthetic fraud is used by organized crime groups to control thousands of fictitious credit card accounts and support luxury lifestyles.

LexisNexis, 2022 mentioned two sorts of methods that are used by attackers to create a synthetic identity:

5.6.1. Manipulated Synthetics

Limited alterations are made to the SSN and other components of Synthetic identities based on genuine identities. These modified identities are frequently used by individuals to conceal prior histories and obtain credit; they may or may not be utilized with evil intent. People with poor credit histories may fabricate identities in order to be granted new credit for honest purchases that they mean to pay back.

5.6.2. Manufactured Synthetics

Although fraudsters piece together bits and pieces of personally identifiable information (PII) from actual persons to generate fake identities, these Synthetic identities were originally formed of valid data constructed from several identities. They are sometimes referred to as "Frankenstein" identities. Recently, they have been constructed using false data, including SSNs that fraudsters select from the same pool of numbers that the SSA currently draws at random to assign SSNs. The account was created using PII that is not associated with any known customers. With the tools we have today, it is challenging to recognize this new type of synthetic.

Financial firms are largely responsible for the load. Customers are not liable for fraud committed against them, so banks, investment firms, and other businesses are the ones who must bear the loss. Other issues exist besides money. The institution is frequently held responsible by customers for ID theft.

5.7. Mail Identity Theft

Mail identity theft happens when criminals target a user's mailbox and take out any mail that contains crucial information. Similar to dumpster diving, a thief may grab a victim's credit card statements, bank records, or anything else that could be used to steal their identity. By filing a change of address to the post office, attackers have occasionally been found to reroute mail without the user's knowledge or consent.

5.7.1. Mail Identity Theft Approaches

Mail identity theft is less technically challenging than database hacking. Knowing how thieves behave may be sufficient to protect their mail from fraudulent operations. There are various typical strategies:[23]

- Attackers re-direct users' mailing by sending a fake change of address request to their mail provider.
- The victim's credit card statement was taken by the perpetrators. Following the theft of such mail, an identity thief can utilize the information to make purchases of products and services. Alternatively, the criminal calls the victims on behalf of a creditor and obtains other sensitive information by using the information from the bill.
- The victims' outgoing correspondence to a credit card firm, for instance, is stolen by identity thieves. This enables them to pay the checks and discover the victim's name, address, and bank account number.
- Attackers may commit theft directly from post office boxes and profit from the knowledge gained before someone comes to call the police. Local post offices can fail to provide the proper security for their mailboxes, which makes postal identity theft easier.

5.8. Real Estate Identity Theft

Real estate is referred to as the land as well as any permanent, whether natural or man-made, structures or improvements related to the property, such as a house. It contrasts with personal property, such as cars, yachts, jewels, furniture, and farm equipment, which is temporally affixed to the land. Attackers, however, pose as the owners of these properties and sell

[23] https://www.inkit.com/blog/mail-identity-theft.

them to the victims for a large sum of money. Some examples of real estate identity theft are discussed below.[24]

5.8.1. Title Deception

The situation when the ownership of property is unclear is known as title deception. The attackers take advantage of this and create duplicate papers for properties that do not belong to them, which they then sell to other people. Property types sold through title deception include:

- The properties that have been vacant for a considerable amount of time.
- The attackers present some bogus properties as their own, but the owners are located abroad.
- Properties where there have been legal issues, unpaid rent, and numerous other obligations that have been outstanding for a long time.
- The attacker sells properties that are in the random place that is depicted or that are not their own.

5.8.2. Pressure to Act Immediately

People purchase in a rush without doing any study on the item's extremely high price because the attackers use urgency tactics and demonstrate that there are only a few apartments remaining, so purchase it immediately. Attackers employ this kind of manufactured buzz to conceal the truth and reality of their ideas and increase sales. The buyer would be rushing through the process and concealing key details.

5.8.3. Selling the Same Unit to Multiple Buyers

The owner usually flees when the same apartment is sold to several different people. This could happen when one person owns the property, and another has power of attorney (PoA) authority, and both of them sold the property to

[24] https://hookfish.in/info/property-frauds-scams-real-estate-investing/.

two different entities by any method, causing conflict and resulting in problems. PoA is a legal document that allows someone else to act on their behalf. One of the two people in this situation has fake identification.

5.8.4. Encroachments

Due to the owner's lack of activity on the property, someone else may have illegally seized ownership of all or a minimal portion of it. Even government property is frequently sold to persons who discover it afterward.

5.9. Driver's License Identity Theft

The user's driver's license information may be stored in a variety of places, including the state department of motor vehicles, the human resources department of their workplace, their doctor's office, or any other location that has copied it for identification purposes. Information may be gathered if any of these locations experience theft of their physical or digital records. In other situations, it is used as identification proof, frequently in combination with other personally identifiable information (PII), to open new accounts, avoid traffic infractions, or even avoid legal action.

According to the Identity Theft Resource Center, since 2017, information from more than 150 million U.S. driver's licenses have been stolen due to a data breach or a failure to safeguard a database. Countless Driver's licenses are additionally taken annually through the pickpocketing of wallets or purses.

The Identity Theft Resource Center claims that when offenders are caught for driving offenses, they display phony driver's licenses to avoid being detained for outstanding warrants. Naturally, when they are summoned to traffic court, they fail to appear, which results in bench warrants that can result in the victim's arrest or summons, as occurred to this woman (Keya Donnell).

Donnell's name was used by a woman when it was convenient, or more particularly when she was being pulled over by police and she mentioned Donnell's name at the time of the traffic stop. A Charlotte/Mecklenburg police officer initiated the woman's arrest. When the officer requested to observe the woman's driver's license, the woman responded that she did not have it with her. She continued by revealing the name and birthdate of

Officer Donnell. Before sending the woman on her way, the officer took the information and issued a citation.

A summons to appear in court was issued to Donnell a few weeks after that citation was written. Donnell was perplexed by what was happening and had to establish her false identity. Donnell had been robbed a few years prior, and her pocketbook had been taken. The credit cards were promptly canceled by Donnell, who believed that was the end of the matter. Currently, it seems the man who robbed her transferred that driver's license to a lady who is now using it or at least provided her with the information on it (Kevin, 2019).

5.10. Senior Identity Theft

Seniors are more susceptible to identity theft schemes because they frequently have higher savings and home equity accumulations, are less likely to constantly monitor their credit and financial accounts and are more trusting in general. According to Matt Cullina, Senior citizens could experience the same kinds of identity theft as everyone else, such as financial identity theft, tax identity theft, and medical identity theft.

June Smith experienced an odd suspicion that the medical bills she had received were false. The hint provided by the 72-year-old New Yorker was a bill for a pregnancy test. Medicare was billed for tens of thousands of dollars' worth of medical treatments under Smith's name using personal information, including her social security number.

5.11. Employment Identity Theft

When a victim's name, SSN, or date of birth is used without their knowledge or agreement to apply for a job, it is considered employment identity theft. If an employee does not disclose the loss of the identification data that was provided during the hiring process, this may occur. For instance, a candidate for a job interview may use false information to pass the interview and be employed for a job for which they are ineligible. False information could also be used by someone purporting to be the victim in order to commit further crimes or steal from victims. According to the National Council on Identity Theft Protection, 2022, a number of circumstances have occurred that could be a symptom of employment identity theft.

5.11.1. Limited-Term Offers

Having a job offer with a limited duration is one situation where someone may be at risk for this kind of offense. A company might, for instance, offer temporary employment for a specific period of time. This person is guilty of employment identity theft if they fail to report the theft of their identity within the authorized time frame.

5.11.2. Inaccurate Credentials

Another instance is when a hiring manager selects a candidate whose resume lists past jobs with erroneous or incomplete credentials. If it is found later on in the process that these credentials are fake or erroneous, this can also be regarded as employment identity theft.

5.11.3. Co-Workers

Without sounding overly cynical, it is much more likely that one of the user's employees will view the user's personal file and utilize it to their advantage than it is that someone will search through dumpsters or the Dark Web. In reality, it is more likely that a worker who has access to users' and other people's private information may do harm to users because of the position he or she has.

5.12. Online Shopping Identity Theft

Online purchasing now offers an unprecedented level of convenience than browsing in person. However, online retail sites may readily compromise users' personal information. Online shopping fraud was actually the second-most commonly reported fraud in 2020, according to the Federal Trade Commission (FTC), costing consumers $246 million. Identity theft is a problem that may affect anyone, according to Robert Westley, CPA/PFS, a member of the AICPA's National CPA Financial Literacy Commission. He added that criminals are getting smarter and leveraging technology to their advantage more and more every single day. According to Hart, 2021a, many Americans fail to take precautions that could keep them safe while making online purchases. Less than half (45%) of those surveyed stated they check their credit card bills or banking applications after making online purchases to make sure the amount charged corresponds to the purchase price they anticipated. 26 percent of respondents admitted to using the same password on various websites.

For instance, a fraudster may use spyware to track their card number and online behavior. Once they are aware of this, they can utilize the user's credit to make purchases and damage the user's credit ratings.

Summary

This chapter discussed the many categories of personal data that criminals utilize to commit identity theft. It is transparent that every piece of information is crucial for fraud by attackers. Identity theft will commonly be a serious problem for everyone, especially for banks, credit card firms, and online retailers. Therefore, each user needs to safeguard their data to prevent access by attackers.

Chapter 6

Tools for Social Engineering Attacks

Although the social engineering attack is considered a non-technical attack, many attackers employ tools for collecting information or attacking the victims. These tools provide an easy way to collect information from the victims without much hard work. Generally, organizations utilize these tools to locate a loophole in their networks, and systems so that they can protect themselves from outside attacks. Many organizations hire penetration testers to test for vulnerabilities or unauthorized access to systems. Penetration testing commonly referred to as pen testing is the process of scanning a computer system, network, web application, or onsite perimeter to identify weaknesses that a malicious attacker could exploit. This chapter discusses the following key tools:

- Social-engineer toolkit (SET)
- Maltego tool
- Nmap (network mapper) tool
- Metasploit tool.

6.1. Social-Engineer Toolkit (SET)

The IT environment may be precisely replicated using social engineering simulation activity, which can also be used to evaluate how sufficiently a company can defend itself against simulated cyberattacks. By accurately simulating the surroundings, the employee can combat potential attacks in realistic environments. The social engineering toolkit is a free and open-source software used for social engineering attacks including phishing, SMS sending, phone spoofing, etc. It is a free application, and it can download and set up a program straight from GitHub.[25]

[25] https://github.com/trustedsec/social-engineer-toolkit.

Dave Kennedy is a programmer who created the social engineering toolkit. This toolkit is used to check cybersecurity risks in organizations all around the globe by security researchers and penetration testers. Utilizing offensive methods on their computers is the purpose of the social engineering toolkit. Additionally, included in this toolkit are custom vector attacks and website vector attacks, which enable phishing attacks and the ability to clone any website. The manual of the SET can be downloaded from Kennedy, 2022.

6.1.1. Features of the Social-Engineer Toolkit

It has several excellent features, such as the ability to send SMS, and fake phone numbers, and assist in the creation of phishing pages by instantaneously replicating the original. The social engineering toolkit has the features listed below:

- The social-engineer toolkit is open source and free.
- The multi-platform social engineering toolkit can be used with Windows, Linux, and UNIX systems.
- There are many different social engineering attack options, including spear phishing attacks, website attacks, infection media generators, mass mailings, attacks based on Arduino, QRcode attacks, attack vectors in PowerShell, and much more.
- The social-engineer toolkit supports integration with third-party modules.
- Access to the platform for fast-track penetration testing is provided through the social-engineer toolkit.

6.1.2. The Social-Engineer Toolkit's Configuration

Downloading and installing this social engineering toolkit is straightforward. The social engineering toolkit can be downloaded from GitHub, as shown in Figure 6.1.

Listing 6.1: Setoolkit Download. $ git clone https://github.com/trustedsec/social−engineer−toolkit setoolkit.

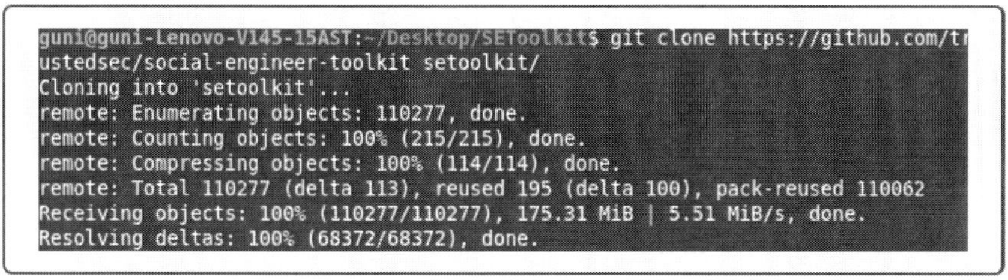

Figure 6.1. Setoolkit is cloned from GitHub in order to be downloaded.

Once the social-engineer toolkit has finished downloading, use the command "cd setoolkit" to access the setoolkit directory. The file structure of the toolkits is shown in Figure 6.2. This toolkit requires the installation of a few prerequisite components in order to operate. As a result, the "pip3" command is used to install the required components.

Listing 6.2: Install the required components $ pip3 install −r requirements. t x t.

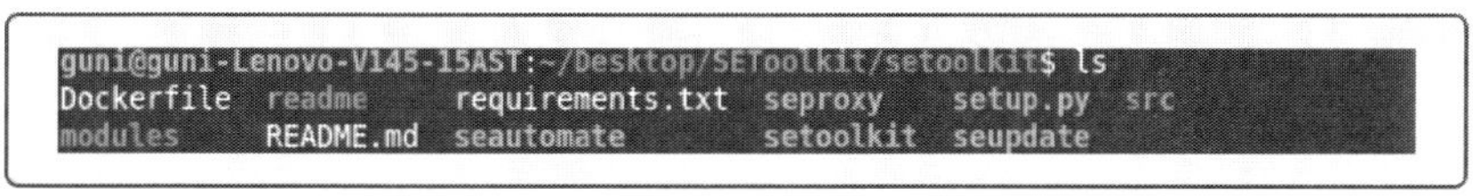

Figure 6.2. Structure of files in setoolkit directors.

All the requirements have been downloaded in the setoolkit. Now it is time to install the setup.py file.

$ sudo python setup.py

6.1.3. Launch the Setoolkit

The social engineering toolkit can now be used after the installation steps have been finished. Type the following command to launch:

$ sudo Setoolkit

Figure 6.3. Download all the necessary components.

Figure 6.4. Install the downloaded setup file.

The home menu of the SET tool is shown in Figure 6.5(a). The user can select from a home menu with a wide range of options after launching the SE toolkit including:

- Social-engineering attacks
- Penetration testing (fast-track)
- Third party modules
- Update the social-engineer toolkit
- Update SET configuration
- Help credits and about
- Exit the social-engineer toolkit.

The first option on the menu is social-engineering attacks, which will be tested in this experiment.

Other options like penetration testing (fast-track): A number of exploits and automated features are present in the attack vectors used in penetration testing (fast-track), which is beneficial to experts in the field. SET has incorporated the vectors from fast-attack track. Each of these attack vectors has been entirely redesigned from the ground up to boost functionality and capability. Third-party modules can be incorporated into SET, as well as third-party modules that are added to the main library modules. To expand the toolkit, new additions or enhancements must be made to the root "modules" folder of SET. First of all, be aware that any additional ".py" files added to the module's directory will instantly be imported into SET under "third party modules."

Update the social-engineer toolkit: Updates SET and all of its modules.

Update SET configuration: Applies any updates made to the set.config file.

Help, credits, and about: This shows all the credits as well as links to the official SET documentation.

Exit the social-engineer toolkit: Exits SET as well as exits any menu from within the modules. In this instance, option 1 is selected.

When the first choice is selected from the home menu, the second menu, which is seen in Figure 6.5(b), opens up and displays a broad variety of attack vectors. This menu includes the following attack vectors:

- Spear-phishing attacks vectors
- Website attacks vectors

- Infectious media generator
- Create a payload and listener
- Mass mailer attack
- Arduino-based vector attack vectors
- Wireless access point attack vectors
- Qrcode generator attack vectors
- Powershell attack vectors
- Third party modules
- Return back to the main menu.

The brief introduction of these attacks vectors is as follows:

1) The first choice is *spear-phishing attacks vectors* which are used to send victim-specific emails in an attempt to trick them as discussed in the previous chapters. Depending on what they have collected, users can send several emails or send them to specific recipients. A user may potentially deliver a malicious attack to the victim using a file format, for instance, a PDF flaw in an effort to weaken the system.
2) The second option is *website attack vectors* which will be tested in this experiment.
3) *Infectious media generator*: A Metasploit-based payload will be created for users by the infectious USB/DVD writer, and he or she will also create an autorun.inf file that, when burned or placed on a USB, will activate an autorun function and, presumably, compromise the system. The devices must be deployed to the physical system in order for this attack vector to work.
4) *Create a payload and listener*: In order to construct a payload, export the exe for users, and generate a listener, the produce payload and listener wrapper for Metasploit is quite straightforward. To properly function, the user would have to download the exe file to the victim's computer and run it.
5) *Mass mailer attack*: users can send several emails with personalized messages to victims using the bulk mailer attack. This approach is typically used to launch a mass phishing assault because users cannot construct payloads with it.

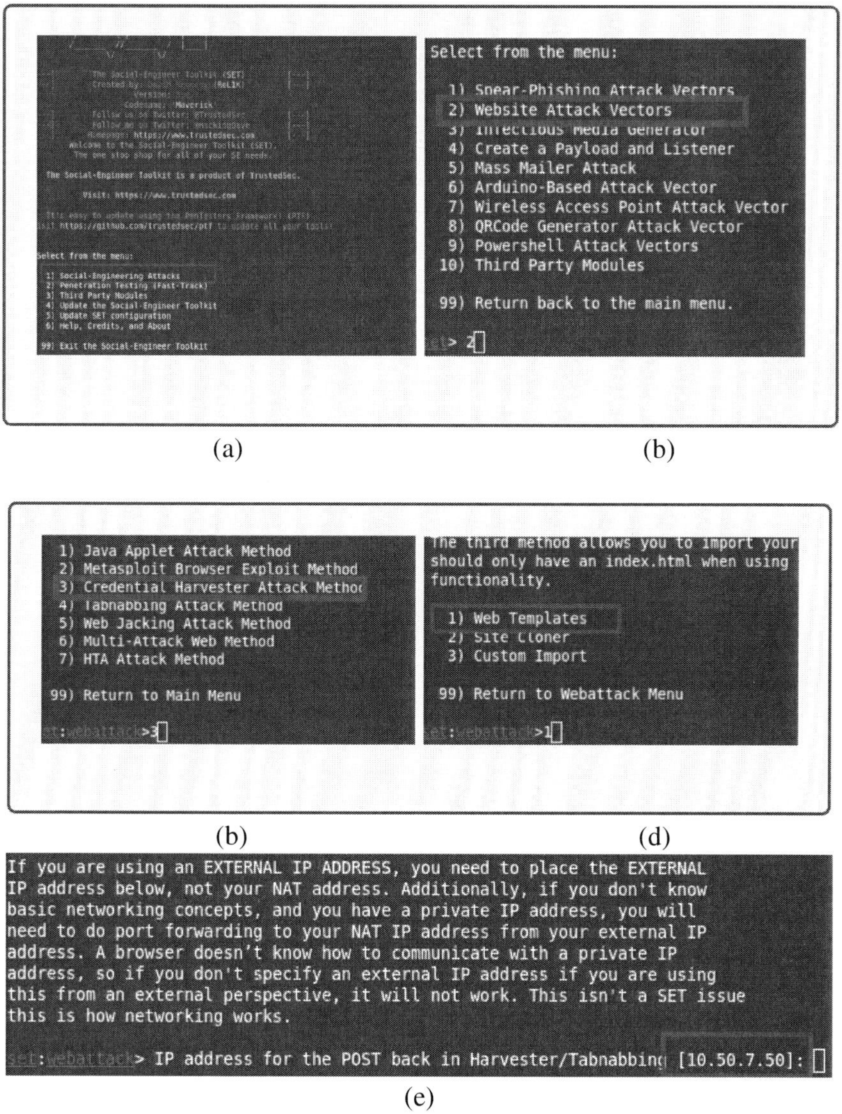

Figure 6.5. (a) SET main menu, (b) List of SEA where website attack vectors selected, (c) List of website attack list where credential harvesting attack method is selected, (d) Three types used for credentials harvesting where web template method is selected, (e) URL of r the fake is generated.

6) *Arduino-based attack vector*: The Arduino-based device is used by this attack vector to program the target device. Users can use Teensy, which has built-in storage and can execute programs

remotely on a physical device. The devices will get beyond any autorun disabled or endpoint protection on the system because they are registered as USB keyboards.

7) *Wireless attack vector*: All DNS requests will be forwarded to the user as a result of creating an access point using the user's wireless card. For the purpose of rerouting traffic to the attacker machine, SET will set up a wireless access point, a DHCP server, and a DNS spoofing service. Once everything is operating as a child process, it will then leave that menu.
8) *Qrcode generator attack vector*: With any URL the user chooses, the Qrcode attack vector will generate a Qrcode for them. When the user has generated the Qrcode, choose a different attack vector in SET and send the Qrcode to their target. For instance, create a Qrcode for the SET Java Applet and mail it to someone.
9) *Powershell attack vector*: It allows users to create Powershell-specific attacks such as shellcode injectors, reverse shells, and bind shells.

It has been seen that many attack vectors are provided by the SET tool. To create a fake website, option 2 is chosen. Then it appears next menu as shown in Figure 6.5(c) where the following options:

- Java applet attack method
- Metasploit browser exploit
- Credential harvester attack method
- Tabnabbing attack method
- Web jacking attack method
- Multi-attack web method
- HTA attack method.

A brief introduction of the website attack's methods is as follows:

1) *Java applet attack method*: The Java applet attack method will fake a Java certificate using a Metasploit-based payload. Thomas Werth's customized Java applet is used to deliver the payload.
2) *Metasploit browser exploit*: The Metasploit browser exploit method allows users to clone a website and use browser-based exploits while importing Metasploit client-side attacks.

3) *Credential harvester attack method*: The credential harvester technique will take advantage of web cloning to collect all the data posted to a website that has a username and password field.
4) *Tabnabbing attack method*: The tabnabbing method will wait for a user to switch to a new tab before refreshing the website.
5) *Web jacking attack method*: This technique uses iframe replacements to make the highlighted URL link look legitimate, but when it is clicked, a window opens, and the malicious link is substituted. If the link replacement is excessively slow or fast, users can change the parameters in the *set_config* file.
6) *Multi-attack web method*: The web attack method will be used to add a combination of attacks using the multi-attack approach. Users can, for instance, use the Java applet, Metasploit browser, and credential harvester/tabnabbing simultaneously to determine which is successful.
7) *HTA attack method*: The HTA attack technique enables replicating a website and do PowerShell injection using HTA files, which may be utilized for Windows-based PowerShell exploitation through the browser. The attacker from a distance can have complete access due to the straightforward HTML application. An HTA often uses the file extension (.hta).

Option 3 (credentials harvester attack method) is chosen from the available options since the intention is to use a fake website to harvest credentials. The information provided to the website will be harvested via online cloning of a website with a login and password field.

Now, three options have appeared including:

- Web templates
- Site cloner
- Custom import.

This option is explained as follows:

1) Using the first approach, SET will be able to import a list of web applications that have already been pre-defined and ready for use.

2) The second approach entirely copies the website of the user's choice and enables the user to apply the attack vectors within the original web application they were trying to copy.
3) The third approach enables the user to import their own website; however, while using the functionality to import a website, the user should only have an index.

Option 1 is chosen for the preset template in order to test the toolkit. Once option 1 has been chosen, a fake website's IP address is displayed, and the software starts to operate as shown in Figure 6.5(e).

The IP address is inserted in the browser, it will appear the fake version of the google page will be displayed to the victims in Figure 6.6. This fake version of the website perhaps tempts them to enter their login and password in the form fields. The credentials are shown as soon as the victim clicks the sign-in, and they are then sent back to the trustworthy website.

Figure 6.6. Fake Google page.

It is transparent that the IP address setoolkit built a Google phishing website. The social engineering toolkits operate in a similar manner. Using a social engineering toolkit, the phishing page will be made. The ID password will be displayed on the terminal where SET is operating as soon as the victim fills it in the appropriate fields.

6.2. Maltego

Maltego is a graphical link analysis open-source intelligence tool (OSINT) used for information collecting. It is difficult and time-consuming to compile all publicly available information using manual methods and search engines. Maltego considerably automates the information-gathering process, allowing users to save a significant amount of time. The software's graphical representation of the data it has mined facilitates the user's analysis of the relationships between the various entities. Maltego employs transformers to retrieve the necessary data.

Maltego provides both infrastructural and personal solutions for investigation. Infrastructure reconnaissance covers domain name system (DNS) information, including name servers, mail exchangers, zone transfer tables, DNS to IP mapping, and related data, and it focuses on the domain. Personal data like email addresses, phone numbers, social networking accounts, links to mutual friends, and so forth are included in personal reconnaissance Poojary, 2012.

6.2.1. Installation

The manual of the Maltego is found in Maltego, 2022. Maltego can be downloaded and installed from their website. On the download page, the version of Maltego needs to be selected. Since Linux (Debian packages) is used, Maltego.v4.3.0.deb is downloaded. Once completed the download, then it installs using the command:

$ sudo dpkg –i Maltego.v4.3.0.deb

Figure 6.7 shows the installation of the Maltego application.

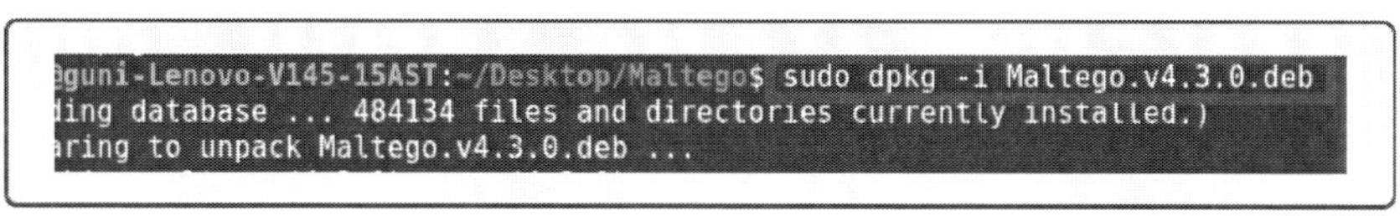

Figure 6.7. Installation of Maltego software.

6.2.2. Launch Maltego

Once the installation is completed, launch Maltego using the command "Maltego" as shown in Figure 6.8.

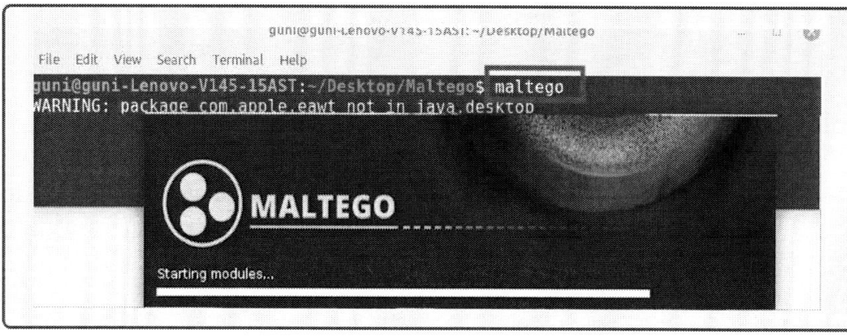

Figure 6.8. Launching Maltego software.

The Maltego homepage will then display once the launch has been completed, as seen in Figure 6.9.

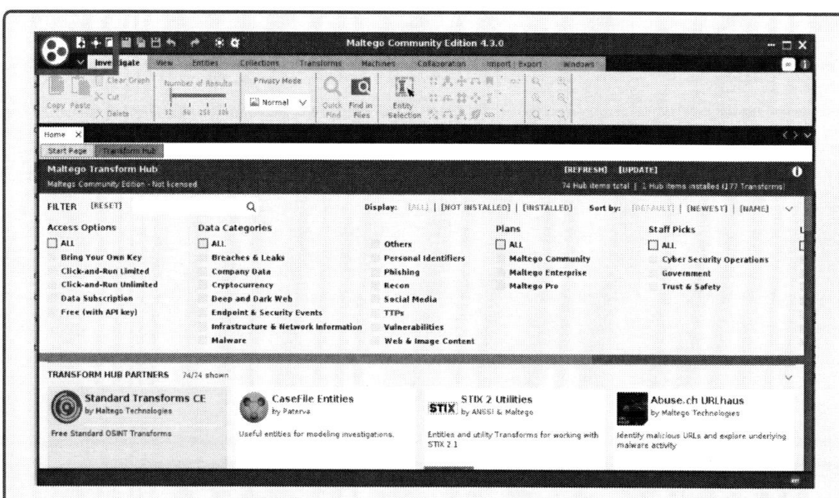

Figure 6.9. Homepage of Maltego software.

On the home page, the Transform Hub is displayed. Transforms are pieces of code that accept an Entity as their input and provide related information in the form of additional Entities as their output. Users can install additional Transforms given by Maltego Technologies and Paterva as well as Transforms from 3rd party Transform providers through the Transform Hub. Transform Hub Items are any of the Transform packages found on the Transform Hub.

Most of the time, users must manually install each transform because they are not pre-installed. The extracted data is then visually displayed on a white canvas. Maltego has a large number of transformations. As a result, users can search through data instantly. An alternative to the commercial version is the free Maltego Community Edition (MCE). The free edition, however, has many limitations and lacks the features and functionality of the paid version. Furthermore, Linux, macOS, and Windows all support Maltego.

The application menu[26] is displayed at the top of the start page as shown in Figure 6.10.

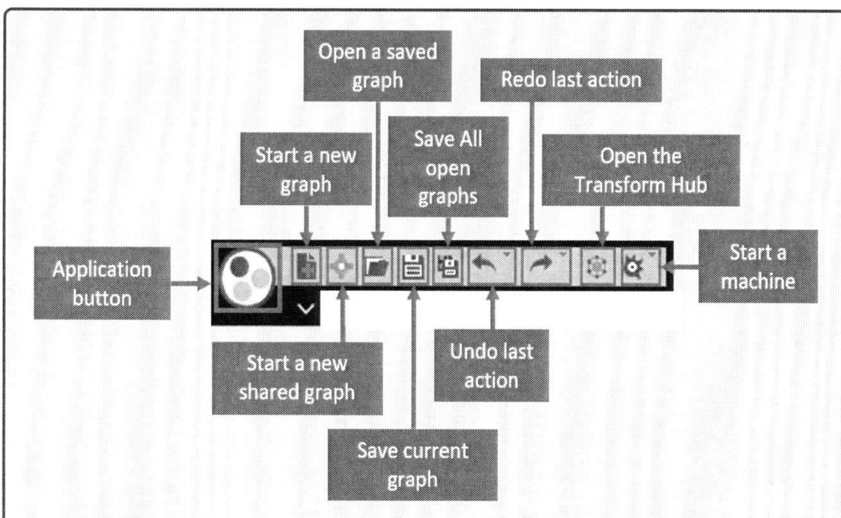

Figure 6.10. Maltego application menu.

[26] https://docs.maltego.com/support/solutions/articles/15000018929-applications-menu.

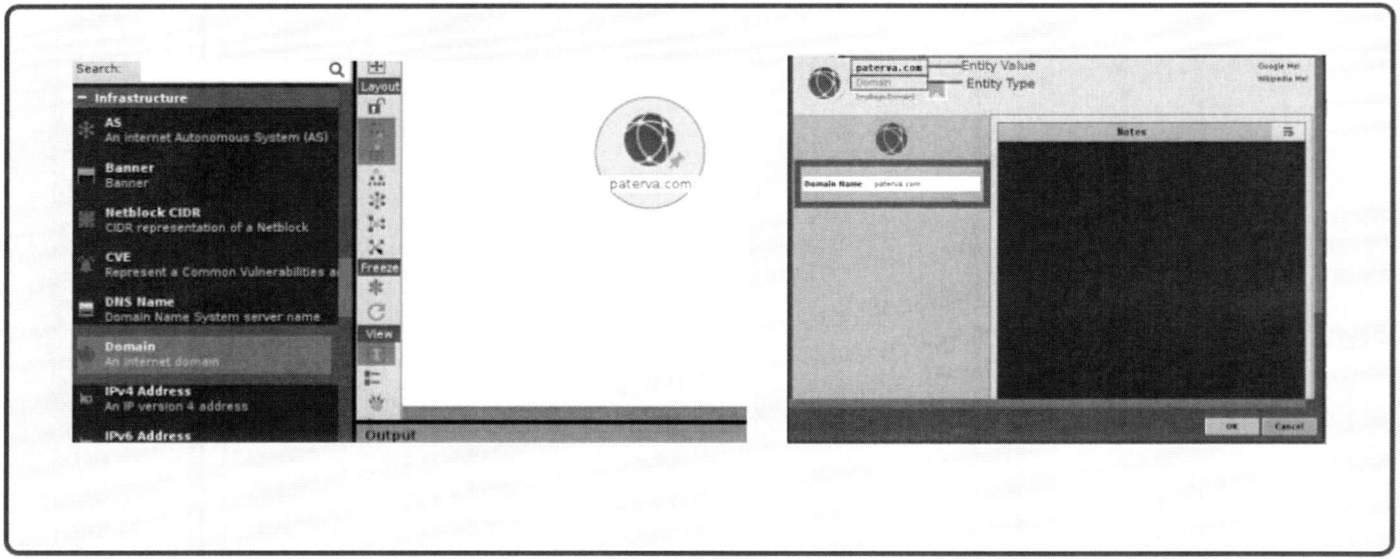

(a) (b)

Figure 6.11. (a) Maltego domain selection, (b) Maltego domain change.

6.2.3. Creating Graphs in Maltego

Graphs are used by Maltego to illustrate the data and information it collects. On the home page's right side, close to the logo, there is a + sign. Users must click the symbol for a new graph page to appear, as seen in Figure 6.11(a). The graph is the masterpiece of Maltego. Following the creation of a new graph, a new page will be generated for it.

It is possible to find many different forms of information in the entity Palette on the left side of the page, including a physical address, a website, a corporate name, an email address, a person's name, a phone number, and many others. Before continuing, it is important to comprehend these three properties of an entity:

- *Type*: The entity is displaying this kind of information.
- *Value*: A graph will always show this field, which is the main piece of data for an entity.
- *Properties*: These are extra fields for the entity's information.

For explanation purposes, the domain entity is selected. To add this domain to the graph page, the user must drag & drop it as shown in Figure 6.11(a). Now the entity type is "domain" the value is "pateva.com" and domain properties are all displayed on the page's right side.

After that, users can double-click a domain to open a new page where they can modify it, as illustrated in Figure 6.11(b) change the domain if they need to change their domain. The user enters the domain they want to use to gather information.

Google is now a domain option for users. The information is then located via the domain's right-click menu. New users almost frequently click on "All Transforms," which brings up a flood of information and perplexes them. Users will end up with a jumble that is difficult to sort through as a result. Instead, it should select each change individually. It can carry out several scans one at a time. Transform first, then examine the outcomes. Next, perform a second transformation, examine the outcomes, and so forth.

For instance, if users wish to gather the email addresses linked to a domain, they first click the plus sign in the all-transforms section, which causes a number of options where they must search for email addresses in the transforms sheet to appear. After selecting the email address option, users should click the run button. The domain's email address will then be scanned (Figure 6.12).

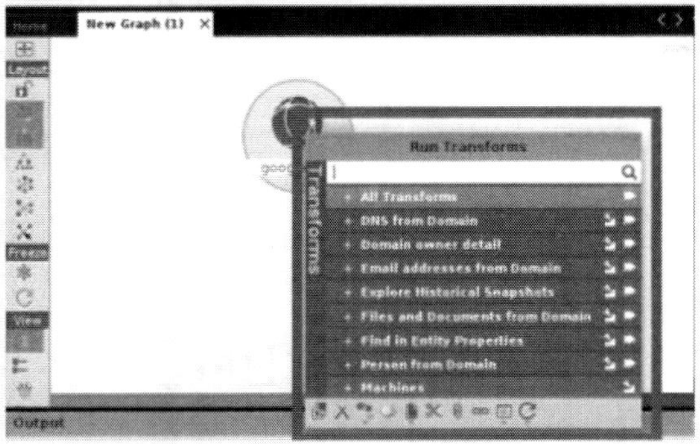

(a)

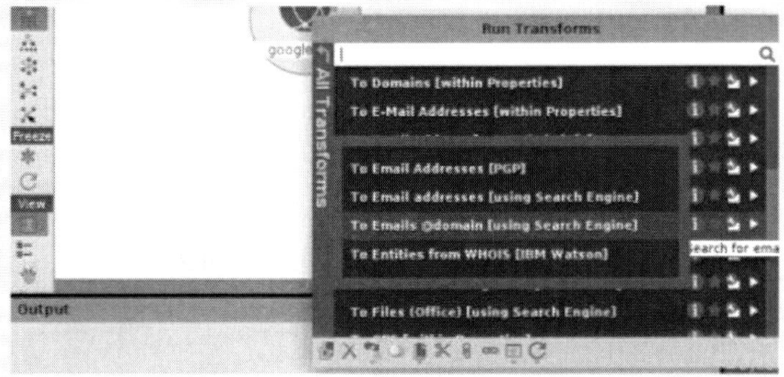

(b)

Figure 6.12. (a) Maltego's all-transforms section, (b) Maltego's email information.

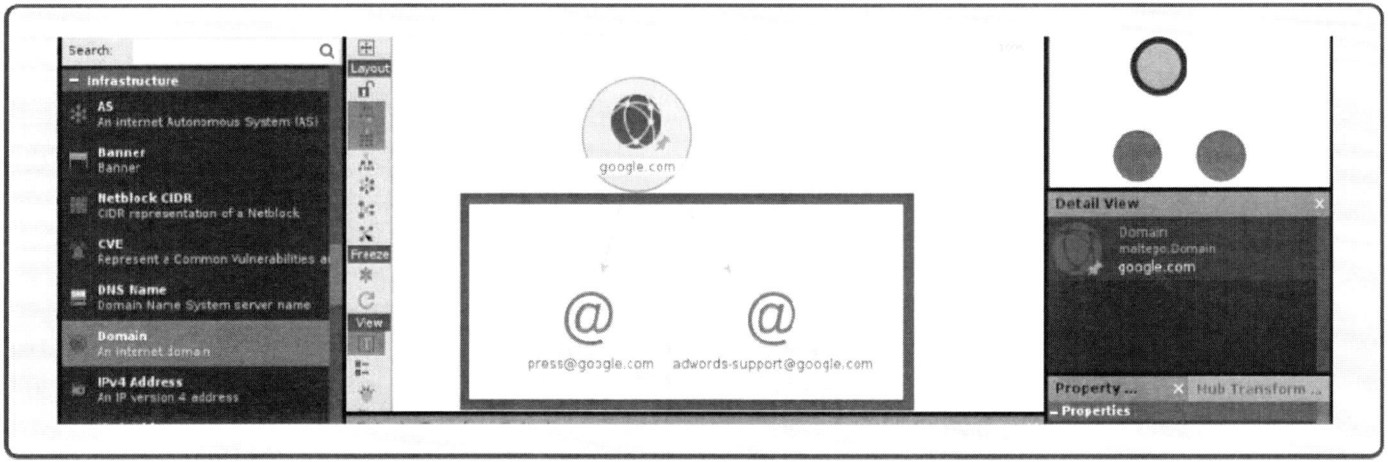

Figure 6.13. All the emails appeared in the domain.

Once completed, the scan then it will show the email address associated with the domain as shown in Figure 6.13. In this way, the users can collect information using Maltego.

6.2.4. Maltego for Attackers

It has been observed that Maltego significantly automates the information-gathering process, enabling users to save a great deal of time. An attacker will try their best to ascertain as much information as they can about the target before beginning an attack. As a result, the attack can be targeted and executed more successfully than it otherwise might be. Additionally, it offers Simple Mail Transfer Protocol (STMP) inquiries, search engine querying possibilities, and other choices. This tool's primary objective is to gather data from WhoIs and DNS.

6.3. Nmap

Nmap, often known as network mapper, is a free and open-source tool used for network mapping, port scanning, and vulnerability analysis. With the aid of this application, the user can discover more about the specifics underlying their connection status. The program analyses the network to which a computer is connected and offers a list of ports, device names, operating systems, and several other identifiers. It is frequently used by IT security companies to mimic the different kinds of attacks that a system might experience. Nmap can be used by attackers to gain access to uncontrolled ports on a system. In order to obtain access, a hacker merely needs to run Nmap on the target machine, seek security holes, and figure out how to exploit them. The working techniques of Nmap are shown in Metasploit. To install the Nmap, use the command:

```
$ sudo apt−get install Nmap
```

Vulnerability scan with Nmap: The most frequent and well-liked CVE detection scripts in the Nmap search engine are Nmap-vulners, vulscan, and vuln. These scripts give the opportunity to learn crucial details about security holes in the system[27]

6.3.1. Nmap Vulners

The most well-known vulnerability scanner currently in use is called Nmap vulners. Let's examine the installation process for this tool and a basic CVE scan. The commands below should be used to install this Nmap tool:

$ cd/usr/share/Nmap/scripts/

$ git clone https://github.com/vulnersCom/Nmap−vulners.git

The syntax to be used to test Nmap-vulnerabilities is quite straightforward, invoking the script with the -script option and specifying the vulnerabilities engine, as illustrated here:

$ Nmap −− script Nmap−vulners/−sV IP Address

or

$Nmap −− script Nmap−vulners/−sV domain name

Figure 6.14 provides data on vulnerabilities of the IP address. Note that it is already included in the standard Nmap NSE (Nmap Scripting Engine) library. The vulnerability will now be examined in the national vulnerability database.[28] The Security Content Automation Protocol (SCAP) is used to represent the National Vulnerability Database (NVD), which is a repository for data on standards-based vulnerability management. The management of vulnerabilities, security assessment, and compliance are all automated thanks to this data.

---

[27] https://github.com/vulnersCom/nmap-vulners.

[28] https://nvd.nist.gov/.

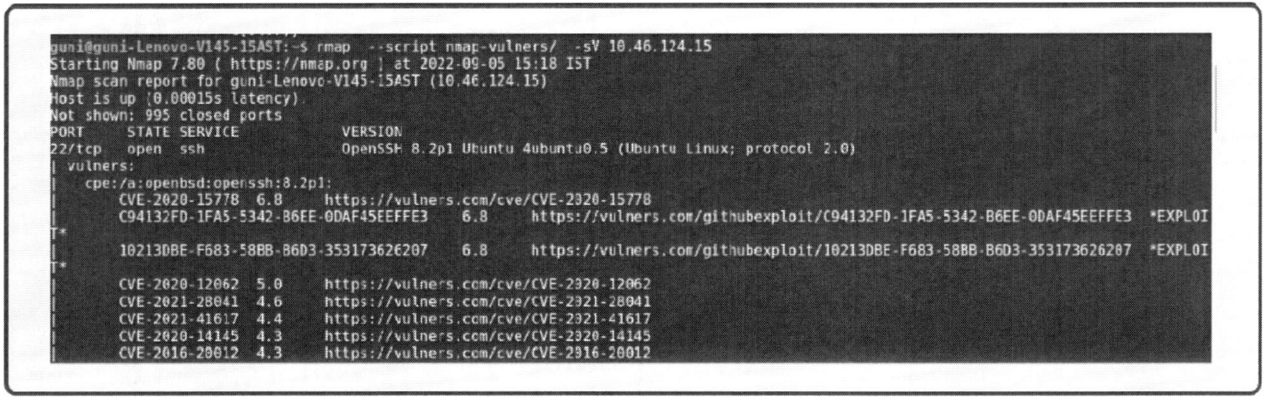

Figure 6.14. Nmap vulners.

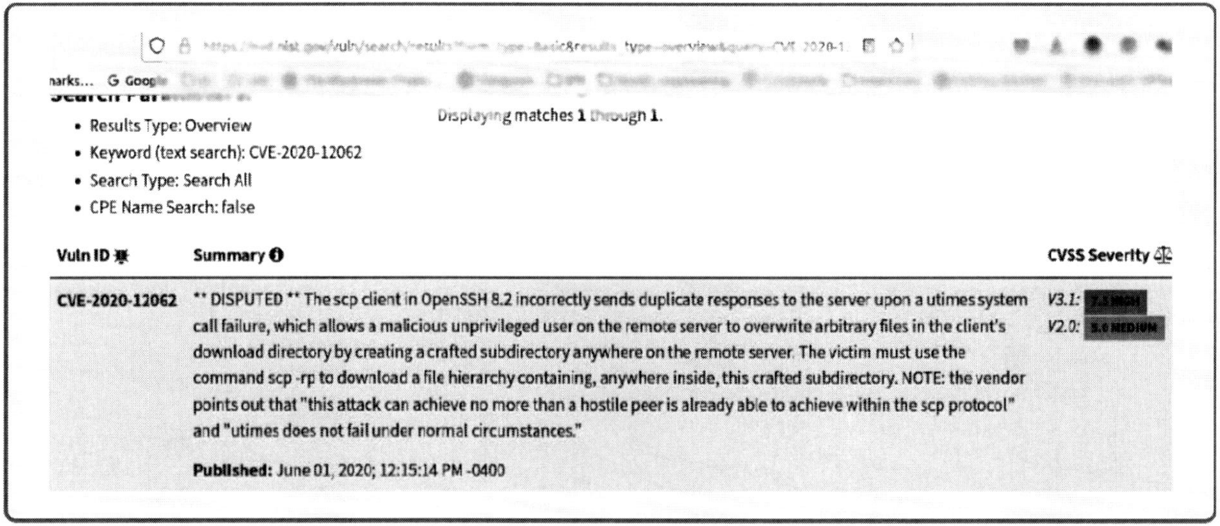

Figure 6.15. NVD report.

The NVD has databases containing product names, security-related software defects, configuration errors, and impact measurements. It also has databases of references to security checklists.

For the example "CVE-2020-12062." Common Vulnerabilities and Exposures is the abbreviation for the CVE. The vulnerability was first reported in the year 2020. The number 12062 is a sequential number given by the Common Vulnerabilities and Exposures (CVE) Numbering Authorities. In addition, the level of vulnerability is shown in the figure. Atlassian, 2022 defined four categories of vulnerabilities as shown in Table 6.1.

An information security vulnerability's severity is represented numerically (0-10) using the Common Vulnerability Scoring System (CVSS). A severity level is included in Atlassian security bulletins. Based on a self-generated CVSS score for each unique vulnerability, this severity level has been determined. An industry-recognized vulnerability metric is CVSS.

Table 6.1. CVSS v3 Atlassian uses the severity rating system

CVSS V3 Score Range	Severity in Advisory
0.1 - 3.9	Low
4.0 - 6.9	Medium
7.0 - 8.9	High
9.0 - 10.0	Critical

Users merely need to replace port numbers, for example 80, with the port they want to scan when adding -p80 after the command to target certain postings. An IP address or domain name should be added by users to the desired IP address or domain name. The remote host's susceptible services' version information can be shown by Nmap using the -sV settings.

Nmap-vulners queries the Vulners exploit database every time the NSE (Nmap Scripting Engine) script is used. As well as here's the expected output:

```
$ Nmap −−script Nmap−vulners/−sV IP Address −p 21−80
```

As can be seen, it was simple to find a number of CVEs, including SSH and BIND vulnerabilities.

6.3.2. Nmap Vuln

NSE scripts are classified according to a set of predetermined categories, to which each script is assigned. Auth, broadcast, brute, default, discovery, dos, exploit, external, fuzzer, intrusive, malware, safe, version, and vuln are some of these categories. The next scan is started against susceptible subdomains with the nmap script vuln. As can see below, the syntax is the same as that of the earlier NSE scripts, with the addition of "vuln" following "-script":

$ nmap ––script vuln IP Address

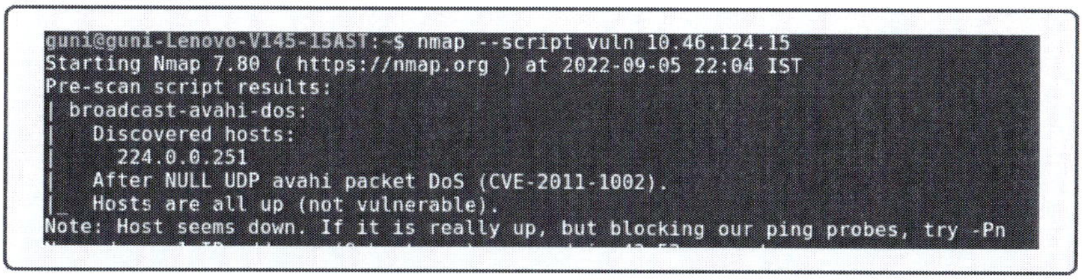

Figure 6.16. Nmap vuln.

The "vuln" category of scripts will be run by this command, and it will only report data if a vulnerability is discovered as shown in Figure 6.16.

6.3.3. Nmap Vulscan

A free and open-source tool called Vulscan is accessible on GitHub. As the simplest and most effective tool for network reconnaissance, Vulscan employs nmap as its primary scanner to scan IP addresses and domains. It is possible to discover more about the target, or domain, with the use of this tool. This may be a website, an IP address, or a domain. The vulscan script and all of the aforementioned databases will be installed using the commands below:

$ git clone https://github.com/scipag/vulscan

$sudo ln -s ‘pwd’/scipag_vulscan/usr/share/nmap/scripts/vulscan

To use vulscan to scan for vulnerabilities, enter the following command:

$ nmap −sV —script=vulscan/vulscan.nse domain name

or

$Nmap −sV −−script=vulscan/vulscan.nse IP Address

The vulscan scan of the target domain for example "example.com" is displayed in Figure 6.17.

Figure 6.17. Nmap vulscan.

It will first begin reporting on the services that are currently offered and comparing them to the vulnerabilities of the Vulscan database. The Vulscan starts executing scripts to seek vulnerabilities in this specific service as soon as it notices that the SSH port is open. It is evident that port 22(File Transfer Protocol (FTP)) is being filtered, making it impossible for Vuls to assess its security. Then, after looking for port 25 (SMTP), tests are performed to determine whether all vulnerabilities in the database should be accepted or rejected. Its purpose is to locate services that may be used to test for every known vulnerability for the service that has been found and is included in the Vuls vulnerabilities database.Once the vulnerability is identified, it is utilized to launch a Metasploit attack against the target IP address. In the part after, Metasploit is explained.

6.4. Metasploit

A framework known as Metasploit is open-source and used for research, offensive security testing, and the detection of threats and vulnerabilities. Security researchers can use it to identify and take advantage of flaws in a variety of systems, networks, and pieces of software. Metasploit by default includes a large number of exploits, but it can also add its own to the library.

6.4.1. Download Metasploit Installer

The installation process for Metasploit is as follows:

Step 1: Download the Metasploit

$ wget http://downloads.metasploit.com/data/releases/metasploit−latest −Linux−x64−installer.run

Step 2: Change the permission

$ chmod +x./metasploit −latest −Linux −x64−installer. run

Step 3: Install the Metasploit

$ sudo ./metasploit −latest −Linux −x64−installer.run

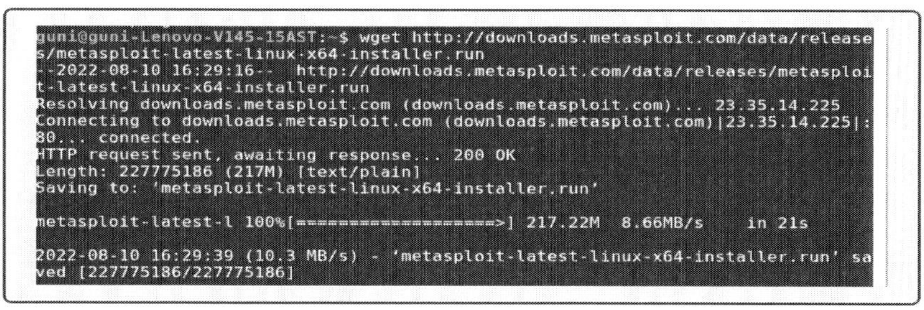

Figure 6.18. Downloading Metasploit.

The configuration of Metasploit begins as soon as the user types the installation command, as seen in Figure 6.19(a). The user will be prompted to choose an installation folder after clicking the Forward button, as shown in Figure 6.19(b). The anti-virus and firewall that are installed on the user's PC will be disabled when the Forward button is clicked, as shown in Figure 6.19(d).Click the Forward button after entering the SSL port in the manner depicted in Figure 6.19(e). The hostname will be requested, as seen in Figure 6.19(f). To begin the installation, click the Forward button at the end as shown in Figure 6.20.

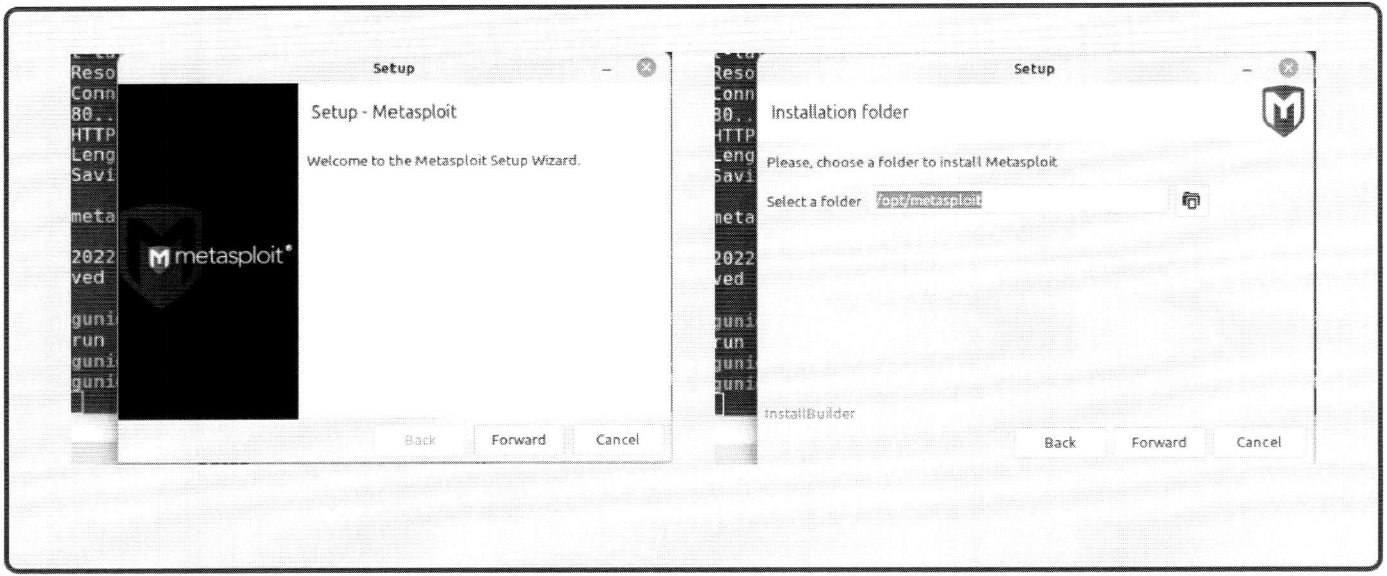

(a) (b)

Figure 6.19. (Continued).

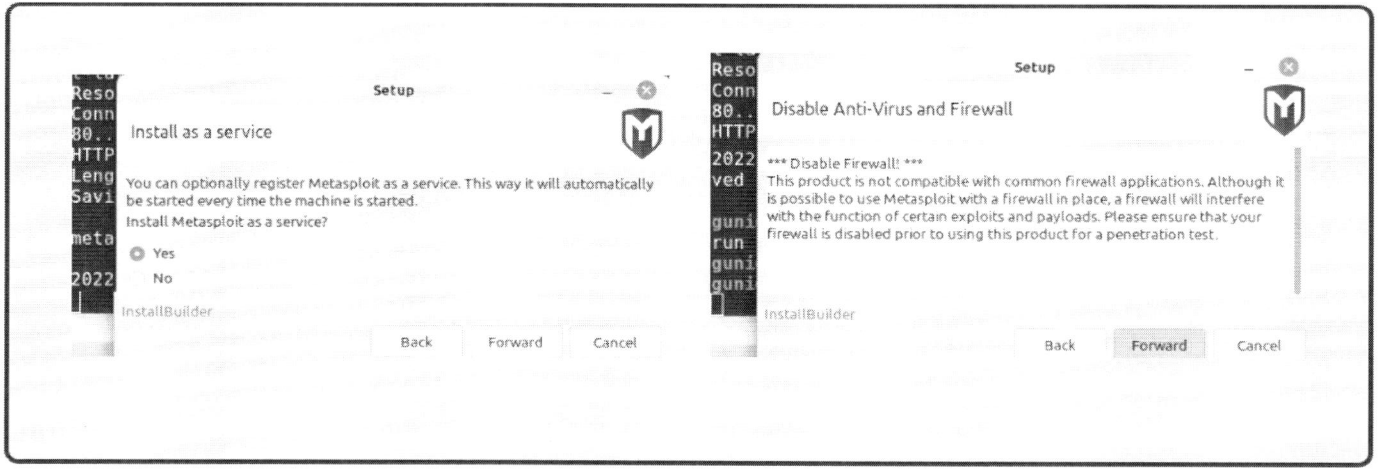

(c) (d)

Figure 6.19. (Continued).

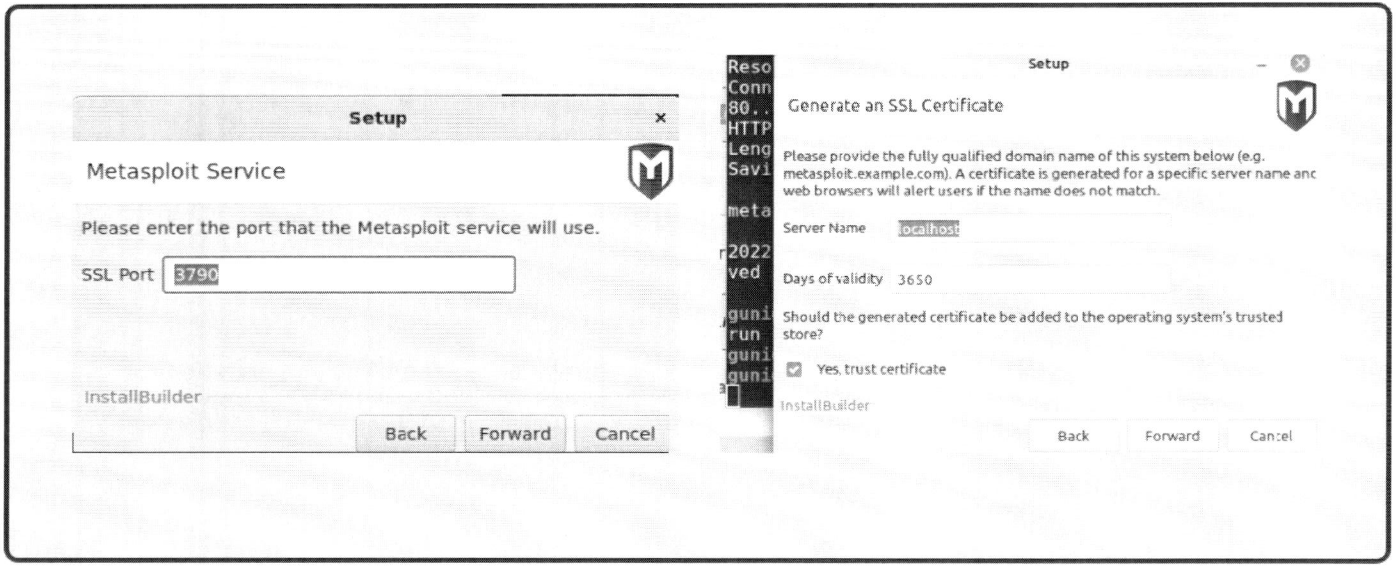

(e) (f)

Figure 6.19. (a) Metasploit start to install, (b) Metasploit installation folder, (c) Metasploit install as service, (d) Metasploit disable the firewall installed, (e) Provides an SSL port, (f) Provides system hostname or localhost.

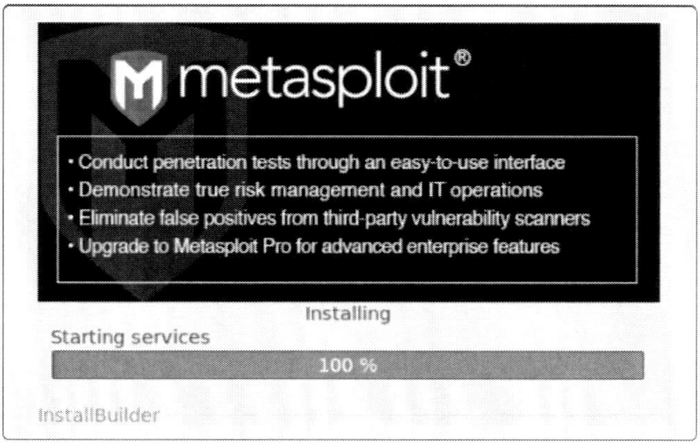

Figure 6.20. Metasploit starts the installation.

6.4.2. Launch the Metasploit

Once the installation is completed, it can be started by typing the command line $ *msfconsole*. The version of Metasploit v6.2.10-dev provides a module as shown in Table 6.2.

Numerous exploits are there in Metasploit, but it must be able to determine which one. Consequently, the "search -h" command is used to assist as shown in Figure 6.22(a). For example, if a window computer is intended to be compromised then it demands SSH details. SSH information is required because Windows-based hacking machines are being built by attackers.

Start by typing the command *search ssh.* There are 72 results returned, including results for Windows and Linux as shown in Figure 6.22(b). However, window ssh is necessary to attack the Windows operating system so the platfrom:windows are included in the command. Type the command in order to do this:

$ search platform:windows name:ssh

$ search platform:windows name:ssh type:post

Now the result only shows the windows SSH to attack as shown in Figure 6.22(c). The next step searches the post-exploitation as shown in Figure 6.22(d). Currently, three posts are displayed where the module *post/windows/manage/install_ssh* is found. With the help of PowerShell, this module installs the OpenSSH server and client on Windows. SSH on Windows can give hackers continuous access to a secure interactive terminal, interactive filesystem access, and port forwarding over SSH.

$ search platform: windows name: ssh type: post

Table 6.2. Metasploit module

Modules	Description	Total
Exploits	Modules for exploiting a vulnerability and delivering a payload. There are remote exploits, local exploits, privilege escalation exploits, client-side exploits, web application exploits, and many others.	2230
Post	Modules for post-exploitation actions such as credential/hash dumping, local privilege escalation, backdoor installation, sensitive data extraction, network traffic tunneling (proxying), keylogging, screen capturing, and many other actions.	398
Payloads	Modules for performing an action during the exploitation, e.g., establishing meterpreter session, reverse shell, executing a command, downloading and executing a program, etc. Payloads can be staged and non-staged.	864
Encoders	Modules for payload encoding and encryption such as base64, XOR, etc. This can help with obfuscation to evade defenses such as Antivirus or network intrusion detection systems (NIDS), endpoint detection and response (EDR), etc.	45
Nops	Modules for generating harmless, benign "No Operation" instructions, e.g., for padding purposes, sliding in memory during exploitation, etc.	11
Evasion	Modules for evading defenses such as Antivirus evasion, AppLocker bypass, software restriction policies (SRP) bypass, etc.	9

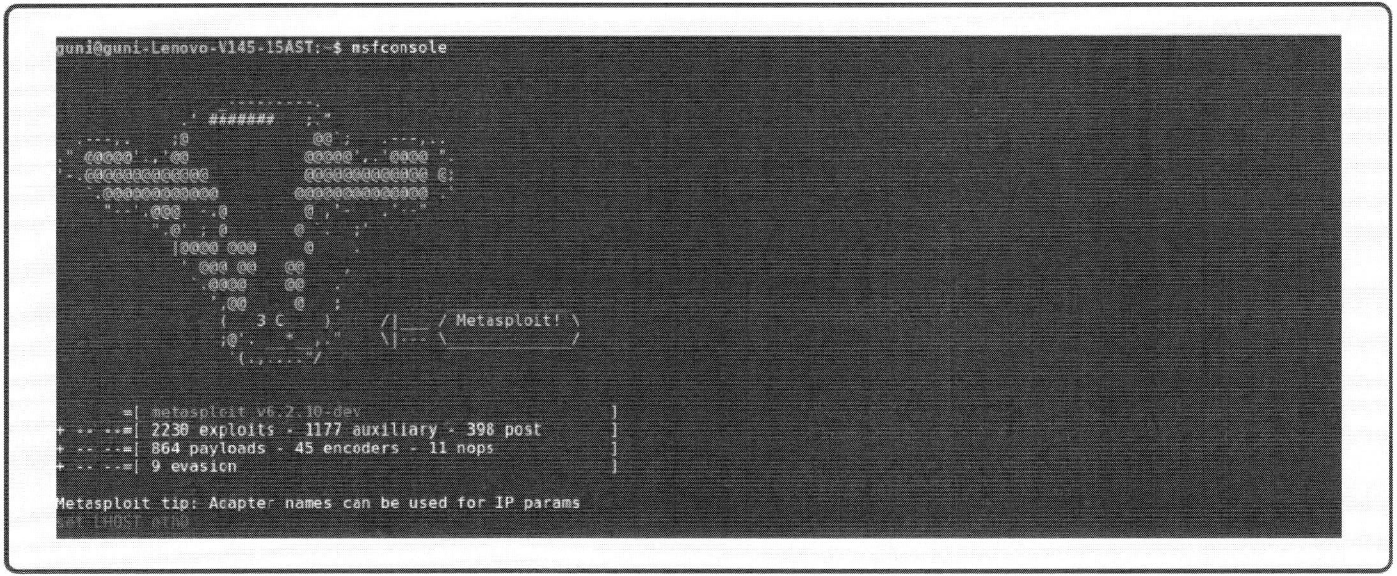

Figure 6.21. Metasploit msfconsole.

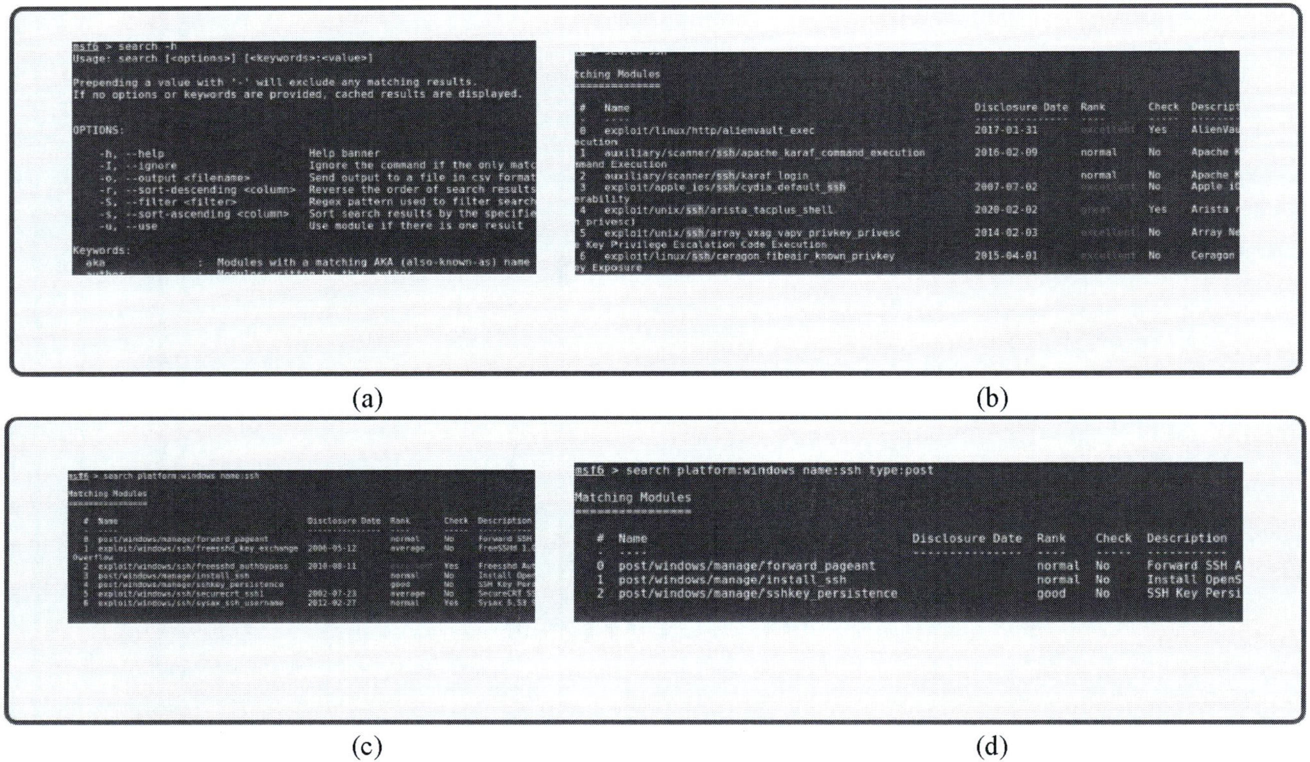

Figure 6.22. (a) Metasploit search help, (b) Metasploit search ssh, (c) Metasploit search platform windows and name ssh, (d) Metasploit search platform window name ssh and exploit post.

Initially, scanning requires the target IP address. It used Nmap to accomplish its objectives and discovered all the FTP-related data, including the FTP's version, vsftpd 2.3.4.

$ Nmap −−script=f t p −vsftpd −backdoor.nse IP Address −p 21

It is now necessary to use a vsftpd 2.3. 4 vulnerability. Enter the command as follows:

$ search name: vsftpd

The result of vsftpd 2.3.4 is shown in Figure 6.23(a). Additionally, Backdoor Command Execution is found, suggesting that command execution may be conceivable. Simply enter the command "use" and the relevant index number to activate the exploit. The current index number is "0," therefore type "use 0" in the command line. It now goes into the details of exploits. Additionally, users can use the info command with the following command to check more information:

$ msf6 > exploit (unix/f t p/vsftpd_234_backdoor) > info

It now needs to examine the options, which refer to the parameters it must provide in order to exploit. Although the Required column in Figure 6.23(c) contains "Yes," the RHOSTS' current setting is empty. So, it must provide the rhosts IP address. There is no need to supply any information if required contains the word "No."

$msf6 > exploit (unix/f t p/vsftpd_234_backdoor) > options

Use "set rhosts IP address" to add the target IP address, as seen in Figure 6.23(d). In general, the most popular variable names in Metasploit are LHOST, RHOST, and SRVHOST. When the attack is successful, the user computer's IP address, or LHOST, is often used to create a reverse connection to the computer. RHOST stands for the IP address of the intended host. The module will also make a connection to SRVHOST in order to obtain additional payload components.

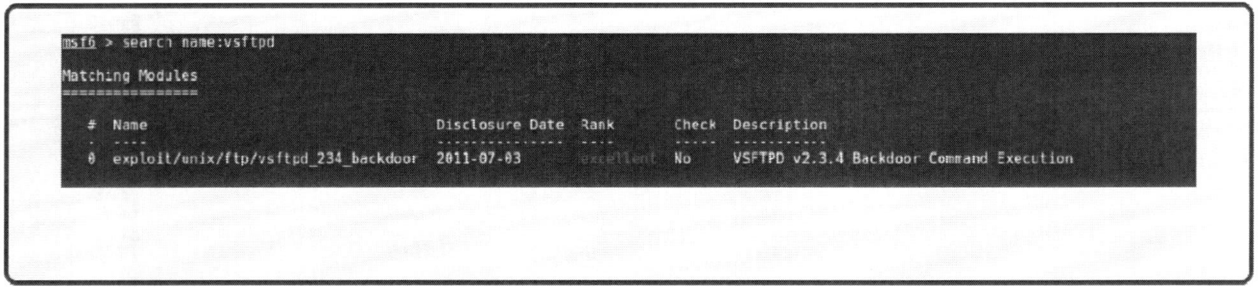

(a)

(b)

Figure 6.23. (Continued).

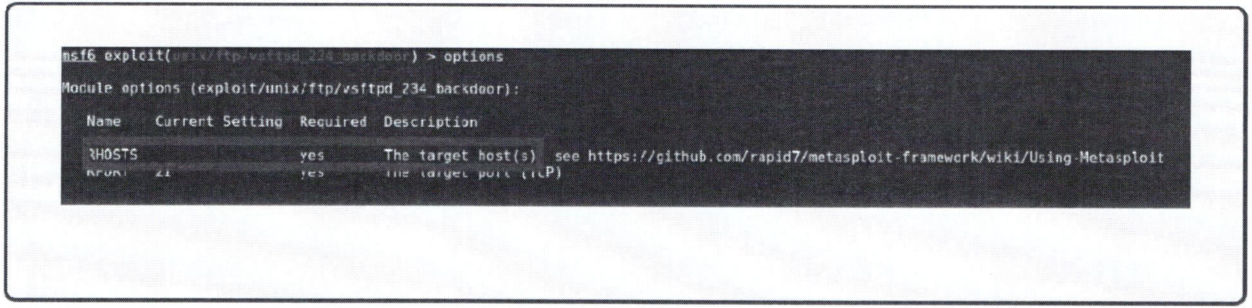

(c)

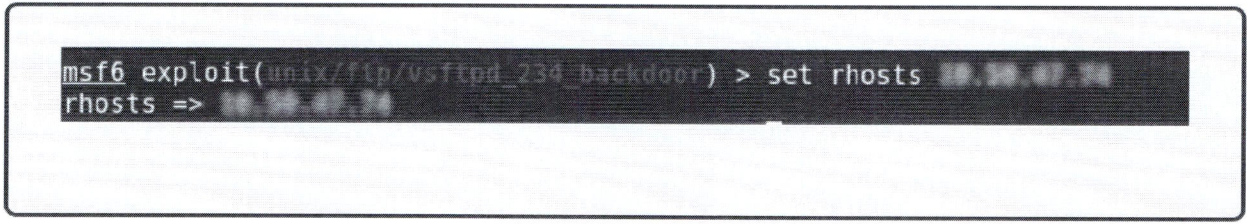

(d)

Figure 6.23. (Continued).

(e)

Figure 6.23. (a) Search the exploits in the vsftpd, (b) Select the exploits, (c) To check the option to give to exploit, (d) IP address is assigned to exploit, (e) Verify whether IP is allotted or not.

Once more, it must confirm whether or not the IP address has been entered. Thus, enter the command option once more. The IP address is successfully placed in the current setting, as seen in Figure 6.23(e). The following command was used to exploit the system:

$ exploit (unix/ftp/vsftpd_234_backdoor) > exploit

However, a screenshot is not displayed for security reasons. It covered the core application of Metasploit. There is still a lot to learn about the robust Metasploit framework. However, now that users are familiar with the foundations of setting up and carrying out an attack, they are ready to begin employing this powerful instrument!

Summary

Several tools for penetration testing were described in this chapter. There are numerous tools available, some of which are mentioned in the book Sonowal, 2022. Although businesses or people can use this tool to address security gaps, criminals utilize this to gather information from the victims.

Chapter 7

Defending against Social Engineering Attacks

Social engineering refers to any action that persuades a person to make a choice that may or may not be in their best interest. Around the world, social engineering is a fairly effective attack strategy used by cybercriminals. Social engineering attacks are successful because they take advantage of one of the biggest security flaws in any organization, namely humans. Human mistakes are the main cause of success in social engineering endeavors. It is human nature to commit mistakes, and technologies are unable to detect novel social engineering attacks. Even the most careful individual can become a victim of one of these expertly designed scams. First, these attackers will research the persons they intend to exploit by gathering personal information and details about their environment in order to execute a more complex and focused social engineering attack. It might be difficult to reduce social engineering attacks. Despite the fact that many professionals or companies are offering preventative steps to slow the spread of social engineering attacks, attackers can get beyond other cybersecurity precautions by simply misleading users. To achieve complete protection, three different sorts of countermeasures are advised by experts:

- Policy and procedures
- Employee awareness
- Technical measures.

7.1. Policy and Procedures

A policy is a set of guidelines or instructions that all employees of a corporation must abide by. Policies provide solutions to queries concerning the actions and motivations of employees. A procedure outlines how a policy should be applied. Procedures are detailed instructions for implementing policy. A policy defines a regulation, and the procedure that goes along with it details who is required to abide by the rule. Having the correct rules, protocols, and processes in place ensures that employees are ready to deal with potentially risky circumstances. Experts from different fields analyze the situation to determine the policies. The policy produces very transparently what is acceptable and unacceptable.

Each employee desires perfection in their work and avoids any sort of dishonesty. The act of declining someone's request creates individuals feeling negative by nature. Requests can come from either attackers or legitimate persons, and in these situations, people may become stupefied. However, if there are transparent procedures in place when a situation starts to deviate from the accepted standards, the employee will be more confident to decline or accept and follow company regulations in a potentially risky condition. As a beginning point for addressing the threat of social engineering against business, take into account this collection of policies. This sample policy document should be used as a reference because it is meant to offer broad advice. It may not take into account every relevant municipal, state, or federal legislation because it is an illegal document.

7.1.1. Email Usage Policy

An organization may decide to create an email policy to make sure that employees use their email in a way that is consistent with the objective of the organization. By examining the situation, several organizations develop policies for their conventions. Despite the fact that each organization's policy will be different, the majority of businesses frequently abide by a few common guides. Numerous businesses have reported being victims of cyberattacks because of email. Therefore, cybersecurity can also be improved at work by having an effective email policy. Even if users use a well-known email provider like Office 365 and their staff is comfortable with email, by establishing rules regarding the transfer of personal information, users can ensure that the organization will suffer less harm in the event that an email is compromised.[29]

Email has become the preferred authentic communication method in the contemporary context. In addition to the circumstance, emails are the primary entry point for most cyberattacks. Any type of organization must therefore have an email policy in order to protect itself from various attacks. Social engineering and phishing emails are two prevalent instances in cyberspace. Using the policy, the employee will comprehend the fraudulent

[29] https://blog.usecure.io/what-is-an-email-policy-and-should-my-company-have-it.

emails and be able to recognize them, allowing the social engineering attack to be mitigated. Workable makes suggestions for what should be covered in the email policy regarding proper and improper email usage.

7.1.1.1. Inappropriate Use of Company Email

Every time an employee uses a company email address, they try to represent their employer. Most of the communication is conducted using email channels. However, many workers are unaware of how to use emails properly, making them easy targets for social engineering scams. Therefore, the following are some of the major policies that employees must not violate:

- Employees must not sign up for services or websites that are illegal, questionable, untrustworthy, or otherwise suspect. These sites frequently host malware that will automatically install (sometimes discreetly) and corrupt an employee's PC, spreading throughout the firm.
- Employees are not permitted to send unsolicited commercial emails. Spammers and phishers frequently send unsolicited bulk emails. Employees often report this type of communication to IT teams because attackers may send fraudulent emails pretending to be employees in order to obtain information.
- Employees must not sign up with their emails for a competitor's services without permission. In some situations, the competitors unlawfully gain trade secrets through industrial espionage.
- Employees must not send content or communications that contain offensive or discriminatory language. It may lead to damage to the organization's reputation.

Employees must not purposefully spam other people's email addresses, including those of their employers. The firms' workplace culture will suffer as a result. Along with spam emails, the crucial message could be concealed.

7.1.1.2. Appropriate Use of Corporate Email

Many employees question what the emails are used for, even though a number of limitations on the company's email are maintained. In general, employees are free to use the company email for purposes relating to business.

The policy for emails does not apply to the following points:

- Employees can communicate with colleagues and customers, both existing and potential. If the employees require any kind of assistance or communication, they can communicate with existing employees.
- Organizations spend a lot of money on internet software to fulfill their objectives. Employees can log on to software they have purchased and are legally entitled to use. Additionally, some of the software that customers are given for usage is legitimate.
- Employees can provide their email addresses to people they meet at conferences, employment fairs, or other corporate events for commercial objectives.
- Employees can join newsletters, platforms, and other online services through their email so that they will get aid in their career development.

7.1.1.3. Personal Use

Although company emails are only used for business-related matters, employees are allowed to use their work email for a limited number of private uses. However, it is strongly advised to utilize their personal emails. In this instance, the user can utilize the company's emails because some trustworthy websites only allow company emails. Employees can use their work email to, for instance:

- Register their work emails for conferences, workshops, certification programs, and conferences as well as for meetings and classes.
- Send emails to friends and family as long as they are free from spam or private information.

Downloading books, guides, and other content for personal use is acceptable as long as it is appropriate and safe.

7.1.1.4. Suggestions on Email Security

Additionally, to the company's confidentiality and data protection policies, employees are always required to abide by this policy. Email is frequently used as a platform for hacker attacks, data breaches, viruses, and other malware. These problems may compromise business equipment's security, legality, and reputation.

Employees must:

- Select a strong password with at least eight characters, including alphabetic, numeric, and special characters.
- Never share the email password with anyone, not even your coworkers or relatives. The attackers may impersonate these characters to steal their credentials.
- Passwords should be kept private and should be remembered rather than written down. Every two months, they change their email password. As explained in the previous chapters, Dumpster is one of the social engineering attacks, where the attackers collect this piece of paper and guess the passwords.
- Avoid opening attachments or links in unsolicited emails, especially those coming from somebody that does not know. The attackers attempt to spread malicious code through the attachments using phishing emails.
- Emails that appear suspect should be reported right away to the appropriate person (often an IT manager). In any situation, the employees get confused about attachments, whether genuine or not.

7.1.1.5. Email Signature

Employers should encourage staff to develop a professional email signature that accurately represents their business. This policy is optional for employees, but by using a proper signature, it provides the recipients with their contact details. Most significantly, the recipients can verify the sender's identity using the information they have received. The recipients can contact the sender directly to learn more about the purpose of the email and if there is any suspicious content. Here is an example of a proper email signature:

[Name of Employee]

[Title of Employee], [Name of Company with a link] [Telephone] | [Business Address]

Employees are allowed to include professional photos, brand logos, and links to films and websites relating to their jobs in their email signatures. They can approach their office manager or their supervisor for assistance if they need it or if they are unsure how to proceed.

7.1.1.6. Disciplinary Action

Employees who violate the current policy will be subject to disciplinary action, which may include termination. Examples of termination grounds include:

- Using an official email address to send private information without permission. Sensitive information may be sent to a third party by an insider who is frequently an attacker.
- Sending disrespectful or offensive emails to company partners, coworkers, or clients. These emails are sent by an insider who desires to harm their company's reputation in order to get revenge.
- Using a business email for illegal purposes.

7.1.2. Internet Usages Policy

Although having access to the Internet at work is a major benefit, it may also result in a significant loss. The organization's internet usage policy describes the rules for how employees are to use the network, equipment, and internet connection of the company. The goal of the policy on internet usage is to prevent inappropriate or unlawful internet use that puts the company's reputation and legal standing in danger. For example, on the internet, an IP address has a significant impact on a business. Using an IP address, the attackers can locate the company's security weaknesses. The organization consequently attaches great attention to its internet usage policy.

7.1.2.1. Inappropriate Internet Usage by Employees

Although employees have access to the internet for their own benefit, they may misuse it to invite attackers in through a backdoor. Employers would be advised to implement an employee Internet usage policy at the workplace to safeguard the organization's assets and maintain Productivity. The following guidelines may be incorporated into the policy.

Therefore, the employees are prohibited from:

- Downloading or publishing pornographic, inflammatory, or unlawful content. These kinds of websites contain malicious software which installs the user's system, which leads to damage to the company's information. To put it another way, these things are offensive to employees, inappropriate, and can promote a hostile work environment.
- Uploading private information to an unauthorized website is strictly prohibited. Many phishing websites are designed to collect information.
- Violating another person's privacy and private information. Employees are not allowed to access the private information of others. Sometimes the attackers impersonate insiders and attempt to access.
- Downloading or uploading movies, music, and other software that is protected by copyright. Damage to the business results from attempting to download or upload via the company's internet. Generally, many real firms prohibit downloading their protected products without paying money for them. However, the attacker creates websites that alert people that they can download these protected products through their website. Malicious malware is placed on users' systems as soon as they use these websites.
- Performing unauthorized or unlawful acts, such as fraud, purchasing or selling illegal items, hacking, and more. Nearly all nations have laws prohibiting these actions. If any activities take place using the company's internet, the government will take Punitive action against any violators, whether they be people or organizations.

Employees are warned to utilize caution when downloading, opening, and running files and software. Inform their supervisor/IT manager/other appropriate people if they are unsure whether a file is secure. Software for data encryption and antivirus may be installed on work PCs. Without permission from management, employees are not permitted to disable or configure firewall settings. If a harmful program infects an employee's device or if their personal data is compromised as a result of improper employee use, the company will not be held liable.

7.1.2.2. Internet Usage by Employees in a Responsible Manner

Employees used the telephone, interoffice mail, and in-person meetings to communicate in the past. However, at the current time, managers and supervisors are able to work from a distance while still communicating with their staff. For the following reasons, the staff is encouraged to utilize the company's internet connection to:

- Communicate with clients and coworkers using the methods designated by the business. By allowing employees to connect electronically, the Internet has expedited the manner that information is exchanged between employees. Time and space constraints are eliminated with electronic communications like email, instant messaging, and video conferencing.
- Carry out their duties using the online resources made available by the business. Businesses can hold meetings and communicate with staff by using Internet connections.
- Look for information they may utilize to enhance their work. Employees are allowed to search for knowledge on the internet, like the Google search engine.
- Access their social media accounts while adhering to social media policies.

It should not restrict its employees' access to websites of their choosing, but it should expect them to use good determination and stay focused on their jobs when using the internet. Any use of their network and connection must adhere to their privacy and confidentiality policy. Employees must abide by the guidelines when using the internet for security reasons, for example:

- The passwords used on various websites are always kept private, as stated above in the email policy.
- Logging into their work accounts only occurs on protected devices. Employees should examine the website's HTTP or HTTPS protocol. Only login if the website is HTTPS-related.
- Use secure passwords when entering websites and services that are essential to their profession.

7.1.2.3. Disciplinary Action

Employees who violate this internet usage policy will be subject to disciplinary action. Serious infractions will result in termination of employment or, if necessary, legal action. Serious offenses include, for instance:

- Stealing from or engaging in other illegal activities via a company's internet connection.
- Causing viruses, worms, or other harmful software to infect their systems.
- Sending disrespectful or abusive emails to their spouses, coworkers, or clients.

7.1.3. Software Usage Policy

The purpose of the software usage policy is to ensure that employees have received proper training on how to use company-owned software in a secure and ethical manner. The attackers frequently employ malicious software to harm the company's system and steal sensitive information. The software usage policy's objective is to prevent improper or unlawful software services that can damage the company's legal standing and reputation.

7.1.3.1. Proper Usage of the Software by Employees

The employee is required to abide by all applicable laws, rules, and guidelines regarding the use of the software. Employees are urged to employ the company's software for the following reasons:

- Use only company-recommended software to carry out their job duties such as words excel, ERP, LMS, teams, zoom, WebEx, and others.
- Allow using the software to solve the research problem or analyze purpose.
- For installing new software, it is compulsory to contact the IT manager.

7.1.3.2. Improper Use of the Software by Employees

One essential component of businesses is software. The software may be used by employees to meet company objectives. As a result, utilizing software is unrestricted in any way, but its appropriate usage requires a policy. However, the following is prohibited for employees in terms of software:

- Employees are forbidden to install software without consulting IT professionals because malicious software can occasionally be deployed either intentionally or accidentally because some employees desire to install third-party software in corporate software to complete their tasks easily.
- Employees are not allowed to install company-licensed software on their personal computers. The software is purchased only to complete company tasks. To purchase the software, the company spends a significant sum of money.
- Avoid using unlicensed software and avoid downloading it. Generally speaking, purchasing software can be pricey. Employees can either search for free solutions or pay for possibly expensive software when they require a new piece of software for their PC. Some individuals are tempted to download pirated or illegal software to avoid these expenses. It has been seen that various challenges have appeared with downloading and using illegal software, including the potential for legal issues, the potential malware infections, and the potential for infecting other devices on the company's network.
- Users are not permitted to eliminate any software that the IT team installed. Some attackers pretend to be corporate employees and make an effort to uninstall the software. The simple explanation is that they wish to seek vengeance on the firm.
- Software may not be distributed by employees to contractors or other outside parties. Companies do not actually own the software they purchase; instead, they do so under a license. They are unable to grant anyone the authority to utilize it except for their own employees.

Any worker who is found to have violated this regulation may face disciplinary action in accordance with the software policy.

7.1.4. Hardware Policy

The term, "company hardware," refers to all types of physical devices, including servers, desktop and laptop computers, handheld electronic devices, process control systems, connecting devices, and telecommunications equipment. All hardware equipment bought by employees or contracted workers on the organization's behalf is and will continue to be considered company property. Utilizing any of these hardware devices requires adherence to all relevant licenses, notifications, contracts, and agreements. The goal of hardware policy is to safeguard the assets of an organization. Proprietary information and hardware are all expensive assets that require protection from theft, failure, loss, damage, and other harm.

7.1.4.1. Proper Use of the Hardware by Employees

Hardware is required to run the software properly. It is impossible to run the software properly or at all if the appropriate hardware is absent or Hardware is worst maintained. It is critical to consider this when making IT system selections, as this can affect how workers work, their productivity, and the bottom line of their firm.

- Utilize the equipment for business purposes. For example, if any employees operate the computer for watching movies, playing games, or other non-useful purposes, then it may harm the working culture.
- Make the appropriate contact with the IT staff if additional hardware is required. With the growth of technology, hardware must also evolve, thus if new upgrading hardware is required, employees must communicate with the IT team to alter or update it.
- The equipment may also be used for research purposes. The apparatus could potentially be utilized for research. Some equipment can be used for study as well as for business. Employees that wish to be researchers can utilize hardware to support the company's development.
- Every piece of equipment needs to be handled with the appropriate care and attention and kept in a setting and condition that promote long life and proper operation.
- All equipment must be logged off correctly and powered down when not in use for long periods of time.

7.1.4.2. Improper Use of the Hardware by Employees

Hardware purchased for business use must not be used in a way that endangers organizations. Every time new hardware is purchased, a functional handbook is included with it so that the employees can use it properly without any damage. An organization has also suggested some criteria in order to use the right hardware:

- Without the permission of the person in charge of IT, no equipment may be transferred. If staffs desire to carry any type of hardware, they must first obtain approval from the IT team. Sometimes the perpetrator impersonates a company employee and seeks to steal equipment that may contain information.
- Without the approval of the IT contract, no equipment may be connected to the network. Attackers attempt to connect their hardware such as computers to the company's network in order to steal information.
- Nothing may be changed to any equipment without the IT person's approval. The IT team is specially assigned to this task, so they know the internal structure of the hardware.
- Any error, loss, or damage must be immediately reported to the IT contact. Employees should alert the IT team if the hardware stops working or shows signs of being harmed in many circumstances.
- When carried away from the office, laptops must be kept safe. Make sure they are always watched over. The risk of theft resulting in the loss of company hardware and data must always be reduced by all personnel. Laptops should not be left unattended outside or in any other unsafe spaces, and special care should be taken to prevent this.

Any organization's hardware is a property; thus, every employee must abide by the rules in order for the business to grow. Appropriate action will be taken against workers who knowingly engage in any type of dishonest behavior on hardware.

7.1.5. Physical Access Policy

The physical security policy's goal is to define the guidelines for providing, controlling, overseeing, and removing physical access to firm information resource facilities. The physical security policy is applicable to everyone who installs, supports, maintains, or is otherwise responsible for the physical security of the company's information resources. Only employees of the company's support staff and contractors whose jobs require access to those facilities may be given access to information resources facilities. Secure and thorough coverage of all areas is required for surveillance cameras.[30] Tailgating, dumpster diving, shoulder surfing, and eavesdropping attacks have already been described as methods for the attacker to physically gain access to the firm and acquire information.

7.1.5.1. Access Cards or Key Access

Physical access controls contribute to the development of best practices for the proper granting, controlling, and monitoring of physical access for all facilities supporting information resources. Many businesses use access cards or key access to determine who has permission and who does not. Access cards and/or keys must be approved by physical security personnel in order to be used to access information resource facilities. The following are some examples of physical access safeguards:

- Physical security professionals are required to periodically check Access cards and/or key access privileges for the facility and eliminate access for anyone who no longer needs it. Sometimes, the attackers try an old employee's access card or key access to access the sensitive area.
- Access cards cannot be transferred to another person without passing through the return process. In the rear situation, the inside employees share their access cards with attackers who are experts in technology and harm their company.
- The proper access and non-disclosure agreements must be signed by each person who is given access to an information resource facility.
- Access will be terminated for lost or stolen access cards and/or keys, which must be reported right away to the appropriate person. In this scenario, if the attackers gain access, they will utilize their access cards to enter the company and engage in unethical behavior. The genuine owner of the card experiences issues if the corporation does an investigation.

---

[30] https://frsecure.com/physical-security-policy-template/.

7.1.5.2. Housekeeping/Cleaning Staff

The organization employs cleaning and housekeeping personnel as well. They are responsible for a range of cleaning tasks, including sweeping, mopping, dusting, and polishing. Ascertain that all rooms are maintained and inspected in accordance with norms, protect the equipment, check for deficiencies, and alert superiors to any damage, deficiencies, or disturbances. On occasion, attackers take advantage of tasks associated with housekeeping, harming the technology and stealing data. In order to not hurt the business, organizations must create policies for them, such as:

- Regular information security awareness training is required for the cleaning and housekeeping employees. The cleaning and housekeeping staff must undergo sufficient and authorized background checks.
- Cleaning services provided by outside parties, or third parties must be certified and licensed. Outside parties or third parties' workers must be watched over or monitored while carrying out their jobs.
- Staff members who perform housekeeping and cleaning duties are required to wear uniforms and badges and be given a special identifier that leaves a record of who entered which areas of the building.
- A specific clearance from security personnel is required if housekeeping or cleaning staff requires access to locations that are prohibited.

7.1.5.3. Policy for Delivery Person

Attackers may pretend to be delivery people in order to gain access to a secure location and try to steal information. The following policies are applied to protect as a result:

- It is necessary to record the steps taken for package delivery and receipt.
- Delivery locations need to be guarded and kept away from the public.
- When the delivery area's internal doors are open, the exterior doors must be locked.
- If not in use, delivery areas must be locked.

- At all times inside delivery areas, unapproved people must be escorted.
- Prior to being placed in interior areas, incoming deliveries must be registered, segregated, and checked for signs of tampering.
- Physical security staff must be informed right away about any indications of tampering found.

7.1.5.4. Disciplinary Actions

Discipline may be taken against those who violate this policy, including the dismissal of workers, termination of contracts with contractors or consultants, dismissal of interns and volunteers, suspension or expulsion of learners, and departure of contractors and consultants from the organization. Additionally, people risk losing their access rights to the company's information resources and facing legal and criminal charges.

7.2. Educating Employees About Social Engineering Attacks

Although the majority of businesses offer a variety of policies to defend employees from social engineering attacks, many workers do not adhere to or comprehend these rules. Employees can defend themselves or comprehend the policies and how they will operate if they are aware of the social engineering attack. Therefore, every organization's principal responsibility is to implement an employee awareness campaign. This program protects businesses from both internal and external attacks. Organizations offer a variety of tools to assist in setting up their staff awareness training programs in order to perform this awareness.

Since social engineering attacks are highly common, there are many resources accessible to train the staff. An organization's social engineer manages a well-known website that provides staff members with all the knowledge they require to be effective social engineer learners. Resources, a structure, specifics, and lectures will all be taught to the employee. In order to train employees, many organizations employ a wide variety of strategies such as materials distribution, videos, interaction with experts, and others.

7.2.1. Awareness Materials

A written document that explains the progression of the subject is used in material-based instruction. Many employees find it convenient to understand materials. The benefit of employing material is that users may easily broadcast themselves, and learners can read at any time. Since the majority of users are occupied with their own activities, they can use it whenever they have free time. These materials can reach clients through a variety of methods. Physical and electronic mediums will be used as a distribution method for awareness materials (Nguyen and Bhatia, 2020). Physical distribution is defined as the process of physical movement of materials from the trainers to the employees. Some of the physical distribution media are as follows:

7.2.1.1. Posters

A visual aid that promotes student learning in the classroom is an instructive poster. The goal of a poster is to grab attention. It has to compete with numerous other posters, especially when being displayed at a poster fair. An infographic-style instructive poster is a great example. An infographic is a grouping of pictures, charts, and sparse text that provides a transparent picture of a subject. Infographics employ eye-catching, captivating pictures, as in the illustration below, to convey information transparently and quickly. Every day, the learners will notice the poster, and the contents will make mental sense to them. The concept is easily understood by the learners in this fashion. An example of the poster is shown in Figure 7.1.

A poster is thought to only have a limited amount of content, while an infographic poster provides learners with a wealth of knowledge. Poster usage provides a number of benefits, including the following:

- A poster can speak for itself without the creator being present. As a result, it is feasible to reach a larger audience than with a time-limited presentation.
- Several posters may be shown simultaneously in the same space so that visitors can view the ones that catch their attention.
- Authors occasionally receive the opportunity to exhibit a poster while providing a brief introduction. More intimate interaction with the audience than while delivering a speech result in an interactive environment.
- Posters can be displayed on many occasions and reused repeatedly.

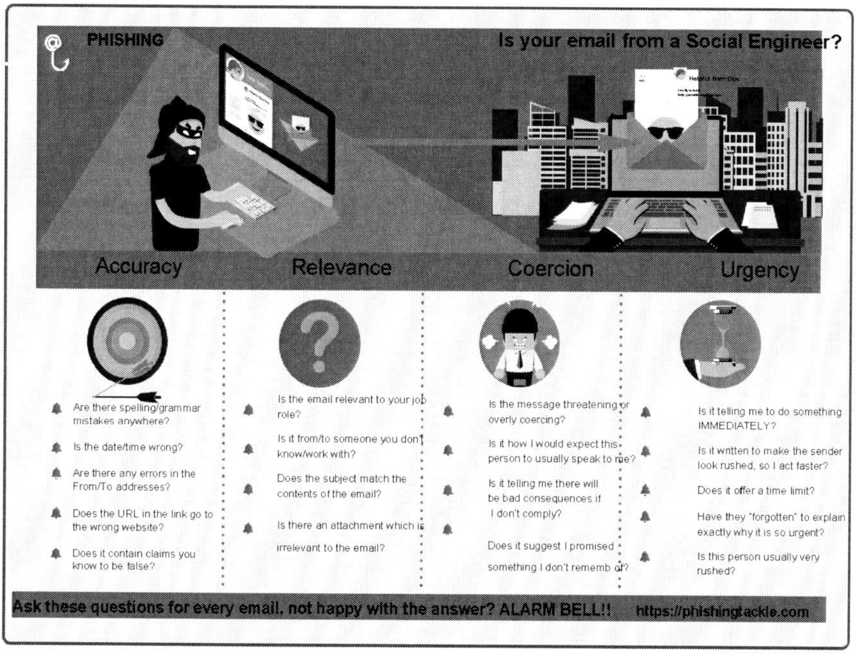

Figure 7.1. Social engineering infographic poster.

The poster has various drawbacks while being utilized in many different sectors. As a result, the following are some drawbacks of posters:

- It will be challenging to make changes or adaptations to a poster once it has been produced; as a result, it is less adaptable than a presentation, which can always be changed.
- Just as with drafting a speech, creating a poster can take some time. However, perfectionism is a product of practice.
- Posters typically call for concise wording that gets right to the point. Making decisions on what must be included or excluded is commonly challenging.

7.2.1.2. Pamphlets

Pamphlets can be made from a single piece of paper that has been printed on both sides and folded into halves, thirds, or fourths, known as a leaflet, or they can be made from a few pages that have been folded in half then saddle stapled at the crease to create a simplc book.

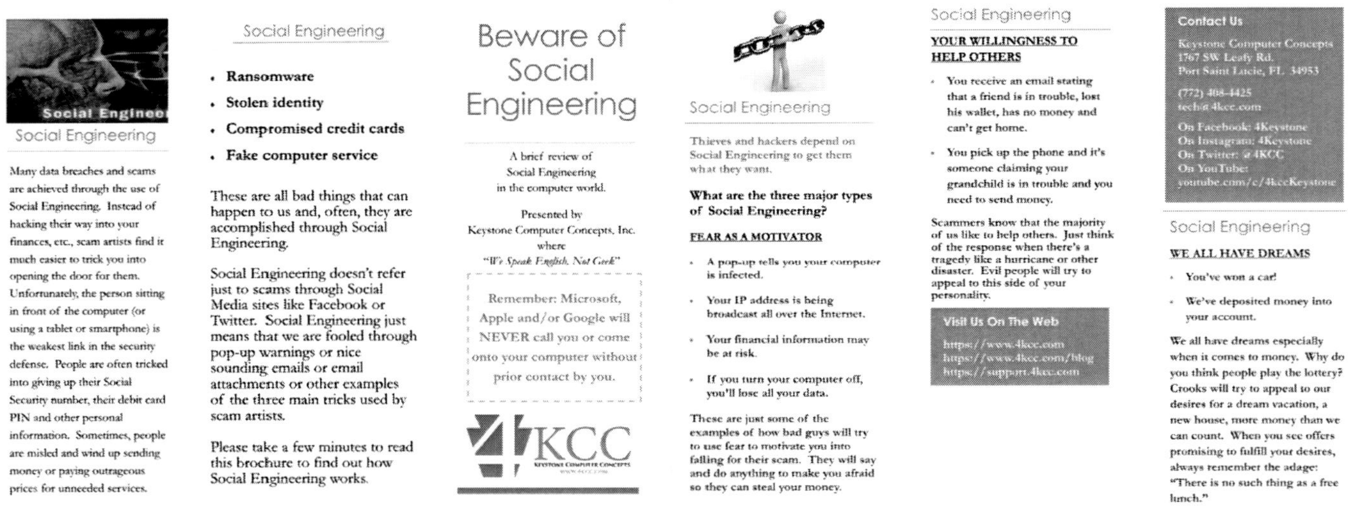

Social Engineering

Many data breaches and scams are achieved through the use of Social Engineering. Instead of hacking their way into your finances, etc., scam artists find it much easier to trick you into opening the door for them. Unfortunately, the person sitting in front of the computer (or using a tablet or smartphone) is the weakest link in the security defense. People are often tricked into giving up their Social Security number, their debit card PIN and other personal information. Sometimes, people are misled and wind up sending money or paying outrageous prices for unneeded services.

Social Engineering

- **Ransomware**
- **Stolen identity**
- **Compromised credit cards**
- **Fake computer service**

These are all bad things that can happen to us and, often, they are accomplished through Social Engineering.

Social Engineering doesn't refer just to scams through Social Media sites like Facebook or Twitter. Social Engineering just means that we are fooled through pop-up warnings or nice sounding emails or email attachments or other examples of the three main tricks used by scam artists.

Please take a few minutes to read this brochure to find out how Social Engineering works.

Beware of Social Engineering

A brief review of Social Engineering in the computer world.

Presented by Keystone Computer Concepts, Inc. where *"We Speak English, Not Geek"*

Remember: Microsoft, Apple and/or Google will NEVER call you or come onto your computer without prior contact by you.

4KCC Keystone Computer Concepts

Social Engineering

Thieves and hackers depend on Social Engineering to get them what they want.

What are the three major types of Social Engineering?

FEAR AS A MOTIVATOR

- A pop-up tells you your computer is infected.
- Your IP address is being broadcast all over the Internet.
- Your financial information may be at risk.
- If you turn your computer off, you'll lose all your data.

These are just some of the examples of how bad guys will try to use fear to motivate you into falling for their scam. They will say and do anything to make you afraid so they can steal your money.

Social Engineering

YOUR WILLINGNESS TO HELP OTHERS

- You receive an email stating that a friend is in trouble, lost his wallet, has no money and can't get home.
- You pick up the phone and it's someone claiming your grandchild is in trouble and you need to send money.

Scammers know that the majority of us like to help others. Just think of the response when there's a tragedy like a hurricane or other disaster. Evil people will try to appeal to this side of your personality.

Visit Us On The Web

https://www.4kcc.com
https://www.4kcc.com/blog
https://support.4kcc.com

Contact Us

Keystone Computer Concepts
1767 SW Leafy Rd.
Port Saint Lucie, FL 34953

(772) 408-4425
tech@4kcc.com

On Facebook: 4Keystone
On Instagram: 4Keystone
On Twitter: @4KCC
On YouTube: youtube.com/c/4kcKeystone

Social Engineering

WE ALL HAVE DREAMS

- You've won a car!
- We've deposited money into your account.

We all have dreams especially when it comes to money. Why do you think people play the lottery? Crooks will try to appeal to our desires for a dream vacation, a new house, more money than we can count. When you see offers promising to fulfill your desires, always remember the adage: "There is no such thing as a free lunch."

Figure 7.2. Social engineering pamphlet.

Figure 7.2 shows the pamphlet on social engineering attacks.[31] Many businesses hand out pamphlet materials to their staff members to raise awareness of social engineering attacks. It is advisable to hand out the brochure to the employees one-on-one, so they can understand it because, in many circumstances, many employees will overlook the poster.

7.2.1.3. Printed Newspapers

News and feature stories on local, national, and international news are frequently published in newspapers. Various IT publications are utilized to present the most recent cyberattack scenarios in various fields. These types of news are used by employees to increase awareness and better comprehend the current social engineering attack scenario. At the very least, readers of the newspaper comprehend the principles of how attackers breach a company's security. Using newspapers has a benefit because current news is published in them. Employees will be able to keep up with the current trend since social engineering attackers employ cutting-edge techniques daily to steal information. Therefore, every organization daily collects these types of news and broadcasts them to employees. The trainers should bring newspapers to their workplace to train their staff.

Due to rising online usage and the fact that many newspapers are now digital, which deliver their information online rather than in a physical version, the number of printed newspapers is currently declining. The content of a printed newspaper and a digital newspaper is the same, whereas the digital newspaper has higher visual quality. The printed newspaper takes longer to get to the readers. The news can be continuously published in digital newspapers.

7.2.1.4. Magazines

Almost all types of organizations, whether small or large, produce a magazine to promote their brand. An all-purpose publication is a magazine. A publication that is published periodically, or at set intervals, is referred to as a periodical. The majority of them are released once every month, although some could also be weekly, fortnightly, bimonthly, or quarterly. A company's magazine typically covers a variety of subjects relating to its events, conferences, workshops, etc. Numerous specialists also write articles about security-related topics. Employees can learn more about cybersecurity by reading the magazine article. Publishing a magazine is one of the best

[31] https://www.4kcc.com/blog/2021/01/08/our-most-popular-brochures/.

ideas because it will inspire employees and teach them a lot about the business.

7.2.2. Electronic Distribution of Materials

The term "electronic distribution" refers to the electronic delivery of materials via the internet, telephone networks, cable systems, servers, satellites, or other public or private access networks or electronic communication mediums. Some of the mediums used by organizations to distribute they're through online are:

7.2.2.1. Blogs

Weblog, a diary, essay, or journal on the web, is reduced to a "blog" in the word. The blog's owner, also referred to as the blogger or author, posts content there. Blogging is the process of updating or writing blogs. Many businesses have blogs to inform their staff and consumers about company news that would be of interest to them, such as new products that are in the works or project progress. In the blog, the security experts may employ to share the concept of social engineering attacks and give tips to avoid them. An example of a social engineering blog is shown in Figure 7.3.

Source: Grimes.

Figure 7.3. Social engineering blog.

Table 7.1. Advantages and disadvantages of blogging

Advantages	Disadvantages
Not much technical expertise is required for configuration. The contents are important for trainers to teach employees.	If the trainers are not experts on social engineering attacks, then it could be based on or include false information.
Social engineering is appearing with new features day by day. updates and new posts are simple and quick.	In the company, trainers have other work, so finding the time to create frequent updates for blogs can become a burden.
If any employees have any doubts, then they can leave comments.	Some comments may be harsh or improper.
There are literally millions of options for readers who wish to read other people's blogs.	There are lots of pretty uninteresting blogs available. Before finding anything worth reading, visitors may have to look through a lot of material.

7.2.2.2. Distribution of Awareness Materials via Social media

The practice of sharing, publishing, and promotional material on different social media platforms is known as social media material distribution. In the current generation, everyone has social media accounts to communicate with their friends, read news, update posts, and videos, etc. It is possible that this material was generated specifically for social media, or that it was previously published content that was reorganized for social media use. Many organizations set up accounts on social media sites like Facebook, Instagram, and Twitter to distribute the necessary knowledge in a way that promotes teamwork and collaboration. Some of the benefits of using social media are listed below:

- Sharing any kind of material, including links and videos, is simple on social media platforms.
- Employees have the option to provide and receive feedback if they have any questions.
- Reminders for events, notifications of new online training courses, and updates to business policy can all be posted by organizations.

Although social media platforms give several benefits for distributing materials, they have some drawbacks:

- It takes time to create and manage social media groups. These social media networks need to be monitored, which takes payroll hours for managers and corporate trainers.

- Large amounts of information are presented to workers all immediately, which may cause cognitive overload. Due to the constant flow of information, they could find it difficult to concentrate on one subject or task.

Instant messaging services are widely utilized to distribute materials in the modern world. With the help of this tool, trainers can set up groups to exchange their resources. It is possible, through audio or video, that people can converse with one another.

7.2.2.3. Learning Management System (LMS)

The LMS was created specifically for training purposes, and it includes a fundamental functional platform that gives administrators access to upload educational materials, teach courses to learners, send out notifications, and share information with authorized users. Behind a secure sign-on procedure, an LMS often runs inside a web browser. All learners and instructors now have convenient access to courses while on the road, and administrators and executives can track student development and make adjustments as a result. The benefits of LMS are as follows:

- An LMS improves the learning materials' adaptability and originality, which improves the employee's experience and promotes teamwork.
- Employees can continue their education on their own using desktops, laptops, and mobile devices.
- A regular learning and skill-building schedule will improve staff performance. The employees' awareness can be improved by regularly providing homework and tests. Evaluating an employee's performance is crucial.
- The capacity to design specialized learning pathways for new and old training programs. It may be able to categorize employees' knowledge of cyberattacks and create a roadmap.
- There is also the option of a video lecture, and it is possible to create a question on the video lecture.
- It is easy to create backup copies and restore information.

Although the LMS is often utilized in many businesses for training purposes, it has certain disadvantages, including the following:

- Some members of the trainers lack the information literacy and information management skills necessary to utilize LMS to assist in teaching in an efficient manner.
- Many learners do not desire to learn from it. They simply use copy paste methods to complete tasks.
- Many instructors find it difficult to plan and construct a variety of learning activities that are suitable for learner requirements and institutional technical capabilities.

7.2.3. Video-Based Training

The term "video-based learning" describes educational activities supported by video. Videos offer a multisensory learning experience unlike any other learning medium since they may integrate camera footage, animation, graphics, text, and voice. Video training must be combined with research-based learning concepts in order to successfully promote learning and behavioral change. This includes but is not limited to strategies including focused practice, recall, spaced Repetition, and learning by doing. Many security organizations create many kinds of videos to explain the concept of social engineering attacks.

7.2.3.1. Instructor-Led Videos for Training

Instructor-led videos are only the virtual equivalent of in-person instruction. A virtual audience hears the instructor, or presenter, on screen. A vast range of training is available through the channels of several third-party organizations, including LinkedIn, Coursera, and Udemy. It has been observed that many specialists also upload videos to YouTube. Users can visit this type of video to educate themselves about social engineering attacks. Once the users complete their videos, then they may receive a certificate for it. An example of an instructor-led video is shown in Figure 7.4.

Source: Ihezukwu.

Figure 7.4. Social engineering instructor-led videos.

Protected Voices: The FBI's Protected Voices initiative offers cybersecurity advice to political campaigns on a variety of subjects, including social engineering, in an effort to reduce the risk of cyber-influence operations aimed at influencing U.S. elections.[32]

7.2.3.2. Animated Videos for Training

Videos or a collection of animations that depict the topics and objects covered in a course are called training animations. Specialized studios will create animation movies for training that are ideal for each training purpose based on the business culture, needs, and course modules. Corporate learners could easily understand training materials that were visualized. More time would be saved by performing this than by scanning everything. This kind of instruction makes complicated subjects easy to understand for learners by using illustrations and simplifications. Whatever the subject, digestible knowledge with a dash of humor is also simpler to remember. As they wait for more pleasure, trainees are more enthusiastic to participate in class when animation is used in training.

Learners can personalize and self-pace their learning experiences with animation for training. Videos make the material understandable for learners. They essentially shorten training periods as a result. A shorter training period enables the personnel to use what they learn in the classroom in the real workplace more quickly. Figure 7.5 shows this kind of video.

[32] https://www.fbi.gov/video-repository/protected-voices-social-engineering-083018.mp4/view.

Figure 7.5. Social engineering animated videos.

7.2.3.3. Movies for Trainers

An excellent approach to communicating and learning is through the movie. It has the power to compel people to take action by inspiring, educating, and raising awareness. People can access it from their laptops or phones while at home, at work, or on the bus. As well as movies are simple to employ in pieces of training, in public gatherings, or classrooms. One of the best movies about social engineering attacks is *Catch Me If You Can* (Figure 7.6). In this movie, a 20-year-old boy named Frank is a talented forger who has impersonated a doctor, lawyer, and pilot. FBI agent Carl Becomes fixated on finding the con artist, who just enjoys the hunt.

Source: IMDB.

Figure 7.6. *Catch Me If You Can* (2002).

7.2.4. Interaction-Based Training Method

The trainer and learners must engage in order for interaction-based training methods to be effective. One can do it using both traditional and modern methods. The online technique involves virtual conference facilities such as Zoom, Team, etc., whereas the physical method employed lectures and required classrooms, seminar halls, etc.

7.2.4.1. Lectures

There are still a number of organizations using this traditional training style. A minimum of one week of security training is required when a new employee joins a company so that they can comprehend some level of a cyberattack. The absence of job pressures during the initial training period allows new hires to focus fully on learning. The learners lack any prior personal experience with cyberattack themes, making them unfamiliar with the subject. Trainers from within or outside the company may attend this seminar. However, when the speaker is a respected authority on the subject and attendees are present to hear what they have to say. Success depends on the knowledge and abilities of the presenter. Question or discussion sessions should be used to ensure learning occurs.

7.2.4.2. Virtual Classrooms

The digital learning space that employees enter to participate in an online course is known as the virtual classroom. Employers and trainers can communicate with one another and participate in learning activities in this setting by using the microphone and web camera on their computers. The distance learning platform, which often contains course materials, homework, examinations, assessments, and other resources to enhance the classroom experience, includes virtual classrooms as one of its components. Online forums and chat rooms may also be used as virtual classrooms, allowing employees and trainers to exchange textual messages.

7.2.4.3. Slides

Trainers commonly use slides while instructing trainees about attention. Trainers generate slides using Microsoft, Libra-office, and latex beamer tools. Trainers spend countless hours preparing presentations and thinking in slides, despite the fact that some people believe these tools to be the most useful and user-friendly ones for developing and presenting visual AIDS. If the trainers are unable to accurately explain anything on the slides, the company will lose money and time. Some of the resources of slides are as follows:

- OWASP Presentation of Social Engineering - OWASP
- Weaponizing data science for social engineering: Automated E2E spear phishing on Twitter - Defcon 23
- Using Social Engineering Tactics for Big Data Espionage - RSA Conference Europe 2012.

Trainers utilize slides to demonstrate concepts both in-person and online. On occasion, they send emails and upload them to corporate websites. Although it is a simple process, staff training offers certain benefits and drawbacks as shown in Table 7.2.

Table 7.2. Slides' advantages and disadvantages

Advantages	**Disadvantages**
Instead of brainstorming, compiling, and concentrating on their content, many trainers generate slides, so they have something to contribute.	Due to the linear format of PowerPoint slides, presenters are forced to condense complicated topics into a list of bullet points that are insufficient to demonstrate the complexity of an issue or facilitate decision-making.
By simply forwarding the slides with a Keystroke, it is simple to present to a large audience while maintaining eye contact, doing away with the requirement for handouts to assist the audience to understand the information.	At present, basic equipment is needed. To show the audience the slides, the instructors will require a computer and projection hardware.

7.2.5. Developing of Security Awareness Program

Cybersecurity training is standard practice in both big, small, and medium businesses. However, claims of an increase in successful cyber-attacks call into question the efficacy of many of the present training programs. While many models for creating Cybersecurity training frameworks for professionals in industry or the public have been put forth, these models frequently neglect to take into account human learning characteristics such as cognitive abilities, learning preferences, and meta-cognition when they are being created. Additionally, a cybersecurity training program's capacity to engage participants is crucial to its success (Chowdhury, Katsikas, and Gkioulos, 2022).

In hybrid CS exercises that include both skilled and unskilled people, Brilingaite, Bukauskas, and Juozapavičius, 2020 propose a framework to assist with the development and assessment of cybersecurity capabilities. Pre-exercise evaluation, pre-exercise training, live exercise, and post-exercise assessment are the four phases of the framework (see Figure 7.7).

Generally, a cybersecurity program combines customized learning needs analysis, design, development, implementation, and evaluation. The ADDIE model is another name for this procedure. Many training methods make use of this concept to instruct learners in cybersecurity.

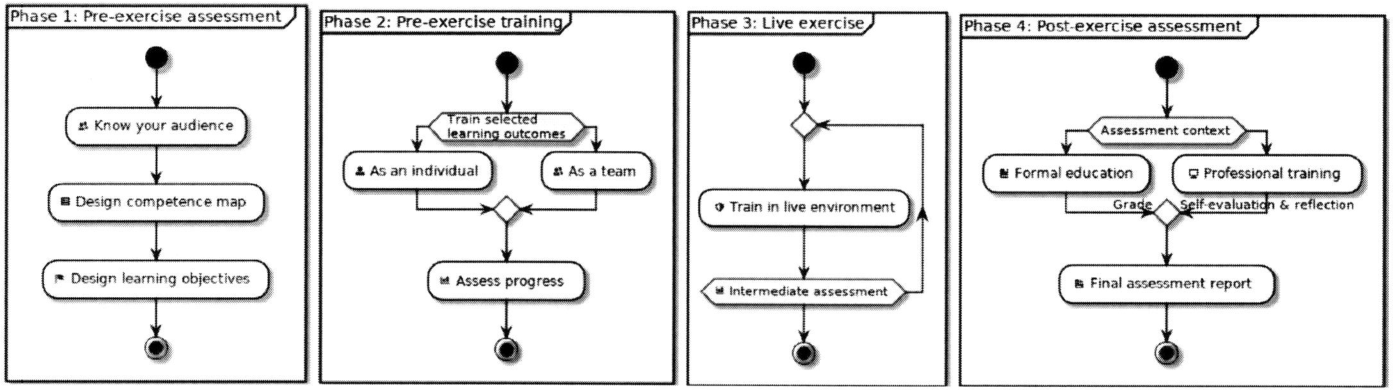

Figure 7.7. The Brilingait et al. framework-based phases for cybersecurity training.

The model's phases are described below:

- *Analysis*: The training specialist outlines the learning objectives, problems such as learner skill level, and the instructional difficulty of social engineering attacks.
- *Design*: To obtain the best design and systematic program creation, the training professional addresses a number of issues. These elements include the following: learning goals, content, exercises, subject analysis, lesson planning, and media.
- *Development*: A storyboard, graphics, and the incorporation of e-learning technology are all part of the blueprint the training specialist uses to produce the material during the design phase.
- *Implementation*: In this phase, protocols are created for instructing both facilitators and learners. The curriculum, learning objectives, delivery strategy, and testing procedures should all be included in facilitator training. As part of their preparation, learners receive instructions on how to register as well as how to use new software and devices. The training specialist also develops the instructional materials and evaluates e-learning.
- *Evaluation*: Throughout the entire design process, there is an ongoing evaluation phase. Its aim is to make sure that all learning objectives will satisfy the listed business requirements. Along with setting goals for on-the-job performance, the training specialist also makes sure that the demands of the company are satisfied.

An ADDIE-model-based cybersecurity workshop gave front-line healthcare workers and nursing learners the information and confidence they required to protect themselves from windows of opportunity for cybercrime (Pears and Konstantinidis, 2021). Participants' knowledge demonstrated a favorable tendency, and their confidence in their ability to employ cybersecurity abilities in daily practice dramatically increased. As recommendations for existing and upcoming curricula, a list of activities for improving cybersecurity in healthcare training is explored.

7.3. Technical Measures

Social engineering by the physical attack can be prevented by adding further levels of security, whereas technological advancements make it very difficult to spot. The technology-based social engineering attack mostly are communicated by phone calls, SMS, emails, and instant messages. One of the most common social engineering attacks that constantly introduce new features is the use of phishing. To counteract the social engineering approach, several researchers are constantly creating a wide range of detection models.

7.3.1. Phone Call Detection Model

The first technology that social engineering attackers utilize is a phone call to trick the victims into disclosing their credentials. Although many different communication avenues are available now, some attackers influence victims over the phone. Vishing refers to the current social engineering phone call attack. In order to mitigate social engineering attacks, phone calls are as follows:

A possible method to track and reduce social engineering (SE) attacks is put forth by Hoeschele and Rogers, 2005 as one of the early models. The SEDA is divided into three sections:

- The first of which is a vocal analysis that turns the entire conversation into text and produces the caller's voice signature.
- The next section of the SEDA is the database, which contains all the caller data and calls records.
- The attack detection processor is the last component. To identify efforts at fraud, this parses the discussion in either voice or text format.

Sandouka, Cullen, and Mann, 2009 looked at the viability of utilizing neural networks to recognize social engineering (SE) attacks in call centers by finding specific characteristics/features of the call or caller that can aid the system in determining whether this is a SE assault. Using this technology in SE has a lot of promise, according to the results they obtained. However, a number of adjustments and enhancements can be made to offer a more effective framework for detecting SE attacks that do not rely solely on keyword filtering but instead extract a set of rules incorporating the psychological characteristics of attackers and/or employees. Other factors may also be taken into account, like call frequency, call length, call time, etc.

7.3.2. Prevent Social Engineering Attacks Using a Whitelist

A whitelist often referred to as an allow list, is a cybersecurity tactic that accepts a certain set of email addresses, IP addresses, domain names, or applications while rejecting all others. A whitelist is a quick and simple tool that IT administrators can use to protect PCs and networks from online threats and improper content that could be harmful.

The whitelist method is widely utilized in the identification of fraudulent applications. Attackers utilize bogus applications to receive data from the victims. As was mentioned in the previous chapter, harmful code is used to generate fake apps by cybercriminals that are intended to steal user data. In order to fool users into downloading them, fake apps are designed to replicate the appearance and functionality of real apps. A third-party program asks users for permission to access their data when they install it. This is used by fake apps to access users' personal data, frequently without their knowledge.

Applocker whitelisting tool is an application whitelisting technology introduced with Microsoft's Windows 7 operating system, and it can be used in Windows 10, Windows 11, and Windows Server 2016 and above. The administrators are able to create rules based on file names, publishers, or file locations that will allow certain files to execute.[33]

Linux systems often come with AppArmor and SE Linux capabilities that can be used to block all apps that are not explicitly whitelisted, and there are also commercial products available.

Whitelisting techniques are used in addition to email, SMS, and URL services to lessen social engineering attacks. It is common practice for spam filters to allow users to "whitelist" specific sender IP addresses, email addresses, or domain names in order to prevent their emails from being rejected or routed to the junk mail bin. These can be manually maintained by the user or system administrator, whereas they can also relate to whitelist services that are externally maintained.

In practice, it is challenging to maintain because of the scale. The whitelist strategies block access to services that are not on the list. The number of emails, SMS messages, and URLs that are generated today makes it challenging to keep them all on the whitelist. As a result, this strategy can only be used if the list contains limited elements. For instance, any firm that

[33] https://docs.microsoft.com/en-us/windows/security/threat-protection/windows-defender-appl i zcation-control/applocker/applocker-overview.

permits communication with only a few SMS numbers, emails, and URLs will receive the best results. In this case, blacklisting is a preferable option.

7.3.3. Prevent Social Engineering Attacks Using a Blacklist

The blacklist is the opposite of a whitelist. It is a simple access control method that denies access to any components on the list, including email addresses, users, passwords, URLs, IP addresses, domain names, file hashes, etc.

Google's Safe Browsing is a well-known web browsing blacklist that is enabled by default in Firefox, Safari, and Chrome. By screening locally, a blacklist in a web browser aims to shield the user from viewing a malicious or dishonest web website.

Mailwasher is email filtering software for Windows that can identify and eliminate spam from a user's email while it is on the mail server, prior to being downloaded to the user's computer. Firetrust, a New Zealand-based business, created Mailwasher. It combines Bayesian filtering with user-defined filters, spam databases, and other techniques.

Sawa et al., 2016 provided a method for spotting social engineering attacks that makes use of natural language processing to spot questionable remarks made by an attacker. Attacks using social engineering either solicit private information or provide directives asking the listener to carry out actions that the speaker is not allowed to. In this method, questions and directives are recognized, and their likely themes are extracted using natural language processing techniques. To evaluate whether a question or command is malicious, each extracted topic is checked against a topic blacklist. Due to the fact that it just depends on the dialogue content, our method is generally adaptable to numerous attack vectors.

7.3.3.1. Greylisting

Greylisting is a technique for spam protection for email users. Any email sent by an unknown sender will be "temporarily rejected" by a mail transfer agent (MTA) utilizing greylisting. If the email is authentic, the sending server will retry after some time, and if sufficient time has passed, the email will be approved. Greylisting works well against spammers' mass emailing programs since they do not queue and reattempt mail delivery as a typical mail transport agent would. Additionally, postponing distribution provides real-time blackhole lists and comparable lists more time to locate and flag the spam source. As a result, compared to before the greylisting delay, these following attempts are more likely to be flagged as spam by other techniques.

7.3.4. Detect Social Engineering Attacks Using the Heuristic Method

A heuristic method is based on using several discriminative traits that can be discovered by comprehending and examining the structure of URLs, emails, web pages, and other things. Effective and accurate classification of social engineering attacks is greatly influenced by the technique used to process these traits.

Attackers trick victims into visiting a false website by sending them a fraudulent URL via email, SMS, or social networking sites. Numerous models were proposed by researchers that use machine learning to examine URLs, emails, or SMS messages in order to determine whether social engineering attacks are occurring. The researchers used many machine learning algorithms to categorize social engineering attacks. Jeeva and Rajsingh, 2016 examine the URL's features and applies both apriori and predictive apriori associative rule mining techniques as shown in Figure.

With the aid of artificial neural networks and multi-layer perceptron (MLP) classifier s in neural networks, Lansley et al., 2020 presented the SEADer++ approach for identifying social engineering attacks. The authors collect features from the chat text, such as URLs, the quantity of misspelled words, verbs, and adjectives like "require," "must," "urgent," etc., during the preprocessing stages. After the features from the real and semi-synthetic datasets were gathered, the method applied to the multi-layer perceptron, Random Forest, and decision tree. The findings above demonstrate that, in comparison to the others, the MLP classifier is more accurate.

Zamir et al., 2020 developed a technique that uses various machine-learning methods to detect phishing websites. In this model, feature selection techniques like IG, GR, Relief-F, and RFE are used to examine the top features. The weakest features are combined into a new feature, while the strongest features are combined into others, following an analysis of the relevance of each feature. All features are altered to their normalized state. Following that, features are supplied to ML classifiers (support vector machine, Naive Bayes, Random Forest, K-nearest neighbor, bagging, and neural network) using principal component analysis (PCA).

Algorithm: Apriori

Rules:

Phishing URLs

Rule 1: *if* {Transport Layer Security = http ∩ Keyword in the path portion of the URL = yes ∩ Top level domain = yes} => *class phishing*(*conf.*, 1).

Rule 2: *if* { Number of slash in URL ≥ 5 ∩ Transport Layer Security = http ∩ Keyword in the path portion of the URL = yes} => *class phishing* (*conf.*, 1).

Rule 3: *if* {Special characters = yes ∩ Transport Layer Security = http ∩ Number of terms in the host name of the URL > 4} => *class phishing* (conf., 1).

Rule 4: *if* {Dot in the host URL > 4 ∩ Transport Layer Security = http ∩ Number of terms in the host name of the URL > 4} => *class phishing* (conf., 1).

Rule 5: *if* {Number of slash in the URL ≥ 5 ∩ Dot in the host URL > 4 ∩ Length of the URL > 75} => *class phishing* (conf., 1).

Rule 6: *if* {*Special Characters* = *yes* ∩ *Transport Layer Security* = *http* ∩ *Top level domain* = *yes* } => *class phishing* (*conf.*, 1).

Rule 7: *if* {*Dot in the host URL* > 4 ∩ *Transport Layer Security* = *http* ∩ *Keyword in the path portion of the URL* = *yes* } => *class phishing* (*conf.*, 1).

Rule 8: *if* {*Special Characters* = *yes* ∩ *Transport Layer Security* = *http* ∩ *Keyword in the path portion of the URL* = *yes* } => *class phishing* (*conf.*, 1).

Rule 9: *if* { *Dot in the host URL* > 4 ∩ *Keyword in the path portion of the URL* = *yes* ∩ *Top level domain* = *yes*} => *class phishing* (*conf.*, 1).

Figure 7.8. Rules extracted for phishing URLs through apriori algorithm.

An anti-phishing model called "SmiDCA" is presented by Sonowal and Kuppusamy, 2018 (Smishing Detection based on Correlation Algorithm). In this model, 39 different features were first derived from the collection of numerous smishing messages from various sources. Dimensionality reduction is a component of the SmiDCA model, and tests using machine learning were run on datasets without (BFSA) and with (AFSA) reduced feature sets. Experiments using datasets in English and other languages have been used to validate the model.

Many artists have utilized YouTube as a promotional platform to submit their music videos, movie trailers, etc., and viewers can leave comments on them. Unfortunately, criminals frequently publish fraudulent website links, advertising, and false information in the comments section, which could spread malware or viruses. In order to maintain social media's flawless operation, these negative remarks must be discovered. In this work, Sharmin and Zaman, 2017 constructed a number of classifier algorithms to distinguish between spam and legal YouTube video comments. Their performance metrics were examined, and the ensemble classifier outperformed a single classifier method when it came to classifying text.

The current research focuses on encountering fake social media profiles. The methods for spotting phony social media profiles can be divided into those that focus on account data analysis and profile analysis. The establishment of false profiles on social networks is thought to harm more people than any other type of cybercrime. Even before the user is informed that a fraudulent profile has been created, this crime must be caught. In addition to discussing the methods for identifying phony social media profiles, this study also discusses the importance of fake identities in advanced persistent threats. Elyusufi, Elyusufi, et al., 2019 will evaluate the effects of three supervised machine learning algorithms: Random Forest (RF), Decision tree (DT-J48), and Naive Bayes in order to create an appropriate prediction of phony or authentic profiles (NB).

7.3.5. Honeypot

Using a virtual trap to entice intruders, honeypots are a type of security technique. Attackers can exploit vulnerabilities in a computer system that has been purposefully infiltrated, allowing researchers to investigate them and strengthen security protocols. The investigation of 40,000 fake accounts by research firm ZeroFOX involved the creation of honeypot accounts, interaction with the impersonators, and observation of the social engineering assault in a sandboxed environment. As a result, the research firm was able to outline the assaults' general structure, indicate their similarities and variations, and gain a clearer understanding of their motivations.[34] Nearly half (48.1%) of all malicious social media impersonators use the brand to lure people looking for promotions while disguising their payload as a phony coupon or giveaway. In their identities, screen aliases, and descriptions, more than 1,000 impersonators used phrases that provide credibility, such as "official," "genuine," "real," "approved," "actual," and "legitimate."

[34] https://www.csoonline.com/article/3177458/honeypot-catches-social-engineering-scams-on-social-media.html.

7.3.6. Important Information on Social Engineering Attacks

Although numerous organizations explain social engineering from their point of view, these are some crucial lessons to teach the staff. According to Irwin, 2021, every information security policy must include a social engineering strategy. They offer the following social engineering preventative strategies that can be used by any organization:

- Employees are aware of the effects of social engineering attacks. Social engineering has a huge effect on business. Every year, social engineering attacks affect many businesses in some way.
- Be wary of incoming calls, visits, or emails from strangers requesting information about staff or other internal matters. Try to confirm a person's identification by getting in touch with the corporation directly if they claim to be from a reliable organization.
- Unless you are assured of a person's authority to possess the information never provide personal information or details about your organization, including its network or structure.
- Try to verify an email request by getting in touch with the business directly if you are suspicious of its legitimacy. Check prior statements for contact information instead of using the contact information listed on a website related to the request. Online communities can also provide information about known phishing attacks.
- Do not open an attachment without proper verification: Even if your antivirus program says the message is clean, do not open an email or email attachment if it sounds suspect. As new viruses are continually being released by attackers, antivirus software may not have the signature. Before opening the attachment, at the very least, get in touch with the person who is said to have sent the message to confirm its validity. However, even messages sent by a trustworthy sender could contain a virus, particularly in the case of forwards. There can be a valid reason if something about the email or the attachment makes the victim uneasy.
- Beware of tailgating. The attacker is frequently seen carrying a clipboard and wearing a tabard. Do not permit anyone inside the building, then, without conducting a thorough investigation.

- Do not rush. Attackers inculcate a sense of urgency so that the victims feel under pressure to respond. Check all emails, SMS messages, and other types of messages carefully before responding to anyone.
- Never divulge private information. Think before supplying critical information, because no respectable company will ever request a customer's password.
- Do not enter information into a bogus website. Check the website's security before submitting any information, even if it appears to be authentic. Examine the website's URL and avoid websites that use HTTP.
- Beware of typosquatting. Pay attention to URLs and typosquatting websites that appear legitimate but have slightly changed web addresses from the original site they are copying.
- Beware of clickjacking. Users are tricked into believing they are clicking on one thing when they are actually clicking on another by an attack known as clickjacking. Therefore, whenever you click something, proceed with caution and let your mouse hover over links to observe where they take you before clicking.

Summary

The three defenses used to lessen the social engineering attack were reviewed in this chapter. The first line of defense is policy, which ensures that staff members are prepared to handle potentially dangerous situations by having the appropriate regulations, protocols, and processes in place. Another defense against a social engineering attempt is raising employee awareness. Although certain social engineering attacks can be challenging to spot since they frequently coincide with new trends in technology channels. To lessen the social engineering onslaught, many experts suggested numerous strategies.

Chapter 8

Laws Governing Social Engineering Attacks

Every firm has its own policies to safeguard its employees and avoid negative publicity. This regulation only applies to the employees who are employed there, yet many internet users are unaware of it. Social engineering has a similar negative impact on common people. Many online users such as students, self-workers, and housewives are frequently preying fall to social engineering attacks. Therefore, there is a requirement for laws that are related to social engineering attacks to protect them. Social engineering attack is an umbrella term, and many cyberattacks employ social engineering tactics to achieve their goal. Therefore, a single law addressing lowering the possibility of a social engineering attack cannot be passed. A social engineering attack's goal is to gather personal data for identity theft, and it can be achieved in many ways. Many nations have laws that determine data protection in an effort to lessen social engineering attacks. Although the term "social engineering attack" is not mentioned in these laws, the application of these laws is connected to social engineering attacks. Therefore, the chapters discuss the following laws:

- Copyright Act
- Telephone Records Act
- Spam Act
- Fraud Act
- Data Protection Act
- Health Insurance Act
- Anti-Phishing Act.

8.1. Copyright Act

Copyright law protects the original works of authorship and allows individuals who use those works without the proper authorization to be sued for damages, court costs, and attorney's fees. Many genuine organizations prevent others from using their identities such as logos, style, text, and quotes because they spend huge amounts of money to design them. Identity is crucial for firms because customers recognize their organizations based on their identity.

Copyright infringement occurs when these proprietary works are used by anyone without the owner's consent. For example, copyright infringement occurs when copies of software are made and sold online without the owner's consent, and it can also occur when content is copied from an online source. A person may be found guilty of copyright infringement if they attempt to use or distribute another person's work without their permission. The copyright gives "exclusive rights" to the owner of the work.

In the cyber-attacks, the attackers commonly employ this copyright content in their emails, SMS, and other communications to convey the impression that they are legitimate businesses. As a result, numerous people divulge their credentials because they believe they got messages from legitimate organizations. Some of the important copyright issues are as follows:

8.1.1. Online Contents

All online content, including text, audio files, video content, and images, is protected by copyright law under the DMCA (Digital Millennium Copyright Act) (Congress, 1998), regardless of whether the content has a copyright sign. This is due to the fact that the attackers utilize the content of an authentic website as the basis for a fraudulent website they create. Visitors to these websites assume they are trustworthy, so they provide their credentials. In some situations, attackers commonly create this kind of website to spread malicious software to victims' PCs.

8.1.2. Trademark

A registered trademark ensures that the brand, name, or logo is owned. It safeguards the owner's brand from unlawful third-party use. Although both copyright and trademarks protect intellectual property, they differ from each other as shown in Table 8.1.

Table 8.1. Copyright vs. trademark

Copyright	**Trademark**
Literary and creative works are protected by copyright	A trademark protects elements that aid in the definition of a company's brand.
Copyright protects books, articles, web material, photographs, paintings, music, and movies, among other things	A trademark protects a person's name, slogan, logo, form, and color, among other examples.
A copyright is granted for a long period of time	A trademark is granted for a relatively limited period of time
Copyright has no symbolic representation to indicate registration whereas some parties use like ©	A trademark used while registration is being processed: ™. When registration is complete, this symbol is used: ®

According to Epps, 2010, in the late 19th century, the first contemporary trademark laws were created. The first complete trademark system in the world was established in France in 1857. The Trademarks Act of 1938 in the United Kingdom altered the system by allowing "intent-to-use" registration, establishing an examination-based procedure, and establishing a system for application publication. Other unique ideas like "related trademarks," consent to use the system, a defense mark system, and a non-claiming right system were included in the 1938 Act, which served as a template for laws of a similar nature worldwide.

A client faces the possibility of suffering legal action for trademark or copyright infringement from another company if they use the logo, or name of that company in a mock social engineering attack. The logo and brand name of a well-known corporation is commonly used by attackers to encourage the victims to believe in their lies, nevertheless. In order to avoid being caught by the legal team, they terminated the connection with the victims after finishing their scam activities.

8.1.3. Cybersquatting

The illegal registration and use of Internet domain names that are identical to or confusingly similar to trademarks, service marks, corporate names, or people's names are known as cybersquatting. The domain name is acquired and used by cybersquatters with the intention of stealing the goodwill of the legitimate trademark owner. To safeguard trademark and business owners against abusive cybersquatting, the federal government and the Internet Corporation for Assigned Names and Numbers have both taken action. One technique that is frequently employed in a cyber cybersquatting attack is typosquatting. Attackers use the trademark of a legitimate website while only slightly altering the domain name of the legitimate website. Phishing attacks frequently exploit cybersquatting to deceive their victims.

The Anticybersquatting Consumer Protection Act (Act, 1999) is the main illustration of the Anticybersquatting Consumer Protection Act (ACPA). Domain name registrations that are identical to or confusingly similar to trademarks or assigned names are forbidden by the federal ACPA. If an illegal user intends to make money off of a unique mark, they may be held accountable to the trademark owner. Additional trademark and service mark matters are governed by additional U.S. legislation, such as the Lanham Act and the Trademark Dilution Revision Act. Owners may also be protected by state legislation.

8.1.4. Software Piracy

The unauthorized use, copying, or distribution of copyrighted software is known as software piracy. According to Koen Jr and Im, 1997, the term "piracy" in its broadest sense refers to three different types of loss.:

- *Commercial piracy*: The unlawful duplication of software with the intention of selling and distributing it.
- *Corporate piracy*: Most of the time it includes a piece of software being distributed across the workplace on several hard drives or put onto a file server that is used by a large number of users. Rarely does it entail duplicating software for direct financial benefit? Consequently, a company may have only acquired one or a few copies of the software, whereas dozens or hundreds of employees may be utilizing those copies. As well as organizations and enterprises, this type of piracy also includes the actions of governmental bodies and educational institutions.
- *Softlifting*: When someone downloads a friend's software or carries a copy of it home from the office for personal use. Many people mistakenly assume that this type of piracy is lawful because it is not done with the intent to profit Financially.

Attackers use pirated software to fuel malware that impersonates legitimate software, as seen in several phishing emails. This software may contain malware such as viruses, adware, or Spyware, not work properly or fail entirely. The Faculty of Engineering at the National University of Singapore (NUS) conducted a Microsoft-commissioned investigation that estimated the connection between software piracy and malware infections. The team investigated and tested several versions of pirated software downloaded from the internet for infection. All websites that include links to download pirated software expose users to many security concerns, and 34% of the downloaded pirated software was packed with malware that infects the computer once the download is complete or when the folder containing the pirated program is opened. The anti-malware software on the machine was disabled by 24% of the harmful programs packaged with pirated software downloads. About 31% of pirated software downloaded did not finish installation but instead redirected traffic to torrent hosting.

Therefore, it is also protected by copyright legislation. Using pirated software could result in fines, and poor press that could harm the company's reputation and ultimately cost the business, as well as civil and even criminal penalties.

8.1.5. Linking

It enables website visitors to go to other websites on the Internet. The user may access another Web page anywhere in the world by just clicking on a word or image on one page or even another page on the same server. The linking of websites or emails often consists of two parts: the visible component, which is visible to users, and the actual part, which hides the website's URL. Information about the actual part is provided by the visible part.

As an illustration, the Paytm website URL is the real link, while the viewable portion displays the Paytm name, logo, and image to provide information about the Paytm website. Attackers take advantage of this linking procedure by using a real firm name or image in the visible portion while hiding a phishing site URL in the hidden portion. Many victims click the link to visit the site but just observe the viewable portion, making them easy targets for social engineering assaults.

8.1.6. Abuse of Law

This law has an interesting event where the assailants abuse it. Typically, the attackers pose as copyright organizations to warn users that they are utilizing protected content and provide a link to contact the original creators. The URL, however, directs them to a fraudulent and phishing website. Following their visit, customers submit their credit card information, install malicious software, and then they make purchases. Due to their fear of copyright legislation, several victims have disclosed their identity or payment.

8.2. Telephone Records and Privacy Protection Act of 2006

In the Telephone Records and Privacy Protection Act of 2006 (Congress.gov, January 12, 2007), pretexting is not permitted unless it is being used by law enforcement or intelligence services to buy, sell, or gain personal phone records. This act covers the following issues:

- Giving a client or employee of a covered organization incorrect or misleading information.
- Presenting a covered entity with documents that are misleading or fraudulent.
- Accessing a covered entity's customer accounts without permission over the Internet or through fraudulent computer-related activities.
- A fine and/or up to 10 years in jail may be imposed if anyone violates this legislation.

This law is crucial in social engineering attacks because the attackers frequently utilize the telephone to communicate with the victims. In the beginning, telephone conversion is used by attackers to persuade users to reveal their credentials. It still has a place in modern society, whereas there are a lot more communication options now. The most considerable advantage of using the telephone to motivate others is that when questions and responses are exchanged in real-time, participants may articulate something more precisely. In many instances, victims mostly ignore email or SMS, and phone calls are considered a true conversion.

Prior to this law's passage, the only prohibited practice in the US under the Gramm-Leach-Bliley Act was the use of pretense to obtain information about a person's finances. The majority of legislators and consumer advocacy organizations argued for the passage of a federal statute even though it was already unlawful in California to use pretexts to receive phone records. The likelihood of criminal prosecution was nonexistent, which led to the widespread sale of fraudulent goods.

The 106th United States Congress passed the Gramm-Leach-Bliley Act (GLBA), [35] often known as the Financial Services Modernization Act (FSMA) of 1999. (1999-2001). The Gramm-Leach-Bliley Act mandates that financial institutions, or businesses that provide consumers with financial goods or services like loans, financial or investment advice, or insurance, disclose to their clients their information-sharing policies and take reasonable steps to protect sensitive information.

Vaden Anderson, 28, was indicted by Ohio authorities in 2008 on charges that he used pretexting to steal private phone records from Sprint/Nextel. The indictment claims that Anderson impersonated a civil subpoena from the U.S. District Court in order to serve the phone company with the records. Anderson may receive a maximum of 10 years in jail and a $250,000 fine if found guilty.[36]

8.3. Fraud Act

Fraud entails providing false information, whether by design or accidentally, to another party in order to obtain something that could not have been given without deceit. As a result, the attackers employ social engineering techniques to commit fraud.

8.3.1. Computer Fraud and Abuse Act of 1986 (CFAA)

The United States enacted the Computer Fraud and Abuse Act (CFAA) in 1986, making it illegal to access a protected computer without authorization.

As per Black, 2001, crimes under the act:

- Acquiring or attempting to acquire any national security information with the purpose of using it against the interests of the United States or to unjustly benefit any foreign country.

[35] https://www.govinfo.gov/content/pkg/PLAW-106publ102/html/PLAW- 106publ102.htm.
[36] https://www.justice.gov/archive/criminal/cybercrime/press-releases/2008/andersonIndcit.pdf.

- Accessing data of a financial institution, credit card company, or consumer reporting agency with the intent to receive information from them.
- Intentional access to a government computer has an impact on how the government uses that machine.
- When someone deliberately uses a federally owned computer without permission, they are able to gain more than just the intention to commit fraud by using the computer.
- Changing, deleting, or causing intentional damage to digital data belonging to another.
- Intentionally entering a computer used for federal purposes and obstructing authorized access to any data or computer services where the loss exceeds $1,000 over the course of a year or requires medical care. The word "loss" nevertheless did not commonly refer to monetary losses. Investors may lose money on a stock, for instance, if stock estimates were changed to make the stock seem more appealing.
- Unauthorized use of passwords.

8.3.2. Fraud Act of 2006

The British Parliament passed the Fraud Act of 2006 (c. 35), which is a law that is applicable to England, Wales, and Northern Ireland. It was passed royal assent on November 8, 2006, and it became effective on January 15, 2007. According to the Act,[37] three types of fraud are considered for criminal offenses: fraud by false representation, fraud by omission to disclose information, and fraud by abuse of position.

- *Section 2 of the Act*: Fraud by false representation occurs when a person makes "any representation as to fact or law. express or implied" that they know to be false or deceptive.
- *Section 3 of the Act*: "Fraud by failing to disclose information" as occurring when someone fails to disclose information to a third party when they are legally required to do so."
- *Section 4 of the Act*: "Fraud by abuse of position" refers to situations in which a person holds a position where they are expected to

[37] https://www.legislation.gov.uk/ukpga/2006/35/contents.

protect another person's financial interests and abuses that position; this includes situations in which the abuse was a covert omission rather than an overt act."

8.3.3. The Indian Penal Code

The official criminal code of India is called the Indian Penal Code (IPC). It is a thorough code that aims to address all important areas of criminal law. The first law commission of India, headed by Thomas Babington Macaulay, and constituted in 1834 as a result of the Charter Act of 1833, made suggestions that served as the basis for the creation of the code. In the early years of the British Raj, in 1862, it became operative in British India. However, it did not immediately apply in the Princely states, which had their own courts and legal systems up until the 1940s. Since then, the Code has undergone several revisions and currently includes more penal statutes.

- *Section 415 is related to cheating*: According to the law, a person is said to "cheat" if they deceive another person in such a way that they coerce them into giving up their property, giving their permission for someone else to keep it, or coercing them into doing something that would harm their body, mind, reputation, or property.
- *Section 416 is related to cheating by personation*: A person is considered to "cheat via personation" if they intentionally represent themselves as someone different than who they actually are, impersonate another person, or intentionally switch one person for another.
- *Section 420 is related to cheating and dishonestly inducing delivery of property*: The punishment for dishonestly causing someone to deliver the property to another person, create, alter, or destroy valuable security, or anything that is signed or sealed and can be changed into a valuable security, is imprisonment of either kind for a term that may be as long as seven years, as well as being subject to a fine.
- *Section 463 is related to fenter*Forgery is the act of making a false document, electronic record, or portion of a document or electronic record with the purpose of misleading the general public or another person, supporting a claim or title, pressuring a person to relinquish

their property, entering into an express or implied contract, or committing fraud.

- *Section 464 is related to making a false document*: Making a fraudulent paper or digital record is defined as:
  - Whoever dishonestly or fraudulently,
    1) Creates, signs, seals, or executes a document or a portion of a document;
    2) Creates or sends any form of electronic record, including a portion of one;
    3) Attaches an electronic signature to any electronic document;
    4) Creates any mark indicating the execution of a document or the legitimacy of the electronic signature with the purpose of making it appear as though such document, portion of the document, electronic record, or electronic signature was made, signed, sealed, executed, transmitted, or affixed by or under the authority of a person who, in his knowledge, did not make, sign, seal, execute, or affix the document.
  - Whoever, without lawful authority, dishonestly or fraudulently modifies a document or an electronic record in any material way after it has been created, signed, or sealed with an electronic signature by himself or by another person, whether that person is alive or dead at the time of the modification.
  - Whoever knowingly or fraudulently induces another person to sign, seal, execute, modify, or affix his electronic signature to any electronic record, knowing that the other person is incapable of doing so due to insanity or intoxication, or that he is unaware of the contents of the document or electronic record or the nature of the alteration due to deception practiced upon him.

8.4. Spam Act

Any unsolicited bulk email is considered spam. Spam is typically transmitted to many users by email, whereas it can also be sent via instant messages, SMS, and social media. Although spam is different from social engineering, some of its campaigns do use social engineering methods like phishing, spear phishing, smishing, or disseminating malicious attachments or links. Some of the spam laws are below:

8.4.1. CAN-SPAM Act of 2003

In 2003, a law known as the Controlling the Assault of Non-Solicited Pornography and Marketing (CAN-SPAM) Act was passed, creating the first national guidelines for sending commercial e-mails in the United States. The Federal Trade Commission (FTC) is mandated by law to carry out the law's enforcement. Conrad Burns, a Republican, proposed the legislation, which was approved by both the House and the Senate during the 108th United States Congress and became law in December 2003.

The recipients are offered the opportunity to discontinue receiving commercial mailings under this law, which also defines the conditions for them. The CAN-SPAM Act also establishes sanctions for breaking the restrictions. Email sent from business to business is not exempt from the law. This implies that all emails, including those advertising a new product line to past clients, must adhere to the law. Mailings that don't follow the law could incur penalties and cost the business money. The following are the primary requirements of the CAN-SPAM Act:

- It is illegal to use a header that contains erroneous or deceptive information.
- It is prohibited to use deceptive subject lines.
- The message should explicitly state that it is intended for advertising purposes.
- Inform the subscribers of the location of their business.
- The unsubscribe link should be prominently shown in the message.
- Describe to clients how they may opt out of receiving emails from the company in the future.
- Even if a company contracts with another company to handle its mailings, it must still fulfill its legal obligations.

The first defendant found guilty by a jury under the terms of the CAN-SPAM Act of 2003 was Jeffrey Brett Goodin of California in January 2007. He was tricking AOL users into providing personal and credit card information by pretending to be the company's billing department and sending thousands of emails to AOL subscribers. He was ordered to serve 70 months in jail despite facing up to 101 years behind bars for the CAN-SPAM violation and eleven other crimes, including wire fraud, the use of credit cards without authorization, and misusing the AOL brand. Goodin started serving his prison sentence right away after being taken into custody for missing a prior court appearance.

8.4.2. Spam Act of 2003

The Australian Parliament passed the Spam Act of 2003 (Cth) to control commercial e-mail and other forms of commercial electronic messaging. The Act prohibits spam, including email spam, some varieties of phone spam, email address harvesting, and other practices.[38]

An overview of this act in simpler terms is provided below:

- This act establishes a system for policing commercial email and other kinds of commercial electronic messaging.
- It is forbidden to send unsolicited commercial electronic messages.
- Commercial electronic messages must contain information about the person or business that provided the message's sending permission.
- A functional unsubscribe feature must be included in all commercial electronic messages.
- An electronic address list produced using address-harvesting software must not be supplied, acquired, or used.
- The main remedies for breaches of this act are civil penalties and injunctions.

8.4.3. Privacy and Electronic Communications (EC Directive) Regulations of 2003

The Privacy and Electronic Communications (EC Directive) Regulations (PECR) is a UK law that carries out the EU's ePrivacy Directive (Directive 2002/58/EC) and establishes privacy rights concerning electronic communications. Anywhere in the European Union, the rules can be applied to a violating company or person. Unsolicited e-mail regulations are

[38] http://www8.austlii.edu.au/cgi-bin/viewdoc/au/legis/cth/consol_act/sa200366/s3.html.

enforced by the Information Commissioner's Office, which also investigates complaints of violations. Depending on the situation, violating an enforcement notice is a crime punishable by a fine of up to £500,000.[39]

The primary distinction between the two is that the GDPR (which will be explained in the following section) refers to the processing of personal data, whilst the PECR relates particularly to electronic marketing and provides provisions on areas:

- Electronic marketing, such as phone calls, SMS messaging, emails, and faxes
- The usage of cookies on websites to monitor visitors
- The safety of open-access electronic communications
- The privacy of users of electronic communications services.

8.4.3.1. Section 66A in the Information Technology Act of 2000

The Information Technology Act (ITA) of 2000 is an Act of the Indian Parliament that was notified on October 17, 2000. It is often referred to as ITA-2000 or the IT Act. It is India's main law addressing electronic commerce and cybercrime. Section 66A in the Information Technology Act, 2000 sanctions using a communication service to send offensive messages, etc. It implies that any individual who sends via a communication device or computer resource,

- Any information that is grossly offensive or has a menacing character;
- Any information that he knows to be false, but uses a computer resource or communication tool to repeatedly incite irritation, discomfort, danger, obstruction, insult, harm, criminal intimidation, animosity, hatred, or ill will;
- Any electronic mail or electronic mail message intended to irritate or inconvenience the addressee or receiver, or to deceive or mislead them regarding the origin of such messages

shall be subject to a fine and a sentence of imprisonment that may extend to three years.

---

[39] https://ico.org.uk/for-organisations/guide-to-pecr/what-are-pecr/.

8.5. Data Protection Act

Data protection is the process of defending sensitive information against loss, tampering, or corruption. In order to steal the data, distort the data, and other things, the attackers typically employ social engineering techniques. As a result, the data protection law is helpful in protecting the data from misuse. Many nations have passed the following data protection laws:

8.5.1. General Data Protection Regulation (GDPR)

The world's strictest privacy and security law is the General Data Protection Regulation (GDPR). Despite being created and adopted by the European Union (EU), 2016, it imposes requirements on organizations worldwide that target or gather information about individuals living in the EU. On May 25, 2018, the rule came into force. Those that break the GDPR's privacy and security regulations will face severe fines that could total tens of millions of dollars.

With the GDPR, Europe is demonstrating its unwavering commitment to data security and privacy at a time when more individuals are committing their personal information to cloud services, and data breaches are occurring on a regular basis. GDPR compliance is a frightening prospect, especially for small and medium-sized businesses, due to the regulation's breadth, scope, and relative lack of specificity (SMEs).

Companies are only allowed to process personally identifiable information (PII) about any individual in accordance with GDPR unless they satisfy at least one of the subsequent six requirements:

- If the person whose personal information is being handled has given their approval.
- Processing is required to carry out a contract with the data subject or to initiate the contract-making process.
- Processing is required to fulfill a legal requirement.
- Processing is required to safeguard a data subject's or another person's vital interests.
- Processing is required to complete work carried out in the public interest or to carry out the controller's official duties.

- Processing is required to further the controller's or a third party's legal interests unless such interests conflict with the subjects' interests, rights, or freedoms.

Additionally, organizations that handle data or extensively monitor data subjects are required to designate a data protection officer (DPO). The DPO is the public face in charge of data governance and making sure the business complies with GDPR. Legal repercussions for violating the GDPR include penalties of up to 20 million euros ($24.26 million) or 4% of the company's annual global revenue. The incumbent of this position must also make sure that proper data protection rules are followed when maintaining personal data.

8.5.2. Data Protection Act of 1998

Personal data is protected in the UK by the Data Protection Act of 1998. All personally identifiable data that a business may have on files, such as names, dates of birth and anniversaries, addresses, and phone numbers, is covered by the Act. On May 23, 2018, the Data Protection Act of 2018 (DPA 2018)[40] replaced it. The EU General Data Protection Regulation (GDPR), which went into effect on May 25, 2018, is supplemented by the DPA 2018. The GDPR dramatically tightens up how personal data is collected, stored, and used.

8.5.3. Protection of Personal Information (APPI)

Japan amended the Act on the Protection of Personal Information (APPI) in 2015 to address significant data breaches. In particular, the significant Benesse Corporation data breach in 2014, in which roughly 29 million pieces of confidential customer information were exposed and sold. Although there is no particular clause in the APPI dealing with data breach reporting, this contains increased criminal penalties for illicit transactions. Instead, in compliance with the APPI, the Policies Concerning the Protection of Personal Information establishes a policy that encourages business owners to voluntarily notify data breaches.

[40] https://www.legislation.gov.uk/ukpga/1998/29/contents.

Kaori Ishii and Taro Komukai hypothesized that the lack of a specific data breach notification requirement to push businesses to improve data security may be explained by the Japanese culture. Leaks are condemned by the general public and the media in Japan, in particular. As a result, data leaks can lead to a loss of consumer confidence, brand value, and eventually income. As an illustration, consider how, following a data leak in 2004, Softbank quickly lost 107 billion yen and Benesse Corporation lost 940,000 clients (Ishii and Komukai, 2016). As a result, the policy's requirement to report data leaks has been followed.

8.5.4. Personal Information Protection Law of the People's Republic of China

The Personal Information Protection Law of the People's Republic of China, also known as the Personal Information Protection Law (PIPL), safeguards the rights and interests of individuals with regard to their personal information, standardizes the handling of such information, and encourages its wise use. It affects the export of personal data from China as well. The PIPL Becomes operative on November 1, 2021, after being adopted on August 20, 2021. Both China's Data Security Law (CSL) and China's Cybersecurity Law (CSL) are related to it, and it builds on both of them ("DSL"). Similar to and partially based on the GDPR of the European Union is the PIPL.

8.5.5. Personal Information Protection and Electronic Documents Act

Canadian law governing data privacy is the Personal Information Protection and Electronic Documents Act (PIPEDA).[41] It sets rules for how businesses in the private sector must gather, use, and disclose personal data. The Act also includes a number of provisions that make using electronic documents easier. To encourage consumer confidence in internet commerce, PIPEDA was enacted into law on April 13, 2000. The act also aimed to persuade the European Union that Canadian privacy laws were sufficient to safeguard the personal data of EU individuals. Section 29 of the PIPEDA mandates that

[41] https://laws-lois.justice.gc.ca/ENG/ACTS/P-8.6/index.html.

Part I of the Act ("Protection of Personal Information in the private Sector") be reviewed by parliament every five years. The first parliamentary review took place in 2007.

Individuals have the right under the act to:

- Understand the rationale behind why a company gathers, uses, or exposes its personal data.
- Anticipate that a company will gather, use, and disclose their personal information in a reasonable and suitable manner, and won't use it for anything outside what they have authorized.
- Aware of who in the company is in charge of maintaining the privacy of their personal data.
- Expect that the company will secure their personal information by adopting the necessary security precautions.
- Anticipate that whatever personal information a company keeps on them will be accurate, complete, and recent.
- Get access to their personal data and request changes if required.
- Believes their privacy rights have not been upheld, and they complain about how an organization manages their personal information.

The act requires organizations to:

- Request permission before collecting, using, or disclosing a person's personal information.
- Provide a product or service to someone even if they object to the gathering, usage, or disclosure of their personal data unless such data is required for the transaction.
- Using ethical and legal methods to receive information.
- Provides clear, comprehensible, and easily accessible personal information policies.

8.5.6. Section 66B in the Information Technology Act of 2000

This law indicates that obtaining computer resources or communication equipment that has been fraudulently taken is illegal. Whoever unlawfully obtains or retains any stolen computer resource or communication device, knowing or having reason to believe that it is a stolen computer resource or communication device, shall be punished with either a term of imprisonment of either description for a term which may extend to three years or with a fine which may extend to rupees one lakh or with both.

8.6. Health Insurance Portability and Accountability Act

The 104th United States Congress passed the Health Insurance Portability and Accountability Act (HIPAA) of 1996 (HIPAA or the Kennedy-Kassebaum Act), which President Bill Clinton signed into law on August 21, 1996. It addressed several constraints on healthcare insurance coverage, updated the flow of healthcare information, and outlined how personally identifiable information kept by healthcare and healthcare insurance businesses should be safeguarded against fraud and theft. To learn more, go to the website (Congress.gov, August 21, 1996). EasyITGuys, 2022 explained the HIPAA which contains five sections or titles:

- *Title I*: Health care access, portability, and renewability. If a person loses their job or changes employment, Title I preserve their health insurance coverage. Additionally, it forbids lifetime coverage caps and the exclusion of certain illnesses and previous conditions from coverage by group health insurance.
- *Title II*: Preventing health care fraud and abuse; administrative simplification; medical liability reform. Title II mandates the development of national standards for the handling of electronic healthcare transactions by the US Department of Health and Human Services (HHS). Additionally, it mandates that healthcare institutions establish safe electronic access to patient records and uphold the HHS privacy standards.
- *Title III*: Tax-related health provisions governing medical savings accounts. Title III contains laws relating to taxes and medical care standards.
- *Title IV*: Application and enforcement of group health insurance requirements. Health insurance reform is further defined in Title IV, which also covers provisions for people who already have problems and those who want to keep their current coverage.

- *Title V*: Revenue offset governing tax deductions for employers. Title V contains laws regarding company-owned life insurance and how persons who lose their US citizenship are treated for tax reasons.

According to the HIPAA Privacy Rule, failing to provide patients with access to their PHI or suffering a healthcare data breach might result in a fine from the Office for Civil Rights (OCR) HHS Office for Civil Rights. The degree of the violation determines the severity of the privacy regulation penalties. There are four groups formed from them:

- Unintentional HIPAA breaches are subject to fines of up to $100 per infraction and a yearly cap of $25,000 for persistent offenses.
- HIPAA infractions are subject to $1,000 reasonable cause fines, with repeat offender's subject to annual fine caps of $100,000.
- A maximum yearly fine of $250,000 is applied to recurrent infractions of willful neglect of HIPAA, but only if the infringement is remedied within a certain time frame.
- A maximum yearly fine of $1.5 million is applied to recurrent infractions of the HIPAA regulations if there is willful neglect and the infringement goes uncorrected.

8.7. Phishing Law

Phishing is a type of social engineering in which an attacker delivers a false such as spoofed, fake, or other deceptive communication intended to deceive a person into giving the attacker critical information or to install harmful software, such as ransomware, on the victim's infrastructure. As a result, social engineering attacks are also covered under anti-phishing laws.

As per the report by Legon, the first legal action was brought by the American Federal Trade Commission (FTC) against a phisher on January 26, 2004. A 17-year-old California teenager is accused of defrauding consumers of their credit card information by using a page that appeared to be from America Online. The FTC claimed that everything is a part of the expanding trend of identity theft. According to the organization, the number of reports of identity theft increased by 88 percent, from roughly 86,000 in 2001 to 162,000 last year. Companies reportedly targeted by phishing schemes in the past several months include Best Buy, UPS, Bank of America, PayPal, and First Union Bank, according to the FTC and Internet security companies.

By tracking down and apprehending phishers, other nations have followed this example. As per the report by Leyden, 2005, Valdir Paulo de Almeida, the leader of one of the biggest phishing criminal networks, was apprehended in Brazil for stealing between US$18 million and US$37 million over the course of two years. In a case related to the U.S. Secret Service Operation Firewall, which targeted infamous "carder" websites, UK authorities convicted two men in June 2005 for their involvement in a phishing fraud.

Eight individuals were detained by the Japanese police in 2006 on suspicion of engaging in phishing fraud by setting up fake Yahoo Japan Web sites and making themselves a profit of 100 million (US$870,000). In 2006, the FBI Operation Cardkeeper made additional arrests, seizing a 16-person gang in both the United States and Europe.

8.7.1. Anti-Phishing Act of 2005

Sen. Leahy, Patrick J of the United States presented the Anti-Phishing Act of 2005 to Congress.gov, on February 28, 2005. This law imposes a fine or up to five years in jail, or both, on anybody caught engaging in fraud or identity theft with knowledge and intent to violate federal or state law:

- Without the consent or authorization of the registered owner of such business develops or arranges for the development of a website or domain name that promotes itself as a legal online business.
- Utilizes that website or domain name to request any person's forms of identification.

Imposes a fine or imprisonment for up to five years, or both, on a person who transmits an electronic mail message intentionally and with the purpose to participate in activities involving fraud or identity theft under Federal or State law:

- Fraudulently claims to be sent by a genuine internet company.
- Involves an internet location tool that refers or links people to a World Wide Web place that falsely claims to belong to or be linked with a reputable online company.

- Requests identification from the receiver.

8.7.2. Section 66C in the Information Technology Act of 2000

Identity theft is a subject of this legislation. This legislation provides for up to three years in jail, a fine of up to one lakh rupees, and additional punishments for anybody found guilty of using another person's electronic signature, password, or other distinctive identifying feature dishonestly or fraudulently.

8.7.3. Section 66D in The Information Technology Act of 2000

This law specified the penalties for exploiting a computer resource to impersonate someone else to cheat. The penalty for using a communication device or computer resource to commit fraud through personation is imprisonment of any kind for a time that may exceed three years, as well as a fine that may exceed one lakh rupees.

8.7.4. Section 71 in the Information Technology Act of 2000

Misrepresentation will be punished under this law. Those who intentionally misrepresent information to the controller or the certifying authority in order to obtain a license or electronic signature certificate, as the case may be, or who omit crucial information from them, shall be punished with up to two years in prison, a fine up to one lakh rupees, or both.

Summary

This chapter discussed the various legal remedies available to those who attempt to manipulate people for their own gain using social engineering attacks. governments adopt a number of laws that, while not directly related to social engineering, are similar to the tactics used in such attacks. Organizations or users can punish the attackers using these laws.

Chapter 9

The Future of Social Engineering Attacks

In social engineering attacks, it has been observed that the attackers use the same methods repeatedly while using various technologies. Future attackers will employ similar strategies while utilizing more cutting-edge technologies. It will become more sophisticated and target more users. In order to slow down the progress of the social engineering attack, artificial intelligence techniques like machine learning, deep learning, and NLP are now being deployed. However, attackers are learning how to get over these defenses and becoming more trendy criminals. Several of the upcoming social engineering attack approaches will be covered in this chapter.[42]

9.1. Deepfake

Today, false media, news, profiles, videos, and other forms of bogus information are a serious concern. With the use of deep learning technology, attackers may easily fabricate information to trick their victims. A deepfake is information produced by artificial intelligence that appears genuinely to be a human. The terms "deep learning" and "fake" are combined to form the term "deepfake," which largely refers to information produced by artificial neural networks, a subset of machine learning. According to Bruce, 2022, deepfake technology is used for a variety of beneficial purposes, including making information more accessible by developing tools like hear and see, generating Synthetic media that can bring historical figures to life in the classroom to make lessons more engaging and interactive, acting as a great resource for independent storytellers to realistically realize the main ideas of comedy or parody at a low cost, and producing avatar experiences for self-expression on social media.

Deepfakes have certain useful uses, but they are also infamous for their unethical and harmful features. As per Gault and Cole, 2022, attackers released two images of US Vice President Joe Biden speaking on two

[42] https://medium.com/unpackai/impact-of-ai-on-social-engineering-e9bd763a77db.

distinct dates, one concerning gas costs and the other from remarks made at a conference using deepfakes technology. Two films were published within a few hours of one another.

The use of deepfakes technology in social engineering attacks has increased recently, and as it advances, more victims may find it difficult to distinguish between real and fake. According to research, artificial intelligence will rule the future of technology. The following is a list of some of the technique's attackers employ for social engineering attacks:

- *CEO fraud*: In the traditional social engineering scam, the attackers pose as CEOs, COOs, or CFOs to create a feeling of urgency and fool workers who are aware of the authority and status of an upper-level executive contacting them by email, SMS, and other channels. Alternatively called a whale phishing attack or CEO fraud. The assault strategies utilizing deepfakes are the most popular. No longer do scammers attempt to convince a worker at a company to send money via a phony email. Through a phone call from someone who sounds like the CEO or CFO, they persuade the recipient. Criminals demanded a fraudulent payment of $243,000 by impersonating a chief executive's voice using deepfakes technology. The CEO of a British energy company believed he was on the phone with his boss, the head of the company's German parent company, who instructed him to wire the money to a Hungarian supplier. According to the company's insurance provider, Euler Hermes Group SA, the caller instructed the executive to pay within an hour and claimed the request was urgent (Stupp 2019).
- *Cyber extortion*: Attackers use deepfake pornography videos of some well-known celebrity-like faces related to celebrities and the bodies of others. This technique is used to blackmail victims. There is a video online of Gal Gadot having sex with her stepbrother. Gadot's body isn't truly her own, and her face is hardly there either. It approximates the way she might seem in an existing pornographic film with an incest subject by switching her face (Cole, 2017). This method is employed by some assailants as retaliation. Although many people (Helen Mort, writer, Professor McGlynn of Durham University, and others) are dealing with these issues, nothing is being done about it. An expert caution that deepfake pornography may turn into a pandemic, as per BBC News. Some attackers use this technique to take revenge.

- *False Information or fake news*: Fake news is currently a major issue on a worldwide scale. Popular people and even government officials are frequently seen spreading false information to sway people's decisions, either knowingly or unconsciously. Fake news typically replicates the format of news media material but not the organizational structure or aim (Botha and Pieterse, 2020). The use of fake news is widespread, including in stock market manipulation, political propaganda, and commercials. Attackers frequently use the voice and faces of well-known news reporters to propagate false information. These news stories were published on social networking sites. Numerous victims can recognize reliable news based on well-known reporters, logos, and other factors. On occasion, they combine malware links with false news to encourage people to click the links. As per Lab, 2022, false Zelenskyy assertions were propagated through a hacked news show and a deepfake video. Hackers broke into a national news program on the Ukraine 24 television network on March 16. Messages that purported to be from Ukrainian President Volodymyr Zelenskyy were displayed on the news ticker of the program. The letters demanded that Ukrainians cease hostilities and lay down their arms while also alleging that Zelenskyy "intended to capture Donbas" but had been unable to do so, thus he had departed Kyiv.

It has been observed that deepfakes are leveraging social engineering attacks to spread daily in numerous fields. Although attackers continue to use social proof to persuade their victims to act, technology is advancing. Individuals are easily persuaded after they observe the videos and listen to the audio of the perfect people. However, the deployment of deepfakes technology by attackers is an intriguing reality. Future deepfakes will become harder to identify as the technology becomes more affordable.

9.2. Social Engineering as a Service

The ready-made toolkits for social engineering are offered on the market, as was covered in the previous chapters. Although many vendors are creating several toolkits for companies, attackers are using them. The version of social engineering assault, such as a phishing toolkit, is also marketed as a component of Software-as-a-Service (SaaS) packages, according to

Svistunova and Yatsenko, 2022. Phishing-as-a-Service (PHaaS) has recently become increasingly well-known. The packages include a wide range of specialized scamming services, from setting up phony websites impersonating well-known brands to starting a focused operation to steal personal information. This involves researching the intended audience, disseminating phishing emails, and giving the client encrypted copies of the stolen data. A total of 1.2 million phishing URLs were blocked in 2021 as a result of the researchers' discovery of 469 unique phishing kits. The top 10 phishing kits they found throughout the course of August 2021 to January 2022, as well as the number of distinct domains where each of these phishing kits was discovered. In total, they found content from phishing kits unboxed on more than 25,000 different distinct domains in October.

For attackers to obtain information without manually doing so, information-collecting tools are a crucial piece of technology. Another tactic that attackers regularly employ is organizational loophole discovery. These kinds of technology will progress and get more complicated.

It has been observed that phishing or social engineering toolkits will become more popular in the future. Attackers will find new toolkits to target large numbers of victims. They will have an effortless technique to assault users as a result. In order to improve their success rate, they will also include artificial intelligence in the toolkit.

9.3. Virtual Customer Assistant (VCA) or Chatbot

Despite the fact that AI has enhanced cybersecurity, it is providing thieves a leg up to launch sophisticated attacks. The use of chatbots is expanding. In a study of 50 respondents by Gartner, 2022 Customer Service and Support (CSS) performed online in January and February 2022, it was discovered that 54% of respondents were employing a chatbot, virtual conversation assistant (VCA), or other conversational AI platform for customer-facing applications. Online users of all kinds can interact with chatbots directly or indirectly. Perhaps it's on Facebook Messenger. Unfortunately, a lot of individuals are unaware they are chatting with a chatbot.

A chatbot, an interactive component, was recently found on an intriguing phishing website (Perez, 2022). As opposed to many phishing websites, this one starts a dialogue before leading the victim step-by-step to the real phishing pages. Future social engineering attacks on communication will make use of chatbots. The fact that chatbots are accessible to clients around the clock is one of their major advantages. Additionally, they answer any inquiries right away. This ensures that clients of any company may resolve their issues at any time, day or night. As a result, the attackers use the chatbot, which serves their needs continuously.

9.4. Web3 and the Metaverse

Web 3.0 (Web3) is the third generation of the evolution of web technologies. It may be predicted that Web 3.0 will alter both (Web 1.0 and Web 2.0) how websites are created and how people engage with them. Web 1.0 was a static information provider where people read webpages but infrequently interacted with them. Web 2.0 was an interactive and social web that enabled user collaboration. As has previously been mentioned through social media sites, Web 2.0 is home to a large number of social engineering operations.

Kerner and Gillis, 2022 claim that the following important Web 3.0 characteristics assist to describe what the third generation of the web will probably be all about:

- *Backdoor*: Contrary to the centralized governance and applications of the previous two web generations, Web 3.0 will be a backdoor. Applications and services will be enabled in Web 3.0 through a distributed mechanism lacking centralized authority.
- *Blockchain-based*: Blockchain enables the creation of backdoor apps and services. Blockchain utilizes a distributed method to spread data and connections among services in contrast to centralized database design. Blockchain can also provide an immutable ledger of transactions and activities in a backdoor setting, aiding in the supply of verified authenticity.
- *Cryptocurrency-enabled*: Utilizing cryptocurrencies in place of fiat money is a crucial component of Web 3.0 services.
- *Autonomous and artificially intelligent*: Web 3.0 will have more automation overall and AI will be mainly responsible for this automation.

According to Schultz., 2022, Web 3.0 poses a variety of particular difficulties and security dangers. Some Web 3.0 risks are merely modernized versions of well-known attacks, such as new phishing techniques or social engineering techniques that aim to cut users off from the contents of their cryptocurrency wallets. Other security issues, such as cleverly manipulating how data on the blockchain is kept and interpreted, are related to the particular technology that underpins Web 3.0.

The possibility of social engineering is one of the major concerns for users who are adjusting to new technologies for the first time. Users who are unfamiliar with technology might frequently end up making poor choices. Web 3.0 is no different. Social engineering attacks are the main source of security problems impacting Web 3.0 users.

Additionally, wallet cloning, which is currently a risk in practice, may develop into a more common attack technique in the future. The hidden key to recovering lost wallets, the seed phrase, is needed for this, and it may be obtained by social engineering, posing as customer service, or duping wallet owners into submitting their information through phony verification procedures (Osborne, 2022).

9.5. Faster Password Guessing

The credentials to the financial website are the main target of the social engineering attack. Phishing emails, SMS messages, and guessing approaches are used to carry out this strategy. However, in the future, the attackers will use deep learning, and machine learning algorithms to predict the passwords. In general, people choose their passwords based on what they find interesting and simple to remember. Once they have all the victim's information, the attackers may utilize AI such as an advanced dictionary attack to predict the actual password. While multi-factor authentication is used by certain businesses, attackers are developing techniques to bypass it.

According to Palmer, 2022, one way for hackers to bypass MFA is to deploy an "adversary-in-the-middle" (AiTM) attack, which combines a phishing scam with a proxy server between the victim and the website they're attempting to login to. As a result, the attackers are able to steal both the password and the session cookie, which gives them access to an extra layer of authentication that they may use, in this example to steal email. Simply put, the user believes they have entered into their account normally. Future multi-factor authentication attacks may employ increasingly sophisticated methods, necessitating the deployment of additional levels of password protection by enterprises.

9.6. Communication Channels

As was covered in the chapters before, communication is crucial in manipulating the victims. At this time, the attackers use SMS, emails, social media, phone calls, and other methods. Due to their usage of profitable materials in emails, SMS, and other communications, individuals have fallen victim to social engineering attacks. In the future, they communicated with the victims using increasingly sophisticated technologies. Additionally, they tweak the information so that the victims would fail to recognize the social engineering attacks.

Virtual reality (VR) and augmented reality (AR) have eagerly risen in importance in recent years. They are reality technologies that either improve or swap out the physical world for a virtual one. With augmented reality (AR), a user's surroundings are enhanced by the addition of digital features to a live view, frequently using a smartphone's camera. Virtual reality is a type of technology that creates synthetic or virtual experiences that are almost real and/or realistic. The development of VR technology began in the 1960s, and it wasn't until the late 1980s that the first commercial VR tools were made available. However, recently, researchers are showing interest in these technologies.

Kaspersky mentioned that, although third-party manufacturers and apps produce and transport the material, AR browsers help with the augmentation process. Given that augmented reality is a relatively new field and means for creating and transmitting verified material are still developing, this poses the issue of dependability. Complex hackers may replace a user's AR with their own, deceiving users or disseminating false information. As a result of the possibility for material to be unreliable, augmented reality systems can be a useful tool for tricking consumers as part of social engineering assaults. Hackers could, for instance, create false signs or displays to mislead users into acting in ways that are advantageous to the hackers.[43]

With the use of machine learning technology, voices, and films may be altered while maintaining their authenticity. A hacker who gains access to motion-tracking data from a VR headset may utilize it to make a digital copy or sometimes referred to as a "deepfake" and therefore compromise VR security.

[43] https://www.kaspersky.com/resource-center/threats/security-and-privacy-risks-of-ar-and-vr.

9.7. Future of the Malicious Software

According to Heine and Luna, 2022, the number of malwares kits and tools that target embedded systems, like DVRs or autos, is now rather low, but that is about to change. The Internet of Things is a sizable, expanding, and highly vulnerable underbelly of the digital universe, as disturbances like the Mirai botnet demonstrate. Take for example ransomware that prevents victims from accessing their home, automobile, or a vital medical device like a dialysis machine. Think about what it would be like if the tools used to create that malware had been released and were widely available online.

- *Increased use of encryption*: As hackers discover new techniques for encrypting their destructive payloads and even entire malware packages, defenders may find it harder to decipher and eliminate this software. The percentage of samples that information security companies can evaluate might significantly decline with the development of more automated, large-scale malware.
- *Attackers surpassing defenders*: Advances in machine learning techniques may enable malware developers to create hundreds of thousands of new versions of their code every day. The number of new variants might overwhelm defenses since each one could have a unique design and new features.
- *The Internet of Unsecure Things (IoUT)*: As IoT grows more pervasive, more crucial systems will be susceptible to manipulation and compromise in exchange for money. As hackers shift their focus from computers and hard drives to vehicles and industrial machinery, the ransomware plague might get even worse.

As per Shankar, 2022, security experts have recently discovered fresh malware that was concealed in James Webb Telescope photographs. The malware, known as "GO#WEBBFUSCATOR," spreads via JWST images as well as phishing emails and malicious documents. Golang, a programming language that can infect Windows, Mac, and Linux computers, is growing in prominence among hacker organizations like Mustang Panda. Golang is used to create viruses. Additionally, Golang executables are more resistant to reverse engineering and analysis.

Summary

Although this chapter demonstrates a few of the tools that attackers frequently utilize, attackers have access to an infinite number of technologies. Generally, the purpose of this chapter is to outline the strategy for upcoming social engineering attacks. Therefore, in order to slow down this attacker's progress, researchers with expertise in social engineering must create new detecting models.

References

Act, Protection (1999). "Anticybersquatting Consumer Protection Act." In: *A. A* 500, p. 1.

Andrews, Michelle (2016). *The Rise of Medical Identity theft*. https://www.consumerreports.org/health/Medical-identity-theft-a1699327549/. Accessed: August 23, 2022.

Arkvik, Isabel (2021). *What is Financial Cybercrime and How to Prevent It?* https://www.visma.com/blog/what-is-Financial-cybercrime-and-how-to-prevent-it/. Accessed: June 20, 2022.

Atlassian (2022). *Severity Levels for Security Issues*. https://www.atlassian.com/trust/security/security-severity-levels. Accessed: September 02, 2022.

Audin, Gary (2009). *Eavesdropping*. https://www.techtarget.com/searchunifiedcommunications/definition/eavesdropping. Accessed: June 26, 2022.

Bahgat, Ahmed (2022). *Types of Malware: Learn How to Protect Yourself Better in 2022*. https://kinsta.com/blog/types-of-malware/. Accessed: May 17, 2022.

Bandura, Albert, Joan E Grusec, and Frances L Menlove (1967). "Some social determinants of self-monitoring reinforcement systems." In: *Journal of Personality and Social Psychology* 5.4, p. 449.

Barracuda (n.d.). *CEO Fraud*. https://www.barracuda.com/glossary/ceo-fraud. Accessed: September 22, 2022.

Bassett, Gabriel, C David Hylender, Philippe Langlois, Alexandre Pinto, and Suzanne Widup (2021). "Data breach investigations report." In: *Verizon DBIR Team, Tech. Rep*.

Berry Law (2022). *Bank Fraud-Definitions & Penalties*. https://jsberrylaw.com/blog/bank-fraud-definition-penalties/. Accessed: May 18, 2022.

Black, Sharon K (2001). *Telecommunications Law in the Internet Age*. Elsevier.

Boston Consulting Group (2019). *Global Wealth 2019 Reigniting Radical Growth*. https://image-src.bcg.com/Images/BCG-Reigniting-Radical-Growth-June-2019_tcm9-222638.pdf. Accessed: April 20, 2022.

Botha, Johnny and Heloise Pieterse (2020). "Fake news and deepfakes: A dangerous threat for 21st century information security." In: *International Conference on Cyber Warfare and Security*, pp. 57–66.

Brilingait˙e, Agn˙e, Linas Bukauskas, and Aušrius Juozapavičius (2020). "A framework for competence development and assessment in hybrid cybersecurity exercises." In: *Computers & Security* 88, p. 101607.

Bruce, Debra (2022). *Applications of Deepfake Technology: Positives and Dangers*. https://www.knowledgenile.com/blogs/applications-of-deepfake-technology-positives-and-dangers/. Accessed: September 19, 2022.

Camenker, B. (2015). *The Big Lie and the Propaganda War.* http://www.massresistance.org/docs/issues/gay_strategies/the_big_lie.html. Accessed: July 02, 2020.

Carlson, Benny (2005). "Social Engineering, 1899-1999: An Odyssey through *The New York Times*." In: *American Studies in Scandinavia* 37.1, pp. 69–94.

Casey, Timothy (2015). "Understanding cyber threat motivations to improve defense." In: *Intel White Paper.*

Chauncey Crail, Dia Adams (2021). *What Is Synthetic Fraud?* https://www.forbes.com/advisor/credit-score/what-is-synthetic-fraud/. Accessed: August 05, 2022.

Chowdhury, Nabin, Sokratis Katsikas, and VasileiOS Gkioulos (2022). "Modeling effective cybersecurity training frameworks: A delphi method-based study." In: *Computers & Security* 113, p. 102551.

Cohen, Karen (2022). *What Is Tailgating? What Is Piggybacking? (The Differences & Risks).* https://www.kelsercorp.com/blog/it-tailgating-piggybacking-differences-risks. Accessed: July 22, 2022.

Cole, Samantha (2017). *AI-Assisted Fake Porn Is Here and We're All Fucked.* https://www.vice.com/en/article/gydydm/gal-gadot-fake-ai-porn. Accessed: 24 September 2022.

Congress, US (1998). "Digital millennium copyright act." In: *Public Law* 105.304, p. 112.

Congress.gov (August 21, 1996). *Text-H.R.3103-104th Congress (1995-1996): Health Insurance Portability and Accountability Act of 1996.* https://www.congress.gov/bill/104th-congress/house-bill/3103/text. Accessed: September 13, 2022.

Congress.gov (February 28, 2005). *S.472-Anti-phishing Act of 2005.* https://www.congress.gov/bill/109th-congress/senate-bill/472. Accessed: July 27, 2022.

Congress.gov (January 12, 2007). *H.R.4709-109th Congress (2005-2006): Telephone Records and Privacy Protection Act of 2006.* https://www.congress.gov/bill/109th-congress/house-bill/4709. Accessed: August 24, 2022.

Consumer Protection Division (2022). *Identity Theft: Income Tax Identity Theft.* https://consumer.georgia.gov/consumer-topics/identity-theft-income-tax-identity-theft. Accessed: August 20, 2022.

Cooke, Trevor (2022). *Smishing Statistics 2022 (SMS Phishing Attacks/Scam Text Messages).* https://earthweb.com/smishing-statistics/. Accessed: June 22, 2022.

Cullina, Matt, Rhode Island (n.d.). *7 Identity Theft Schemes That Target Seniors.* https://www.FTC.gov/sites/default/files/documents/public_comments/FTC-seeks-public-input-how-identity-theft-impacts-senior-citizens-project-no.p065411-00009%C2%A0/00009-83187.pdf. Accessed: August 06, 2022.

DiGiulio, Sarah (2019). Why compliments make us feel so good-and how to get better at giving them. *NBC News.* https://www.nbcnews.com/better/lifestyle/why-compliments-make-us-feel-so-good-how-get-better-ncna1062546. Accessed: July 18, 2022.

EasyITGuys (2022). *Health Insurance Portability and Accountability Act (HIPAA).* https://www.easyitguys.com/health-insurance-portability-and-accountability-act-hipaa/. Accessed: Accessed August 13, 2022.

Ekran (2022). *7 Best Practices to Secure System Administrators' Privileged Accounts.* https://www.ekransystem.com/en/blog/system-server-administrators. Accessed: July 04, 2022.

Elyusufi, Yasyn, Zakaria Elyusufi, M'hamed Ait Kbir. (2019). "Social networks fake profiles detection using machine learning algorithms." In: *The Proceedings of the Third International Conference on Smart City Applications*. Springer, pp. 30–40.

Epps, Thomalyn (2010). "Trademark Law : How We Got to Where We Are In: *J. Contemp. Legal Issues* 19, p. 3.

European Union (EU) (2016). *General Data Protection Regulation (GDPR).* https://eur-lex.europa.eu/eli/reg/2016/679/oj. Accessed: August 29, 2022.

FBI (n.d.). *Protected Voices: Social Engineering*. https://www.fbi.gov/video-repository/protected-voices-social-engineering-083018.mp4/view. Accessed: May 05, 2022.

FirstOrion (2020). *Infographic: 2020 Scam Call Report*. https://firstorion.com/infographic-2020-scam-call-report/. Accessed: June 22, 2022.

Freedman, Jonathan L and Scott C Fraser (1966). "Compliance without pressure : the foot-in-the-door technique." In: *Journal of Personality and Social Psychology* 4.2, p. 195.

Gartner (2022). *Gartner Predicts Chatbots Will Become a Primary Customer Service Channel Within Five Years*. https://www.gartner.com/en/newsroom/press-releases/2022-07-27-gartner-predicts-chatbots-will-become-a-primary-customer-service-channel-within-five-years. Accessed: September 26, 2022.

Gault, Matthew and Samantha Cole (2022). *Is Joe Biden Dead, Replaced by 10 Different Deepfake Body Doubles? An Investigation*. https://www.vice.com/en/article/wxnn54/is-joe-biden-dead-replaced-by-10-different-deepfake-body-doubles-an-investigation. Accessed: September 24, 2022.

Gillett, Rachel (2016). Meet the job seeker who has been impersonating a Postmates delivery guy to get his 'resume' to major tech companies. *Business Insider*. https://www.businessinsider.in/careers/meet-the-job-seeker-who-has-been-impersonating-a-postmates-delivery-guy-to-get-his-resume-to-major-tech-companies/articleshow/54725270.Cms. Accessed: June 30, 2022.

Grimes, Roger (2022). *Answer 4 Simple Questions To Avoid a Social Engineering Attack*. https://blog.knowbe4.com/answer-4-questions-to-avoid-a-social-engineering-attack. Accessed: August 17, 2022.

Gui, Valentin (2019). *Social Proof: Different Types of Social Proof Plug-ins With 20+ Examples and Benefits*. https://prooffactor.com/blog/social-proof/. Accessed: June 23, 2022.

Hart, Megan (2021a). *Identity Theft a Risk to Consumers as Online Purchases Increase*. https://www.journalofaccountancy.com/news/2021/jan/identity-theft-attempts.html. Accessed: September 02, 2022.

Hart, Robert (2021b). *TripAdvisor Took Down Nearly 1 Million Fake Reviews Last Year*. https://www.forbes.com/sites/roberthart/2021/10/27/TripAdvisor-took-down-nearly-1-million-fake-reviews-last-year/?sh=577b60f62fa0. Accessed: August 02,2022.

Heine, Luke and Brian de Luna (2022). *What is the Future of the Malware Markets?* https://www.newamerica.org/in-depth/malware-markets/what-future-malware-markets/. Accessed: September 28, 2022.

Hoeschele, Michael and Marcus Rogers (2005). "Detecting social engineering." In: *IFIP International Conference on Digital Forensics*. Springer, pp. 67–77.

Holland, Michael (2012). *5 Types of Authority Available to Managers*. https://www.bishophouse.com/new-leader/5-types-of-authority-available-to-managers/. Accessed: July 11, 2022.

Ihezukwu, Stephanie (n.d.). *Cybersecurity Awareness: Social Engineering*. https://www.linkedin.com/learning/cybersecurity-awareness-social-engineering-14308872/. Accessed: August 17, 2022.

Indeed Editorial Team (2021). *What Is Scarcity Marketing? (Plus 10 Tactics To Increase Sales)*. https://www.indeed.com/career-advice/career-development/scarcity-marketing. Accessed: June 20, 2022.

Infosightinc (n.d.). *What is Impersonation in Social Engineering?* https://mysecurityawareness.com/article.php?article=384&title=what-is-impersonation-in-social-engineering#.YujJWjVBzeQ. Accessed: Aug 02, 2022.

Ionos (2020). *Shoulder surfing- an underestimated threat?* https://www.ionos.com/digitalguide/server/security/shoulder-surfing/. Accessed: July 21, 2022.

Irani, Danesh, Marco Balduzzi, Davide Balzarotti, Engin Kirda, and Calton Pu (2011). "Reverse social engineering attacks in online social networks." In: *International Conference on Detection of Intrusions and Malware, and Vulnerability Assessment*. Springer, pp. 55–74.

Irwin, Luke (2021). *5 Ways to Prevent Social Engineering Attacks*. https://www.grcelearning.com/blog/5-ways-to-mitigate-social-engineering-attacks. Accessed: June 06, 2022.

Ishii, Kaori and Taro Komukai (2016). "A Comparative Legal Study on Data breaches in Japan, the U.S., and the U.K." In: *Technology and Intimacy: Choice or Coercion*. Ed. by David Kreps, Gordon Fletcher, and Marie Griffiths. Cham: Springer International Publishing, pp. 86–105. isbn: 978-3-319-44805-3.

Jacoby, Ari (2022). *A New Frontier of Fraud: Synthetic Identity Fraud*. https://www.paymentsjournal.com/a-new-frontier-of-fraud-Synthetic-identity-fraud/. Accessed: May 16, 2022.

Javelin Strategy & Research (2021). *Child Identity Fraud Web Deception and Loss*. https://javelinstrategy.com/research/child-identity-fraud-web-deception-and-loss. Accessed: August 15, 2022.

Jeeva, S Carolin and Elijah Blessing Rajsingh (2016). "Intelligent phishing URL detection using association rule mining." In: *Human-centric Computing and Information Sciences* 6.1, pp. 1–19.

Johansen, Alison Grace (2021). *5 Child Identity Theft Facts You Need to Know*. https://www.lifelock.com/learn/identity-theft-resources/child-identity-theft-facts-you-need-to-know. Accessed: August 26, 2022.

Kaplan, David A. (2006). *Suspicions and Spies in Silicon Valley*. https://www.newsweek.com/suspicions-and-spies-silicon-valley-109827. Accessed: July 27, 2022.

Kennedy, David (2022). *SET User Manual Made for SET 6.0*. https://raw.githubusercontent.com/trustedsec/social-engineer-toolkit/master/readme/User_Manual.pdf. Accessed: August 08, 2022.

Kennedy, Kevin. (2019). *Identity Theft: Stolen Driver's License Becomes a Nightmare For Triad Woman*. Accessed: July 16, 2022.

Kerner, Sean Michael and Alexander S. Gillis (2022). *Web 3.0 (Web3)*. https://www.techtarget.com/whatis/definition/web-30. Accessed: September 27, 2022.

Kleut, Jennifer van der (2021). *Identity Theft: What Is It and How to Avoid It*. https://us.norton.com/internetsecurity-id-theft-what-is-identity-theft.html. Accessed: June 13, 2022.

Koen Jr, Clifford M and Jin H Im (1997). "Software piracy and its Legal implications." In: *Information & Management* 31.5, pp. 265–272.

Koorsen Fire & Security (2021). *Types of Access Control Key Cards*. https://blog.koorsen.com/types-of-access-control-key-cards. Accessed: August 30, 2022.

Krebs, Brian (2019). *Legal Threats Make Powerful Phishing Lures*. https://krebsonsecurity.com/2019/05/legal-threats-make-powerful-phishing-lures/. Accessed: July 17, 2022.

Kreimer, Ivan (2020). *3 Ways to Increase Your Conversion Rate with Data-Driven Marketing*. https://www.campaignmonitor.com/blog/email-marketing/3-ways-to-increase-conversion-rate-with-data-driven-marketing/. Accessed: June 20, 2022.

Kwiatkowski, Ivan, Fãl'lix Aime and Pierre Delcher (2019). *Holy Water: Ongoing Targeted Water-Holing Attack in Asia*. https://securelist.com/holy-water-ongoing-targeted-water-holing-attack-in-asia/96311/. Accessed: July 29, 2022.

Lab, Digital Forensic Research (2022). *Russian War Report: Hacked News Program and Deepfake Video Spread False Zelenskyy Claims*. https://www.atlanticcouncil.org/blogs/new-atlanticist/russian-war-report-hacked-news-program-and-deepfake-video-spread-false-zelenskyy-claims/. Accessed: September 22, 2022.

Lansley, Merton, Francois Mouton, SteliOS Kapetanakis, and Nikolaos Polatidis (2020). "SEADer++: social engineering attack detection in online environments using machine learning." In: *Journal of Information and Telecommunication* 4.3, pp. 346–362.

Legon, Jeordan (2004). *Phishing' Scams Reel in Your Identity*. http://edition.cnn.com/2003/TECH/internet/07/21/phishing.scam/index.html. Accessed: June 20, 2022.

LexisNexis (2022). *Synthetic Identity Fraud is a Complex and Growing Challenge*. https://risk.lexisnexis.com/insights-resources/article/Synthetic-identity-fraud. Accessed: August 15, 2022.

Leyden, John (2005). *Brazilian Cops Net 'Phishing Kingpin'*. https://www.theregister.com/2005/03/21/brazil_phishing_arrest/. Accessed: August 28, 2022.

Maltego (2022). *Maltego Desktop Application Guide*. https://docs.maltego.com/support/solutions/articles/15000008703-client-requirements. Accessed, August 05, 2022.

McLeod, AS (2018). Asch-Conformity Experiment. *Simply Psychology*, 28.

Mitnick, Kevin D and William L Simon (2003). *The Art of Deception: Controlling the Human Element of Security*. John Wiley & Sons.

Mouton, Francois, Louise Leenen, and H.S. Venter (2016). "Social engineering attack examples, templates and scenariOS." In: *Computers & Security* 59, 186–209. iSSN: 0167-4048. doi: https://doi.org/10.1016/j.cose.2016.03.004. URL: https://www.sciencedirect.com/science/article/pii/S0167404816300268.

Mouton, Francois, Louise Leenen, Mercia M Malan, and HS Venter (2014). "Towards an ontological model defining the social engineering domain." In: *IFIP International Conference on Human Choice and Computers*. Springer, pp. 266–279.

National Council on Identity theft Protection (2022). *What is Employment Identity theft and How Can it Occur*. https://identitytheft.org/types/employment/. Accessed: August 16, 2022.

Nguyen, Thai and Sajal Bhatia (2020). "Higher education social engineering attack scenario, awareness & training model." In: *Journal of The Colloquium for Information Systems Security Education*. Vol. 8. 1, pp. 8–8.

Osborne, Charlie (2022). *Social Engineering Attacks to Dominate Web3, the Metaverse*. https://www.zdnet.com/article/social-engineering-attacks-to-dominate-web3-metaverse-services/. Accessed: September 27, 2022.

Palmer, Danny (2022). *Hackers are finding ways around multi-factor authentication. Here's what to watch for*. https://www.zdnet.com/article/hackers-are-finding-ways-around-multi-factor-authentication-heres-what-to-watch-for/. Accessed: September 25, 2022.

Pears, Matthew and Stathis Th Konstantinidis (2021). "Cybersecurity training in the healthcare workforce–utilization of the ADDIE model." In: *2021 IEEE Global Engineering Education Conference (EDUCON)*. IEEE, pp. 1674–1681.

Pemberton, Chris (2016). *Tap Into The Marketing Power of Sms*. https://www.gartner.com/en/marketing/insights/articles/tap-into-the-marketing-power-of-sms. Accessed: September 20, 2022.

Perez, Adrian (2022). *Interactive Phishing: Using Chatbot-like Web Applications to Harvest Information*. https://www.trustwave.com/en-us/resources/blogs/spiderlabs-blog/interactive-phishing-using-chatbot-like-web-applications-to-harvest-information/. Accessed: September 26, 2022.

PhishingTackle (n.d.). *Social Engineering Email Alarm Bells Infographic*. https://phishingtackle.com/social-engineering-alarm-bells-pdf/. Accessed: August 16, 2022.

Poojary, Karthik (2012). *Maltego tutorial*. https://www.computerweekly.com/tip/Maltego-tutorial-Part-1-Information-gathering?_gl=1*yum706*_ga*MTc2MDgzNDI0Mi4xNjU1NzUxNzE0*_ga_TQKE4GS5P9*MTY2MDAyODIyNy4zOC4xLjE2NjAwMjgyMzEuMA..&_ga=2.226312154.1332626072.1660028232-1760834242.655751714. Accessed: August 10, 2022.

Proofpoint (2019). *2019 Human Factor: Today's Cyber Attacks Target People-How to Keep Them Safe*. https://www.proofpoint.com/us/resources/webinars/human-factor-2019. Accessed: May 20, 2022.

Ratha, Nalini K., Jonathan H. Connell, and Ruud M. Bolle (2001). "Enhancing security and privacy in biometrics-based authentication systems." In: *IBM Systems Journal* 40.3, pp. 614–634.

Regan, Dennis T. (1971). "Effects of a favor and liking on compliance." In: *Journal of Experimental Social psychology* 7.6, pp. 627–639. iSSN: 0022-1031. doi: https://doi.org/10.1016/0022-1031(71)90025-4. URL: https://www.sciencedirect.com/science/article/pii/0022103171900254.

Sachdev, Ameet and Tribune Staff Reporter (2001). *P&G admits Unilever garbage search.* https://www.chicagotribune.com/news/ct-xpm-2001-09-01-0109010181-story.html. Accessed: July 21, 2022.

Sahlins, Marshall (2013). *Stone Age Economics*. Routledge.

Sandouka, Hanan, Andrea J Cullen, and Ian Mann (2009). "Social engineering detection using neural networks." In: *2009 International Conference on CyberWorlds*. IEEE, pp. 273–278.

Sawa, Yuki, Ram Bhakta, Ian G Harris, and Christopher Hadnagy (2016). "Detection of social engineering attacks through natural language processing of conversations." In: *2016 IEEE Tenth International Conference on Semantic Computing (ICSC)*. IEEE, pp. 262–265.

Schultz., Jaeson (2022). *On the Radar: Securing Web 3.0, the Metaverse and beyond.* https://blog.talosintelligence.com/2022/02/securing-web-3.0-metaverse-and-beyond.html. Accessed: September 27, 2022.

Shankar, Siddharth (2022). Hackers now using James Webb Space Telescope's images to hide malware. *Times Now News*. https://www.timesnownews.com/technology-science/hackers-now-using-james-webb-space-telescopes-images-to-hide-malware-article-93901757. Accessed: September 29, 2022.

Sharmin, Sadia and Zakia Zaman (2017). "Spam detection in social media employing machine learning tool for text mining." In: *2017 13th International Conference on Signal-Image Technology & Internet-Based Systems (SITIS)*. IEEE, pp. 137–142.

SlickText (2022). *44 Mind-Blowing SMS Marketing and Texting Statistics*. https://www.slicktext.com/blog/2018/11/44-mind-blowing-SMS-marketing-and-texting-statistics/. Accessed: June 22, 2022.

Social-Engineer (n.d.). *Security Through Education*. https://www.social-engineer.org/. Accessed: August 17, 2022.

Sonowal, Gunikhan (2022). "Phishing Kits." In: *Phishing and Communication Channels: A Guide to Identifying and Mitigating Phishing Attacks*. Berkeley, CA: Apress, pp. 115–135. ISBN: 978-1-4842-7744-7. doi: 10. 1007/978-1-4842-7744-7_6. URL: https://doi.org/10.1007/978-1-4842-7744-7_6.

Sonowal, Gunikhan and KS Kuppusamy (2018). "SmiDCA: an anti-smishing model with machine learning approach." In: *The Computer Journal* 61.8, pp. 1143–1157.

Staff, Dark Reading (2020). *Employees Aware of Emailed Threats Open Suspicious Messages*. https://www.darkreading.com/attacks-breaches/employees-aware-of-emailed-threats-open-suspicious-messages. Accessed: June 30, 2022.

Statista Research Department (2022a). *Number of data breaches in the United States from 2013 to 2019, by industry*. https://www.statista.com/statistics/273572/number-of-data-breaches-in-the-united-states-by-business/. Accessed: July 04, 2022.

Statista Research Department (2022b). *Share of Instagram influencers involved in fraud worldwide from 2019 to 2021, by number of followers*. https://www.statista.com/statistics/1250681/share-of-Instagram-influencers-involved-in-fraud-worldwide/. Accessed: Aug 02, 2022.

Stouffer, Clare (2021). *What is pretexting? Definition, examples, prevention tips*. https://us.norton.com/internetsecurity-online-scams-what-is-pretexting.html. Accessed: July 29,2022.

Stupp, Catherine (2019). *Fraudsters Used AI to Mimic CEO's Voice in Unusual Cybercrime Case.* https://www.wsj.com/articles/fraudsters-use-ai-to-mimic-CEOs-voice-in-unusual-cybercrime-case-11567157402. Accessed: September 23, 2022.

Sugawara, Sho K., Satoshi Tanaka, Shuntaro Okazaki, Katsumi Watanabe, and Norihiro Sadato (Nov. 2012). "Social Rewards Enhance Offline Improvements in Motor Skill." In: *PLOS ONE* 7.11, pp. 1–6. doi: 10.1371/journal.pone.0048174. URL: https://doi.org/10.1371/journal.pone.0048174.

Svistunova, Olga and Anton Yatsenko (2022). *Phishing-kit market: What's inside "off-the-shelf" phishing packages.* https://securelist.com/phishing-kit-market-whats-inside-off-the-shelf-phishing-packages/106149/. Accessed: September 25, 2022.

The Hindu (2022). *Cyberattack forces Iran steel company to halt production.* https://www.thehindu.com/sci-tech/technology/cyberattack-forces-iran-steel-company-to-halt-production/article65570230.ece. Accessed: July 02, 2022.

The Hindu Business Line (2021). *Phishing scammers increasingly targeting users through messenger apps.* https://www.thehindubusineSSLine.com/info-tech/phishing-scammers-increasingly-targeting-users-through-messenger-apps-report/article35377937.ece. Accessed: July 29, 2022.

Thomas, Ian (2021). *IRONSCALES Releases Findings from State of Cybersecurity Survey.* https://ironscales.com/blog/ironscales-releases-findings-from-state-of-cybersecurity-survey/. Accessed: June 22, 2022.

Truecaller (2021). *Truecaller Insights 2021 U.S. Spam & Scam report.* https://truecaller.blog/2021/06/28/us-spam-scam-report-21/. Accessed: June 22, 2022.

Vidwans, Ranjeet (n.d.). *Top 10 Phishing Attack Statistics That Should Scare You.* https://www.clearedin.com/blog/phishing-attack-statistics. Accessed: June 22, 2022.

Wang, Zuoguang, Hongsong Zhu, Peipei Liu, and Limin Sun (2021). "Social engineering in cybersecurity: a domain ontology and knowledge graph application examples." In: *Cybersecurity* 4.1, pp. 1–21.

Weisman, Steve (2016). *When identity thieves commit crimes in your name.* https://www.wkyc.com/article/news/nation-now/when-identity-thieves-commit-crimes-in-your-name/95-208200357. Accessed: August 12, 2022.

Workable (n.d.). *Corporate email usage policy template.* https://resources.workable.com/email-usage-policy-template. Accessed: August 14, 2022.

Zaharia, Andra (2015). *Insider Advice: 12 Cyber Security Tips for Bloggers.* https://heimdalsecurity.com/blog/insider-advice-12-cyber-security-tips-for-bloggers/. Accessed: July 06, 2022.

Zamir, Ammara, Hikmat Ullah Khan, Tassawar Iqbal, Nazish Yousaf, Farah Aslam, Almas Anjum, and Maryam Hamdani (2020). "Phishing web site detection using diverse machine learning algorithms." In: *The Electronic Library* 38.1, pp. 65–80.

Zhang, Ellen (2018). *What is Fileless Malware (or a Non-Malware Attack)? Definition and Best Practices for Fileless Malware Protection.* https://digitalguardian.com/blog/what-Fileless-malware-or-non-malware-attack-definition-and-best-practices-Fileless-malware. Accessed: June 28, 2022.

Index

Author's Contact Information

Gunikhan Sonowal
Assistant Professor,
Faculty of Computer Technology,
Assam Down Town University,
Guwahati, Assam 781026, India
gunikhan.sonowal@gmail.com